YORK MEDIEVAL PRESS

York Medieval Press is published by the University of York's Centre for Medieval Studies in association with Boydell & Brewer Limited. Our objective is the promotion of innovative scholarship and fresh criticism on medieval culture. We have a special commitment to interdisciplinary study, in line with the Centre's belief that the future of Medieval Studies lies in those areas in which its major constituent disciplines at once inform and challenge each other.

All enquiries of an editorial kind, including suggestions for monographs and essay collections, should be addressed to: The Director, University of York, Centre for Medieval Studies, The King's Manor, York, YO1 7EP (E-mail: lah1@york.ac.uk).

Publications of York Medieval Press are listed at the back of this volume.

RITES OF PASSAGE

CULTURES OF TRANSITION IN THE
FOURTEENTH CENTURY

Edited by
Nicola F. McDonald and W. M. Ormrod

YORK MEDIEVAL PRESS

First published 2004

A York Medieval Press publication
in association with The Boydell Press
an imprint of Boydell & Brewer Ltd
PO Box 9   Woodbridge   Suffolk IP12 3DF UK
and of Boydell & Brewer Inc.
668 Mount Hope Avenue   Rochester   NY 14620   USA
website: www.boydellandbrewer.co.uk
and with the
Centre for Medieval Studies, University of York

ISBN 1 903153 15 8

A CIP catalogue record for this book is available
from the British Library

Library of Congress Cataloging-in-Publication Data
Rites of passage : cultures of transition in the fourteen century / edited by
Nicola F. McDonald and W.M. Ormrod.
    p. cm.
Includes bibliographical references and index.
    ISBN 1–903153–15–8 (hardback : alk. paper)
1. Civilization, Medieval – 14th century.   I. McDonald, Nicola.
II. Ormrod, W. M., 1957–
CB365.R58 2004
392.1′5′0940902–dc22   2004004688

Printed in Great Britain by
Antony Rowe Ltd, Chippenham, Wiltshire

CONTENTS

CONTRIBUTORS

Joel Burden	University of Newcastle upon Tyne
P. H. Cullum	University of Huddersfield
Isabel Davis	University of York
Jane Gilbert	University College, London
Sarah Kay	University of Cambridge
Nicola F. McDonald	University of York
W. M. Ormrod	University of York
Helen Phillips	Cardiff University
Miri Rubin	Queen Mary, University of London
Sharon Wells	University of York

PREFACE

'Rites of Passage' was the theme of the Second York Interdisciplinary Conference on the Fourteenth Century, organized by Dr P.J.P. Goldberg (to whom we owe the theme) and the editors of this volume and held at the Centre for Medieval Studies, University of York, in July 2001. This occasional series of conferences is intended to draw together scholars working in different disciplines in order to share information, ideas, methodologies and problems relating to the field of fourteenth-century studies. The event proved as productive as its predecessor, and demonstrated once again the special value of the interdisciplinary and multi-disciplinary approaches promoted by the Centre for Medieval Studies at York.

All the contributors to this volume presented papers at the 2001 conference, and most of the articles published here comprise revised versions of those papers. We are especially grateful to all the delegates (including those who gave papers not included here) for the intellectual stimulation of the conference and for the encouragement and commitment that has led to publication. This is a fitting place to express our special thanks to Jeremy Goldberg for his leadership within the conference and his guidance in publication planning, Louise Harrison for administrative support, to Isabel Davis for assistance with copy-editing, and to Caroline Palmer at Boydell & Brewer for her usual enthusiasm and support.

Nicola McDonald
Mark Ormrod

Introduction: Rites of Passage

Miri Rubin

The articles collected in this volume consider a varied and rich array of ritual-ized events and actions in the lives of late medieval people. They do so by test-ing the concept of *rite de passage*, which is now frequently used both in academic discussion and in daily parlance. The term was created in 1907 or 1908 by Arnold Van Gennep (1873–1957), the German-born and naturalized Savoyard folklorist and linguist. Van Gennep saw the life of an individual in any society as a series of passages 'from one age to another or from one occu-pation to another'.[1] The rites which attracted his attention were those 'that accompany transitions from one situation to another and from one cosmic or social world to another'.[2] As a folklorist, Van Gennep was acquainted with the variety of European and extra-European practices related to kinship and the life-cycle. His intuition led him to believe that these might be fitted into cat-egories, and that an underlying structure may be identified in life-cycle rituals:

> Since the goal is the same, it follows of necessity that the ways of attaining it should be at least analogous, if not identical in detail.[3]

Van Gennep was eager to bring clarity to the study of these rituals of passage and transition, to make them easy to understand. The anthropology of his day recognized multiple overlapping characteristics of ritual: direct and indirect, positive and negative, contagionist or dynamic, sympathetic or animistic.[4] To these Van Gennep added a diachronic axis, the sense of unfolding: what we might, these days, call narrative structure for a lifetime of change. Passage, journey, transition are some of the spatial images central to an understanding of *rites de passage* and to the method involved in applying the term – to the past, the present or the future.

---

[1] A. Van Gennep, *The Rites of Passage*, trans. M. B. Vizedom and G. L. Caffee (London, 1960), pp. 2–3; N. Belmont, *Arnold Van Gennep: The Creator of French Ethnography*, trans. D. Coltman (Chicago, 1979), pp. 1–9. For a critique of the use of anthropo-logical theories of ritual see P. Buc, *The Dangers of Ritual: Between Early Medieval Texts and Social Scientific Theory* (Princeton, NJ, 2001). Buc, is particularly critical of histo-rians who are unaware of the intellectual roots and implications of categories devel-oped in the social sciences and applied in their historical work.

[2] Van Gennep, *Rites of Passage*, p. 13.

[3] Ibid., p. 3.

[4] Ibid., p. 9.

Based on his study of a multitude of customs, artifacts and texts, Van Gennep identified three crucial stages in the making of *rites de passage*: separation, transition and incorporation.[5] This schema is so general as to include procedures which last years, months, days or even just a few minutes; but they all possess an element of marking and demarcation. Maurice Bloch has described ritual as

> a dramatic commentary on life, which represents it as a mixture of two elements, pure and impure. The task of ritual is to separate the two so that the impure can be eliminated in order that the true – pure – can emerge.[6]

Thus, where child-birth is seen as polluting, churching is a *rite de passage* which allows women to return to a state of purity and re-enter society after bearing a child. The mother experiences: *separation* soon after conception, with the reduction of sexual availability to her husband and entry into an increasingly feminine sphere which offers advice and support;[7] *transition* within the birth space and in a feminine circle during labour; and finally *aggregation*, through the process of churching and re-incorporation into the community.[8] Similar temporal variety of the liminal stage characterizes the *rite de passage* of young Tamil Brahmin women in south India, of the Aiyar people, who experienced it over years. During the transition into womanhood, knowledge about sexuality and marriage was conveyed by a combination of song, dance and jokes which led on to the stage of marriage, but only ended when the woman delivered a son.[9] Once this occurred, the songs deemed appropriate were devotional, thanksgiving chants for the safe delivery of the child.[10]

The stage of separation can be associated with images of symbolic death, particularly in rites of initiation like those experienced in the Poro Bush society of Liberia. There a boy is thrown over the community's perimeter wall, only to be caught by a man on the other side, who throws a log to the ground in imitation of the sound of a falling body. The boy was dead to the world and his kin, led by wailing women, mourned his death.[11] The transitional period lasts

5   Ibid., p. 11. Tripartite schemes have been formative in European social thought, see for example G. Duby, *The Three Orders: Feudal Society Imagined*, trans. A. Goldhammer (Chicago, 1980), esp. the introduction, pp. 1–9.
6   M. Bloch, 'Religion and Ritual', in *The Social Science Encyclopedia*, ed. A. Kuper and J. Kuper, 2nd edn (London, 1996), pp. 732–6 (pp. 734–5).
7   For a study that sees greater male involvement in this sphere see U. Rublack, 'Pregnancy, Childbirth and the Female Body in Early Modern Germany', *Past and Present* 150 (1996), 83–110.
8   S. Karrant-Nunn, 'A Women's Rite: Churching and the Reformation of Ritual', in *Problems in the Historical Anthropology of Early Modern Europe*, ed. R. Po-chia Hsia and R. W. Scribner, Wolfenbuetteler Studien 78 (Wiesbaden, 1997), pp. 111–38 (pp. 128–30).
9   V. K. Duvvury, *Play, Symbolism, and Ritual: A Study of Tamil Brahmin Women's Rites of Passage* (New York, 1991), pp. 213–14.
10 Ibid., pp. 217–18.
11 R. Raphael, *The Men from the Boys: Rites of Passage in Male America* (Lincoln, NE, 1988), pp. 4–5.

between four and eight years and includes ceremonies of circumcision, scarification and training in hunting. The last stage, that of incorporation, includes cleansing, receipt of new clothes, the licence to marry and re-birth as a new person with a new name.[12] Arunta youth in Australia lay on green boughs over an open fire, and had their heads bitten unto bleeding to encourage hair-growth, before re-birth as a man. One may similarly consider the veiling ceremony of a medieval anchoress in these terms. In its images, two *rites de passage* – marriage and death – merged. The postulant's separation stage was a death to the world through the requiem section of the mass. She was thus separated from her maidenhood and prepared for emergence as the betrothed and then wedded bride of Christ.[13]

The messages conveyed by *rites de passage* diverge greatly according to the underlying intent and mood of the institution surrounding them. This is a point made clear in Joel Burden's article in this volume, on the burial of Edward II (1327). Context is shown to determine the meaning and political impact of the ritual of royal burial. For the burial of a deposed king was vastly different in shape, as well as in meaning, from that of a king who had died peacefully in his bed. The display of regalia and the replacement of the mutilated body by an idealized mannequin aimed to mask the violence of the king's death and to support the new ruler, Edward III, the dead king's son. Nancy Bradley Warren's study of late medieval English female monasticism compares Franciscan and Benedictine veiling ceremonies.[14] The Benedictine profession, as laid out in the Barking Ordinal, has the priest or prelate as recipient ritual actor; the abbess only removes the postulant's clothes, while the priest blesses the habit and veil in a ritual role of father as well as substitute bridegroom.[15] Yet it is instructive that the English verse translation of the Benedictine rule includes an invocation of Mary as the postulant takes her vow:

> Unto mary, cristes moder dere,
> And to al halows of heuyn clere.[16]

---

[12] T. A. Leemon, *The Rites of Passage in a Student Culture: A Study in the Dynamics of Transition* (New York, 1972), pp. 8–10.

[13] M. Rubin, 'An English Anchorite: The Making, Unmaking and Remaking of Christine Carpenter', in *Pragmatic Utopias: Essays for Barrie Dobson*, ed. R. Horrox and S. Rees Jones (Cambridge, 2001), pp. 204–23. On historians' use of anthropological concepts see P. Burke, *History and Social Theory* (Cambridge, 1992), pp. 38–43; M. Rubin, 'What is Cultural History Now?', in *What is History Now?*, ed. D. Cannadine (Basingstoke, 2002), pp. 80–94 (pp. 86–9).

[14] N. B. Warren, *Spiritual Economies: Female Monasticism in Later Medieval England* (Philadelphia, PA, 2001), pp. 3–30.

[15] *The Ordinale and Customary of the Benedictine Nuns of Barking Abbey*, ed. J. B. L. Tolhurst, Henry Bradshaw Society 65–6 (London, 1927–8), II, 353–5.

[16] 'The Northern Metrical Version of the Rule of St Benet', in *Three Middle-English Versions of the Rule of St. Benet and Two Contemporary Rituals for the Ordination of Nuns*, ed. E. Kock, EETS OS 120 (London, 1902), pp. 48–118 (p. 108, ll. 2137–8).

The Franciscan order had the entrant offer herself to Mary, Francis and St Clare, through the hands of the abbess: 'make þey pofessioun in hondes of þe Abbesse bifore alle þe couent'.[17] The Brigittine script is even more explicit about the agency of the abbess and the sisters, as well as of the postulant. It is extensive, inasmuch as it begins with the ceremony of delivery into the abbess's hands:

> And than that suster schal fal down to kysse the abbes fete, whiche in nowyse sche schal suffer, but rather put down her ryght hande, that sche may kesse that.[18]

On the eighth day the postulant enters her name into the register of the house, saying 'I delyuer and betake ȝour reuerent moderhode, thys wrytyng, writen at myne instaunce in thys omen registre.'[19] In as much as she enters relationships with the divine, these are experienced through the 'wombe of mary'.[20] These variations in tone and gesture – priest/father and Mary/abbess – underpin and express the differing styles of the convents. The Benedictine, Franciscan and Brigittine orders each held differing assumptions about female agency and the purpose of women in religious life, as well as quite distinct patterns of power within the convent. These affected the shape of their veiling *rites de passage*.

The stage of the *rite de passage* that has probably attracted most attention from scholars, is the period of transition, the *liminal* stage. Patricia Cullum's article in this collection, on the rituals of entry into clerical orders, demonstrates that the transitional stage in clerical formation – entry into the minor orders – could be extended or contracted according to a variety of personal circumstances. The liminal stage was treated with particular energy and imagination by the British anthropologists Victor and Edith Turner and their many students.[21] Their approach to ritual emphasizes the social context and the movement of participants between social categories. It has frequently been invoked by medieval historians and students of religion. Medievalists have contributed to a critique of its assumptions: scholars like Caroline Bynum, and the contributors to the volume edited by Kathleen Ashley, *Victor Turner and the Construction of Cultural Criticism*.[22] According to the Turners, it is during the

[17] 'The Rewle of Sustris Menouresses Enclosid', in *A Fifteenth-Century Courtesy Book and Two Franciscan Rules*, ed. R. W. Chambers and W. W. Seton, EETS OS 148 (London, 1914), pp. 81–119 (p. 83).
[18] *Rewyll of Seynt Sauioure*, ed. J. Hogg, Salzburger Studien zur Anglistik und Amerikanistik 6 (Salzburg, 1980), p. 98, ll. 16–19.
[19] Ibid., p. 98, ll. 4–5.
[20] *The Myroure of Oure Ladye*, ed. J. H. Blunt, EETS ES 19 (London, 1873), p. 238.
[21] J. Holm and J. Bowker, 'Introduction: Raising the Issues', in *Rites of Passage*, ed. J. Holm and J. Bowker (London, 1994), pp. 1–9 (pp. 3–4).
[22] *Victor Turner and the Construction of Cultural Criticism*, ed. K. M. Ashley (Bloomington, IN, 1990); *Gender and Religion: On the Complexity of Symbols*, ed. C. W. Bynum, S. Harrell and P. Richman (Boston, MA, 1986).

liminal stage that those ideas, sentiments and facts that had been hitherto for the neophyte bound up in habitual and conventional configurations, which are accepted unthinkingly, are resolved into their constituents.[23] This suspended state of journeying, full of self-awareness, was often characterized by ludic elements; thus the carnivalesque and the liminal often converge. The carnivalesque and the licentious dominate the *rite de passage* experienced by young Australians after the completion of their equivalent to 'A-level' examinations: in Queensland and Victoria whole beaches are turned during Schoolies' Week into a free zone of drink, sex, dance and drugs.[24] Tens of thousands leave home towards the beaches for what seems to be a very long party.

During the liminal stage something is experienced through the disaggregation of normal functions, expectations and procedures, through the shedding of status, vocation and even gender, and entry into a state which Turner named *communitas*. This is meant to be a state of spontaneity and joy, experienced apart from institutional structures. The liminal, a state of betwixt and between, between all times and places, allows some human essence to be experienced, which is individual, but illuminated by the appreciation that it can be shared and experienced by every human. This is *communitas*, reduction of human sensation to essence.[25] *Communitas* is a concept that medievalists have found most alluring, but it is none the less rather nebulous. John Bossy attempted to use *communitas* in his exploration of the mass as a social institution.[26] In it a core element of ritual is isolated: the intense awareness of being bound together in a community of shared experience, shared humanity. The authors of a collection of essays on *rites de passage* bring the example of the Live Aid Concert in 1986 and the words of Bob Geldof:

> Everyone came on for the finale. There was tremendous feeling of oneness on the stage [. . .] Now everyone was singing. [On the way home . . .] people walked over to the car and hugged me [. . .] Some cried, 'Oh Bob, oh Bob', not sneering, not uncontrollable, just something shared and understood [. . .] I wasn't sure what had happened in England, or everywhere else, but 'I knew' cynicism and greed and selfishness had been eliminated for a moment. It felt good. A lot of people rediscovered something in themselves.[27]

This colourful description of behaviour out of the ordinary begs the question: if this is *communitas*, how long does it last?

23 V. Turner, *The Forest of Symbols* (Ithaca, NY, 1967), p. 105.
24 H. P. M. Winchester, P. McGuirk and K. Everett, 'Schoolies' Week as Rite of Passage: A Study of Celebration and Control', in *Embodied Geographies: Spaces, Bodies and Rites of Passage*, ed. E. Kenworthy Teather (London, 1999), pp. 59–77.
25 V. Turner, *Dramas, Fields and Metaphors: Symbolic Action in Human Society* (Ithaca, NY, 1974), pp. 231–71.
26 J. Bossy, 'The Mass as a Social Institution, 1200–1700', *Past and Present* 100 (1983), 29–61.
27 B. Geldof, *Is That It?* (London, 1986), p. 310.

The Turners identified within Van Gennep's schemas not only the rituals of an individual life, but a template applicable to whole societies. They emphasized the danger of situations of liminality, as an individual or group inhabits space between or apart from clearly defined roles and responsibilities. Sharon Wells here shows the Arthurian court to have been suspended in a state of enduring liminality, displayed in irresponsibility, 'somewhat out-of-control, moody'. Jane Gilbert deftly analyses in her contribution to this volume the figure of the restless dead, Alceste in Chaucer's *Legend of Good Women*. Here is a being who returns and revisits, and thus unsettles and overwhelms, retarding ritual mourning and closure. In this state of indeterminacy – often experienced as a crisis – individuals and groups are moved to extraordinary actions; here creativity can emerge.[28] By concentrating on the liminal stage, the Turners theorized a state – *liminoid* – which could be applied outside *rites de passage*: to a pilgrimage, to leisure activities generally, to states of being, such as an anchorite or a holy person. Isabel Davis's article in this volume points out, through the analysis of rites of entry into chivalry, the importance of travel and itinerancy before the elevation into knighthood.

Why are *rites de passage* effective, if effective they are? Classical anthropology, following Durkheim, has postulated the state of ritual as one of enhanced being, of cognitive awareness, of sense perceptions induced by drugs, pain, rhythm or through costume, gazing into mirrors, masks[29] – a state of hyper-receptiveness. This ritual state was essential for the periodic inscription of crucial knowledge of the 'rules of conduct which prescribe how a man should conduct himself with sacred things'.[30] Thus rituals serve to keep alive something that is beyond them, and which they represent, like religious belief.[31] Moving from ritual to *rites de passage*, Raymond Firth attempted to be more precise about the social impact of initiation rituals:

> [. . .] by bringing the person into formal and explicit relation with his kindred, [it] confronts him with some of his basic social ties, re-affirms them and thus makes patent to him his status against the days when he will have to adopt them in earnest.[32]

Rituals and daily reality are intricately linked. The anthropological thinker who has most affected historians – Clifford Geertz, always passionate and impassioning – shows ritual to be as 'messy' as daily life is. Geertz sees not a unique territory for ritual, but continuity in perception and use of symbols

---

[28] Van Gennep, *Rites of Passage*, p. 128; S. Lavie, K. Narayan and R. Rosaldo, 'Introduction: Creativity in Anthropology', in *Creativity/Anthropology*, ed. S. Lavie, K. Narayan and R. Rosaldo (Ithaca, NY, 1993), pp. 1–8.

[29] B. Myerhoff, 'Rites of Passage: Process and Paradox', in *Celebration: Studies in Festivities and Ritual*, ed. V. Turner (Washington, DC, 1982), pp. 109–35 (pp. 111–13).

[30] E. Durkheim, *The Elementary Forms of Religious Life*, trans. K. E. Fields (New York, 1995), p. 38.

[31] For the full discussion see ibid., pp. 21–44.

[32] R. Firth, *Tikopia Ritual and Belief* (London, 1967), p. 437.

between the ritual and the 'mundane', a distinction which he encourages us to dispel:

> In a ritual, the world as lived and the world as imagined, fused under the agency of a single set of symbolic forms, turn out to be the same world.[33]

The habitual understanding of *rites de passage* which couples biological development and ritual moment – as in baptism, circumcision or churching – forces a question: what do we make of rituals in which the biological moment of change and the related ritual are separate in time?[34] Mark Ormrod's article focuses on a related problem: the dilemma posed by the king-making ritual that emphasizes virility and adult leadership in cases when the king was a mere infant. He analyses the efforts which were invested in late medieval England by the political elite in the creation of reassuring devices and additional stages of ritual progress for the maturing infant-king, as in the case of Henry VI, who was crowned at the age of nine months.

Inasmuch as 'the mundane order' is always one of conflict and competition – power inequality based on age, gender, ethnicity – ritual should also be the arena for dramatisation of conflict. Whereas the critique of ethnographic authority and the move towards more interpretative, reflective and less structural understandings of ritual in the last two decades has meant that schemas such as *rites de passage* have become less commonly used, the very notion that personality and subjectivity are constructed through public, social and linguistic experiences is one which we still find to be attractive. It intersects neatly with many of the assumptions of those studying the making of gender; it offers occasion for the examination of the operation of power; and it also invites psychoanalytic reading of ritual. Reg Hook's analysis of the circumcision rites of the Gisu of Uganda emphasizes not the power of the father, which is relatively weak among the Gisu where property devolves through mother and sisters, but that of the ancestors, of the elder men, over the boy. Maurice Bloch developed the concept of 'rebounding violence', whereby initiation rites turned 'prey' into 'hunter', as the weak and dependent, the possibly resentful, were transformed so as to turn their violence against animals, women and enemies.[35] The circumcision of adolescent Gisu is linked to the channelling of feelings of bitterness, envy and hatred (*lirima*), into martial aggression and perhaps even into sexual aggression in marriage.[36] Suzette Heald's reading of the ritual emphasizes the separation of boys from

[33] C. Geertz, *The Interpretation of Cultures* (New York, 1973), pp. 87–125 (p. 112).

[34] On Bar Mitzvah see V. Crapanzano, 'Rite of Return', in *Hermes's Dilemma and Hamlet's Desire: On the Epistemology of Interpretation* (Cambridge, MA, 1992), pp. 260–80 (pp. 261–2).

[35] M. Bloch, *Prey into Hunter: The Politics of Religious Experience* (Cambridge, 1992), p. 6.

[36] R. H. Hook, 'Psychoanalysis as Context', in *Anthropology and Psychoanalysis: An Encounter through Culture*, ed. S. Heald and A. Deluz (London, 1994), pp. 225–38; (pp. 230–1); S. Heald, 'Every Man a Hero: Oedipal Themes in Gisu Circumcision', in *Anthropology and Psychoanalysis*, ed. Heald and Deluz, pp. 184–210.

women, the construction of a fierce inter-generational incest taboo, and the making into a tribal hero of every growing boy.

Separation from womenfolk is thus central to initiation *rites de passage*, and it can be identified in the case of late medieval men en route to ordination. Separation is realized in stages, following the series of steps from lower orders – in which clerics can marry – to ordination to priesthood, which requires men to be unmarried and sexually clean. But even in the lower orders, men were separated from the female sphere of nurture, which is also a vernacular sphere, and were introduced into Latin learning, male company and the discourse of celibacy. All these changes are associated with pain. Rita Copeland has demonstrated the link between Latin pedagogy, discipline and pain. This is the price young men paid for entry into a world of power and privilege which often involved policing and regulation of the very vernacular sphere of childhood.[37]

Pain is associated with coming of age in many *rites de passage*. Hazing and genital mutilation of boys have been interpreted as punishment and deterrence against desire for the mother, as well as an expression of envy of women: genital bleeding as mock menstruation; raised scars around the nipples (among the Kwoma of New Guinea) as the drawing of a breast on the young man's chest.[38] Initiation rituals allow parents and ancestors to bear heavily upon individuals – be it the young man, the teenage cleric or the postulant nun.[39]

How does coercion affect our understanding of *rites de passage*? Ritual participation might be secured through fear (the Poro Bush Society boys were shown trays of fingers and toes cut off from errant members).[40] In tracing coercion we may wish to draw distinctions between rites that are utterly expected in a given society – say baptism, confession and communion for a medieval Christian – and those that were chosen, say ordination, veiling, entry into political office. But we are surely also aware that these 'choices' were often made before any experience of the life-style in question, as in the case of celibacy and enclosure. As Mark Ormrod shows, there was a real tension between the dynastic logic of succession and the expectation that the ritual agent fit the ritual promise of coronation. In the case of succession of the very young – as in the case of Henry VI – that tension demanded careful management and political support for the ritual of coronation. But even in less spectacular settings, can choices ever be taken freely within a ritual

[37] R. Copeland, *Pedagogy, Intellectuals, and Dissent in the Later Middle Ages* (Cambridge, 2001), pp. 51–98.

[38] Raphael, *The Men from the Boys*, p. 9.

[39] For further insights into initiation see B. Lincoln, *Emerging from the Chrysalis: Studies in Rituals of Women's Initiation* (Cambridge, MA, 1981); J. L. Brain, 'Homage to Neptune: Shipboard Initiation Rites', *Proceedings of the American Philosophical Society* 125 (1981), 128–33.

[40] Raphael, *The Men from the Boys*, p. 13.

frame? How should the individual's commitment to it and the nature of her participation be situated within the ritual field: as a necessary component, as a redundant one, or as an emergent one?

The notion of the emergent ritual actor is an interesting one and I am led to think about it within the Jewish tradition. In orthodox Judaism, 613 rules regulate all aspects of daily life. Of course most people do not adhere to all, but the Jew is seen as emerging from ritualized practice. By setting intention aside, by the sheer rhythms of ritualized life, the ritual is expected to make the Jew, by forming good habits and thoughts. This is a process of continuous emergence.

Emergence raises the issue of depth and length of ritual effect; in what sense should we think of the effect of ritual as limited in time, as wearing off? James W. Fernandez has addressed this question of ritual 'evaporation' in his study of the *Bwiti* religion developed by the Fang people in Gabon. Their rites are enacted in waterside chapels, embracing in syncretic manner native and Christian ideas, natural and sympathetic magic. They are performed on week-ends by migrant workers returning to wells and beaches for re-engagement with communal life, with a cosmology equally reflected in space, food, clothes and gender relations. Their experiences are what Fernandez calls synesthetic – involving all the senses – and from them participants are expected to come away strong and able to maintain a state of purity for another period of hard work in an alien city. The rite offers balm against the pollution of work, competition and quarrels:

> Where there was failing sense of the past, cosmic and human origins have been vividly revitalised. Where there was a decentering in Fang village experience, a sense of peripherality, there has emerged a vital center of activity, the Bwiti chapel.[41]

Here Fernandez will have us perceive effect, but limited effect; as if the energy of *Bwiti* can only charge the bodies and minds for a while. As it wore off, the preferred nurturing ethical community weakened, and so men and women returned to the *Bwiti* chapel for more. The prominence of return and iteration intersects fruitfully with Sarah Kay's reflection on the *moment de conclure* in Froissart's romance writings. Memory of pain and the anticipation of death, which are ever the stuff of ritual action, are shown also to produce poetic creative impulses.

These reflections on effect and on agency are meant to raise ambiguities in our understanding of the degree of detachment or absorption, acceptance or doubt, involvement or apathy, which ritual actors experience and know within *rites de passage*. Those of us who work historically are attuned to difference and variety, to the nuance of the specific, to the particular event

---

[41] J. W. Fernandez, *Bwiti: An Ethnography of the Religious Imagination in Africa* (Princeton, NJ, 1982), p. 565 and more generally pp. 565–73.

situated within wide grids of traditions and systems of meaning. We are particularly attuned, as the articles collected here show, to issues of gender difference, access to resources, to the determinants of freedom and health and well-being. Theories of culture and most ways of apprehending *rites de passage* and ritual more generally, fail to guide us towards historical observation which is capable of incorporating variation. Don Handelman has suggested the use of the term 'ritual of transformation' rather than 'rite of passage'. In such ritual seven characteristic traits should be considered, among them levels of coercion and awareness affecting the participants.[42] While envisaging a wider field of outcomes than Van Gennep did, and a less benign effect of ritual action than Turner did, Handelman leaves historians with ample scope to explore further the many meanings of symbols and the varying experiences which may be inhabited within a single ritual.

Moments of agency and resistance, like those displayed in the voice of Alceste, brought to us by Jane Gilbert, are accorded little space in the theories of ritual. Thick ethnographic description often dwells on symbolic connections and distances itself from the full import of what is 'going on'. A laudable exception to this is the impressive work of Caroline Humphrey and James Laidlaw on the Jain rites of worship.[43] Their dense theoretical reflection is based on ethnography experienced in west India, over a number of years, among the Jain.[44] When Humphrey and Laidlaw observed the Jain ritual of *puja*, they noticed that those who had not prepared properly for it (by washing, by changing clothes), and who were therefore barred from touching the idol at the centre, none the less entered the temple, stood in front of the idol offering it fruit, laying a flower, dropping some rice grains or bringing some sandalwood powder.[45] They accommodated and created ritual forms, using their bodies and mundane materials.

This attention to the body is full of ethical implications of interest to those who apply ethnographic method to historical events. Dominick La Capra may have been somewhat melodramatic in asking 'What about the cat?' in his critique of Robert Darnton's influential analysis of the 'great cat massacre', but his comment spurs us to awareness of the bodies involved in ritual, and especially in *rites de passage*.[46] In this volume Joel Burden never loses sight of

---

[42] D. Handelman, *Models and Mirrors: Towards an Anthropology of Public Events* (Cambridge, 1990), pp. 23–41.
[43] C. Humphrey and J. A. Laidlaw, *The Archetypal Actions of Ritual: A Theory of Ritual Illustrated by the Jain Rite of Worship* (Oxford, 1994).
[44] Their observations and conclusions display several points of similarity with my own study of Eucharistic rituals and symbols in the later Middle Ages, M. Rubin, *Corpus Christi: The Eucharist in Late Medieval Culture* (Cambridge, 1991).
[45] Ibid., p. 118.
[46] D. La Capra, 'Chartier, Darnton, and the Great Symbol Massacre', *Journal of Modern History* 60 (1988), 95–112. For similar thoughts see R. Rappaport, *Ritual and Religion in the Making of Humanity* (Cambridge, 1999), who calls for a return to 'acts' in ritual, to what was 'going on'.

the dead king's body and its matching effigy, while Sharon Wells places boys and men around tables in late medieval halls, with a challenging immediacy in exploring the experiences that turned men into boys and some pages into knights.

Studying ritual historically *is* an ethnographic exercise, despite the fact that it does not involve participation. Historical ethnography is best applied through the reading of texts about practice alongside normative materials such as ordinals, sacramentaries, processionals, manuals of all kinds. What arises from such evidence, as it did for Humphrey and Laidlaw, is the realization that ritual experience is full of what historians have tended to see as 'error', 'abuse', 'lack'. Ritual is messy, it is full of 'noise' and awkwardness: spilt wine, spectacles left behind, rain on the parade, stage-fright, loss of the script. Yet to see in these rituals failure is to miss the very nature of ritual.[47] None of these are signs of decay, loss of tradition or indifference. Rather, out of the variety of unpredictable and emergent forms social drama arises: the shouts of parishioners – 'raise it higher!' – at the elevation of the host, or the jostling for position in Corpus Christi processions, are revealing moments of high ritual awareness, the creative re-working of scripts by participants.

Every ritual 'deficit' offers an opportunity. Henry V's unerring sense of ritual and presentation led him to initiate a second burial for Richard II, and this time a burial fit for a king. Into the vacuum of rumour and silence created by the first ignominious burial he inserted a rich and generous ritual that was not only a burial, but a proclamation of his power and confidence.[48] This is highly reminiscent of the ways in which people who were deemed unworthy of reception of communion – those who had not confessed and done penance – none the less partook in the ritual virtues of the mass through the merits of seeing it, praying to the host and venerating it 'spiritually'.[49] Levels and meanings of participation should perhaps be seen as an unfolding and rolling array of possibilities around inherited procedures more or less codified – orally or in written form – which allows participants to invent and embroider and test the terms of their participation. This is true even of *rites de passage*, or better, rites of transformation which, as we have seen, encompass all rituals.

This volume thus continues the work of exploring medieval lives through concepts that aim at comparison. The sources used by the contributors range from episcopal registers to liturgical books, from royal wardrobe accounts to chronicles. They consider dreams and memory, poetry and images, artefacts and gestures. The historical and the poetical meet in rich moments of significance and signification. To work through *rites de passage* is also an engagement

---

[47] Humphrey and Laidlaw, *The Archetypal Actions of Ritual*, p. 140.

[48] See P. Strohm, *England's Empty Throne: Usurpation and the Language of Legitimation, 1399–1422* (London, 1998), pp. 101–27.

[49] Rubin, *Corpus Christi*, pp. 63–77.

with a century of exploration on the nature of human creativity which we may approach through history and texts, traces of action and sentiment.

By steering away from the normative weight of ritual we may now be led to appreciate the creative, resistant, optative, indifferent or frustrated moods of participation. When rituals are presented through literary formulation – by Froissart, Chaucer, Gower – the insight presented in Helen Phillips' article is of particular use: that ritual is cast differently according to genres. From such texts, culture may appear as 'contested, temporal and emergent',[50] as 'a clash of meanings in borderlands'.[51] The formalized aspects of ritual behaviour are a backdrop for the 'creative tendency to break the established patterns and create new forms'.[52] It is also necessary to consider the simple recognition that 'perfunctory ritual may be pleasant but also meaningless'.[53] These realizations offer much to students of the Middle Ages in their search for experience, identity and meanings in collective as well as private lives of the past. Since, as Marshall Sahlins has recently suggested, from that which is most formalized and stylized – the work of history upon each individual in the form of ritual endowment and expectations – a location for the individual as the agent of historic forms, as the maker of meanings, as a historically driven psyche, may emerge.[54]

---

[50] J. Clifford, 'Introduction: Partial Truths', in *Writing Culture: The Poetics and Politics of Ethnography*, ed. J. Clifford and G. E. Marcus (Berkley, CA, 1986), pp. 1–26 (p. 15) as 'an inscription of communicative processes that exist historically, between subjects in relations of power'.

[51] S. B. Ortner, *The Fate of 'Culture': Geertz and Beyond* (Berkeley, CA, 1999), pp. 1–13 (p. 11).

[52] C. A. LaLonde, *William Faulkner and the Rites of Passage* (Macon, GA, 1996), p. 7.

[53] S. Kimball, 'Introduction', in Van Gennep, *Rites of Passage*, p. xvii.

[54] M. Sahlins, *Culture in Practice: Selected Essays* (New York, 2000), pp. 293–351.

Re-writing a Rite of Passage:
The Peculiar Funeral of Edward II

Joel Burden

Since Arnold Van Gennep first discussed his ideas on 'rites of passage' at the beginning of the twentieth century, it has come to be recognized that ritual, when deployed in particular types of social or political context, functions as a mechanism for mediating changes of status or the transferral of authority.[1] In essence, ritual plays a double trick, acting not only on the individual or individuals at the centre of the ritual, but also manipulating the perspective of those situated on the periphery of the ritual who observe a 'seeming transformation' taking place. In the medieval period, the transforming aspect of ritual lent it a particular importance within the greatest of the royal rites of passage, that which was associated with the accession of a king. At the centre of this royal rite of passage were the rituals of coronation, with the act of consecration located at the very heart of the process. However, by the fourteenth century, the burgeoning ritual associated with the burial of a king had also come to acquire symbolic significance for the process of legitimating the royal authority of the dead king's successor.[2]

To understand how a royal funeral might have worked as a mechanism for legitimating royal authority, it is helpful to turn to the work of a second social theorist of the early twentieth century, Max Weber. Weber outlined three criteria he saw as essential to the effective operation of a legitimation process.[3] Legitimating activities should first conform to the dictates of tradition and custom, should secondly present an appearance of legality and should thirdly emphasize the charisma of leadership.[4] Weber's tri-partite formula not only acknowledges that legitimating activities have a tendency to become ritualized, it also goes further by elucidating a fundamental aspect of the way in which political ritual works on participants and spectators alike. This is to

---

[1] A. Van Gennep, *The Rites of Passage*, trans. M. B. Vizedom and G. L. Caffee (Chicago, 1960).

[2] E. A. R. Brown, 'The Ceremonial of Royal Succession in Capetian France: The Funeral of Philip V', *Speculum* 55 (1980), 266–93.

[3] *Max Weber*, ed. H. H. Gerth and C. Wright Mills (London, 1970), pp. 77–9.

[4] On charisma, see C. Geertz, 'Centers, Kings and Charisma: Reflections on the Symbolics of Power', in *Culture and its Creators: Essays in Honour of Edward Shils*, ed. J. Ben-David and T. N. Clark (Chicago, 1977), pp. 150–71.

demonstrate that the power of ritual as a mechanism for legitimating authority resides primarily in its representation of normative appearances, rather than its safeguarding of actual principles or practices. Paradoxically, the apparent conservatism of ritual practices will often veil a reality in which ritual traditions are not static, but continually reproduced. Weber's analysis therefore modifies our understanding of rites of passage within the political domain by demonstrating that the power of rituals resides in the fact that they are at once both 'age-old and ever-changing'. It is this tension at the heart of ritual that is key to understanding why royal rituals in the past were not simply picturesque adjuncts to the political process, but instead comprised a fundamental aspect of politics in themselves.

The funeral of Edward II discussed in this chapter provides an interesting example of the way in which a rite of passage could perform an overt political function through the manipulation of public perceptions of normality. Edward's funeral in December 1327 has long been viewed as somewhat unusual and to some extent innovative in its features. His peculiar status in death as a dead *deposed* king, together with the unique circumstances in which he was buried, combined to create a highly unorthodox ritual environment for a royal funeral to take place. Yet, what is particularly striking about the funeral of Edward II is the extent to which the tenor of the visual imagery deployed within the ritual performance was at variance with the actual political realities on the ground. While the introduction of innovatory elements into the funeral ritual undoubtedly responded to the peculiarities of the situation, the purpose which these innovatory elements seem to have served was not to highlight the fact that Edward had died as a deposed king, but actually to obscure the irregular circumstances of Edward's funeral through the vigorous representation of a false image of normal political succession.

The story of Edward II's funeral sheds an illuminating light on the role of ritual as a mechanism for helping to establish the royal authority of an underage king whose accession occurred against a background of constitutional impropriety and seeming regicide. It also illustrates the importance of studying ritual in action rather than in the abstract, in order to understand its dynamic aspect within the political process of royal succession. Finally, analysis of Edward's funeral serves to underline the importance of the visual dimensions of ritual action in the past for communicating meanings to ritual participants and spectators alike.[5]

Edward II was deposed in January 1327 following his capitulation and surrender to an insurrectionary baronial force led by his estranged wife Queen

5 J. F. Burden, 'Rituals of Royalty: Prescription, Politics and Practice in English Coronation and Royal Funeral Rituals' (unpublished D.Phil. dissertation, University of York, 1999), pp. 10–23, analyses theoretical approaches to the study of ritualized behaviour developed in the social sciences as a basis for developing new historical understandings of the ways in which medieval royal rituals communicated political meaning to contemporary participants and spectators.

Isabella of France and her lover Roger Mortimer, earl of March.[6] The twin processes of Edward's deposition and his son's accession as Edward III were completed with considerable rapidity. However, the details of these events in January 1327 are confused and at times contradictory in surviving contemporary accounts of proceedings. As demonstrated by Clare Valente in her research on the deposition process, there existed fundamental unease within the political community at the implications of Edward II's forced removal from the throne, an unprecedented event in post-Norman Conquest England.[7] Whilst a forceful rhetoric for deposing the king was advanced in Parliament and on the streets of London on 12–13 January, by the time homage was formally withdrawn from the king, at Kenilworth on 20 or 21 January, the language of deposition had evolved into a language of voluntary abdication. Effectively, Edward II's enforced departure from the throne was represented to an uneasy and divided political elite as being altogether less than a deposition. In turn the process through which this ending was achieved was itself reformulated in the writing of official political memory to suggest that Edward's 'voluntary abdication' of the throne had actually precipitated a political crisis in January 1327 rather than help bring it to a close.

Between January and April 1327, Edward was held at Kenilworth Castle in the custody of his cousin Henry, earl of Lancaster. He was then removed to the custody of Thomas Berkeley and John Maltravers at Berkeley Castle near Bristol, where he remained imprisoned until his death on 21 September 1327. Throughout his captivity, Edward II posed something of a latent threat to the new regime as a focus for political opposition. Edward's imprisonment both coincided with and contributed towards a more general climate of political unrest within the kingdom. There were several incidents of civil disturbance during the spring and summer of 1327, some of which were clearly directed at freeing the king, and, in the case of the Thomas Dunheved conspiracy, may briefly have succeeded in this aim.[8] Also contributing to a deterioration in the political climate was the humiliating failure of Edward III's first campaign against the Scots in the summer of 1327. This disastrous summer campaign sapped

---

[6] M. McKisack, *The Fourteenth Century, 1307–1399* (Oxford, 1959), pp. 83–95; N. Fryde, *The Tyranny and Fall of Edward II, 1321–1326* (Cambridge, 1979), pp. 195–206.

[7] C. Valente, 'The Deposition and Abdication of Edward II', *English Historical Review* 103 (1998), 852–81.

[8] T. F. Tout, 'The Captivity and Death of Edward of Carnarvon', *Bulletin of the John Rylands Library* 6 (1921–2), 69–114. The active resistance of Despenser supporters continued in South Wales until March 1327, while a conspiracy to free the deposed king was also foiled in Buckinghamshire around this time. See Fryde, *Tyranny and Fall*, p. 202. Resistance to enforced service in the campaign against the Scots played a role in provoking the Dunheved rising. Meanwhile the *Historia Roffensis* mentions the outbreak of urban unrest at this time, including major disturbances at Canterbury in mid-March and at Rochester in June. See R. M. Haines, *Archbishop John Stratford: Political Revolutionary and Champion of the Liberties of the English Church, ca. 1275/80–1348* (Toronto, 1986), pp. 190–1.

the moral authority of a new royal regime that had made much of Edward II's own humiliating military failures fighting the Scots, notably at Bannockburn in 1314. More seriously, the 1327 campaign considerably eroded the financial reserves inherited by the new government and necessitated the summoning of a parliament at Lincoln in the early autumn of 1327. Here, Edward III's minority government faced criticism of its poor performance at the same time as it sought to levy new subsidies to meet an escalating Scottish threat.[9]

It was against this disturbed political background that an order was almost certainly issued for the murder of Edward II at Berkeley Castle. The immediate occasion of Edward's death was probably word of a new rising in Wales in the late summer of 1327. Roger Mortimer was apprised of this Welsh conspiracy in a letter sent to him by William Shalford, his deputy in Wales, on 7 September. Shalford warned Mortimer that the plot aimed to release Edward II and advised him to devise a 'suitable remedy' to meet the threat.[10] Three weeks later it was officially announced at the Parliament at Lincoln that Edward II had died of natural causes at Berkeley Castle on 21 September. Unsurprisingly, it was widely assumed by contemporary and later commentators that the deposed king had in fact been quietly murdered.[11]

Narrative descriptions of the treatment of Edward II's corpse after death are almost entirely lacking. However, surviving government accounts provide relatively detailed information concerning the care of Edward's corpse during the three months that separated his death and eventual burial. Additionally, they provide further details relating to the supply and carriage of various paraphernalia for use at the king's funeral, from the great wardrobe in London to Gloucester Abbey where the interment took place.

Edward's body was eviscerated and embalmed at Berkeley and his heart was placed in a specially manufactured silver casket that would eventually be buried with the body of Queen Isabella at the Grey Friars' Church in Newgate, London, in 1358.[12] Initially the embalmed corpse remained in the custody of Thomas Berkeley and John Maltravers at Berkeley Castle. Adam Murimuth records that various local dignitaries from Bristol and Gloucester viewed the royal corpse at this time, suggesting that it did not bear obvious marks of any violence done to it.[13] On 21 October, a full month after his death,

[9] R. Nicholson, *Edward III and the Scots: The Formative Years of a Military Career, 1327–1335* (Oxford, 1965), pp. 15–41; Fryde, *Tyranny and Fall*, pp. 209–14.
[10] Tout, 'Captivity and Death', pp. 89–90.
[11] Ibid., pp. 86–92. See also A. Gransden, *Historical Writing in England, Vol. II: c. 1307 to the Early Sixteenth Century* (London, 1982), pp. 38–42.
[12] S. A. Moore, 'Documents Relating to the Death and Burial of King Edward II', *Archaeologia* 50 (1887), 215–26; F. D. Blackley, 'The Tomb of Isabella of France, Wife of Edward II of England', *International Society for the Study of Church Monuments Bulletin* 8 (1983), 161–4.
[13] *Adae Murimuth, continuatio chronicarum Robertus de Avesbury de gesta mirabilibus Regis Edwardi Tertii*, ed. E. M. Thompson, Rolls Series 93 (1889), 54–5. Murimuth reports that the corpse could only be viewed 'superficially'.

Edward's corpse was delivered into the custody of the Benedictine Abbey of St Peter in Gloucester. Here it remained for a further two months, prior to the eventual interment of the king at the abbey in the presence of Edward III and Queen Isabella on Sunday 20 December 1327.

Edward II's funeral was undoubtedly a splendid affair. Again the main source of evidence for the occasion is the surviving enrolled and particular accounts relating to the supply and carriage of items from the great wardrobe in London to Gloucester for use at the funeral.[14] The accounts suggest that Edward II's corpse was interred in his consecration robes, comprising the linen coif, shirt, tunic and gloves worn by the king on the day of his coronation in 1308. A wooden funeral effigy made in likeness of the dead king was manufactured specially for use in the funeral and this was adorned with a copper crown that was also made for the occasion.[15] Edward's funeral is the earliest occasion on which a funeral effigy is known to have been employed at a royal funeral.[16] A further set of items supplied by the great wardrobe in London was also drawn from the robes and regalia that Edward II had used at his coronation. As these were returned to the great wardrobe after the completion of the funeral it is to be presumed these items were used to adorn the effigy as occurred in later English and French royal funerals. These further coronation robes and regalia supplied to Gloucester for use at the funeral consisted of a mantle, tunic, dalmatic and girdle, pairs of buskins, sandals and spurs, a cap of estate, a crown of silver-gilt, a sceptre and a rod, two silver-gilt fleurons and a silver-gilt ring.[17]

The coffin, presumably surmounted with the effigy, was placed in an elaborate hearse which incorporated a prominent display of royal heraldry. Four great gilt lions provided by the king's painter stood at each side of the hearse wearing mantles displaying the royal arms of England. Royal leopards were also emblazoned in gilt on the harnesses of the horses, which wore special gilded coverings. Charges appear in the accounts for the use of gold leaf to decorate four standards and twenty pennants for the funeral, although it is not clear what was depicted on these items. In addition to the four gilded

[14] London, Public Record Office (hereafter PRO), E 361/3 and E 101/383/3.

[15] PRO, E 101/383/3, m. 6. 'Item cuidam magistro cindenti et formanti quamdam ymaginem de ligno ad similitudinem dicti domini Regis Edwardi deffuncti ex convencione in grosso, xl s. Item in una corona de cupro pro eadem ymagine empta cum factura et deauracione eiusdem, vii s. viii d.'

[16] W. H. St John Hope, 'On the Funeral Effigies of the Kings and Queens of England', *Archaeologia* 60 (1907), 517–70 (pp. 526–8) suggests the possible use of a funeral effigy at the funeral of Henry III in 1272. Subsequent commentators have rejected this theory. See R. E. Giesey, *The Royal Funeral Ceremony in Renaissance France* (Geneva, 1960), p. 81; J. Litten, 'The Funeral Effigy: Its Function and Purpose', in *The Funeral Effigies of Westminster Abbey*, ed. A. Harvey and R. Mortimer (Woodbridge, 1994), pp. 3–19; P. Lindley, 'Ritual, Regicide and Representation: The Murder of Edward II and the Origin of the Royal Funeral Effigy in England', in *Gothic to Renaissance: Essays on Sculpture in England*, ed. P. Lindley (Stamford, 1995), pp. 97–112.

[17] PRO, E 361/3, r. 8.

lions, the hearse incorporated four standing figures of the evangelists. Outside of the hearse were placed eight figures of angels holding golden censers and a further two figures of lions rampant.[18] There was a clear expectation that the obsequies for the dead king would be well attended by mourners as a charge is recorded for the manufacture of barriers from four great pieces of oak to resist the pressure of crowds gathering around the royal corpse.[19]

Edward II's funeral manifested several unusual or innovatory aspects, most notably as the first known occasion on which a funeral effigy was used within royal funeral rituals, establishing a tradition in English and French royal funeral practice that would persist for well over two hundred years. However, while innovative elements within Edward II's funeral cannot be denied, there were also many continuities running through the occasion that linked it to past practice and located it within a ritual framework that was otherwise remarkably conventional. Before examining the 'invention' of the funeral effigy tradition, it is important to discuss two other seemingly peculiar aspects of the funeral arrangements in 1327 which could lead historians to lend undue weight to an interpretation of the funeral as standing outside of established royal ritual tradition. These features of Edward's funeral were the three-month delay that separated the death and burial of the king and the choice of Gloucester Abbey as the burial church for his royal remains.

Although medieval embalming techniques were relatively primitive, the three-month interval which lapsed between death and burial of Edward II was not exceptional by the standards of fourteenth-century English royalty. The bodies of Edward I, John of Eltham, Isabella of France, Philippa of Hainault, the Black Prince and John of Gaunt all remained unburied for equivalent or longer periods of time. While the reason for the delay in 1327 is not made clear in the records, it is unlikely this delay reflected neglect or lack of interest on the part of the new government in the carrying through of arrangements. If Murimuth's account of the viewing of Edward's body by civic officials from Bristol and Gloucester is to be believed, then it also seems implausible that delaying the funeral was intended to provide an excuse for not displaying the corpse publicly, though this was a practice observed within the funerals of a number of Edward's royal predecessors. In reality, the probable cause of the postponement was not a need to conceal any hideous disfigurement of the corpse but a more prosaic requirement to allow time for Edward III and Queen Isabella to attend the funeral in person.[20] French royal

---

[18] PRO, E 101/383/3. See Tout, 'Captivity and Death', pp. 94–5; Moore, 'Death and Burial', p. 221.
[19] PRO, E 101/624/14, printed in Moore, 'Death and Burial', p. 226.
[20] W. M. Ormrod, 'The Personal Religion of Edward III', *Speculum* 64 (1989), 849–77 (pp. 867–8), remarks on Edward III's assiduous attendance of the funerals of his friends and relatives.

ritual convention at this time demanded that a new king attend the funeral of his predecessor as a means of cementing his new acquisition of royal authority.[21] Such a convention would undoubtedly have been familiar to the French Isabella, who had lost a father, two brothers and a nephew as kings of France in the space of just thirteen years. During much of the autumn of 1327, the new king and his government were preoccupied with the peace negotiations with the Scots that took place at Nottingham and led eventually to the sealing of the Treaty of Northampton in the following year. Additionally, the geographical dispersion of relevant organs of government at this juncture may have inhibited the efficiency with which the various arrangements for the funeral could be made, although it is worth observing that the resultant delay in completing the funeral arrangements was put to some positive effect with the government eventually organizing a notably splendid ritual occasion.[22]

While the delay to the funeral of Edward II was less remarkable than is sometimes supposed, the choice of Gloucester Abbey as his place of interment was more surprising. According to an official history of Gloucester Abbey, written towards the end of the fourteenth century, Edward was buried at Gloucester because it was the only local religious house prepared to receive his corpse.[23] However, these retrospective sentiments do not fit with the evidence of the royal records which indicate quite clearly that the minority government of Edward III took an active interest in the care of his father's body throughout the period between his death and burial. The unusual selection of Gloucester as a royal burial site was also made with full government knowledge and approval. The choice of Gloucester Abbey was certainly peculiar, particularly as there is no reason to suppose that Edward II had a personal interest in the Benedictine abbey. Indeed, the king's religious tastes veered more towards the mendicant orders, as illustrated in his patronage of the Dominican friary at King's Langley, Hertfordshire.[24] Regrettably, it is not possible to identify Edward's own preferred place of burial, so in the absence of other evidence it is probably best to presume that Gloucester was chosen at the behest of the new royal government as the most suitable place of burial for Edward within a relatively close radius of Berkeley Castle.

It is unfortunate that Edward's unusual failure among medieval English kings to denote his preferred place of burial has encouraged historians to assume that Westminster Abbey ought therefore to have been his natural resting place. If Gloucester was selected on grounds of practicality, this decision

---

[21] E. A. R. Brown, 'The Ceremonial of Royal Succession in Capetian France. The Double Funeral of Louis X', *Traditio* 34 (1978), 227–71.

[22] Tout, 'Captivity and Death', p. 94. The court and council were variously located in Yorkshire, Lincolnshire and Nottinghamshire, the wardrobe and exchequer had recently been moved to York, while the great wardrobe remained in London.

[23] *Historia et cartularium monasterii Sancti Petri Gloucestriae*, ed. W. H. Hart, 3 vols., Rolls Series 33 (1863–7), I, 44–5. See Tout, 'Captivity and Death', pp. 92–4.

[24] *A History of the King's Works: The Middle Ages*, ed. R. A. Brown, H. M. Colvin and A. J. Taylor, 2 vols. (London, 1963), II, 970–7.

does not necessarily imply any conscious desire to 'deny' Edward burial at Westminster Abbey. On a personal level, Edward II may have had good reason for preferring not to be buried alongside his warlike father at Westminster, not least because he enjoyed notably bad relations with the monastic house over the course of his reign.[25] Moreover, Gloucester Abbey was not in itself an inappropriate place for a royal burial. The abbey already housed the tomb of William the Conqueror's eldest son, Robert Curthose, duke of Normandy, and it had also witnessed the only post-Conquest coronation not to be staged in Westminster Abbey, when the young Henry III was crowned at Gloucester in 1216. Furthermore, Edward's body was interred in a highly prestigious position within the Abbey choir on the north side of the High Altar, a position that explicitly acknowledged his high status in death.

When the deposed Richard II was interred at King's Langley in 1400, instead of beside his beloved first queen in their completed double tomb in Westminster Abbey, it could be argued that the misplaced burial of Richard symbolically de-legitimized his kingship by denying him his chosen place within the recognized royal pantheon of the Plantagenet dynasty.[26] Nevertheless, while a tradition of royal burial at Westminster Abbey had clearly developed by the early fourteenth century, reflected in the burial there of both Henry III and Edward I, it remains doubtful whether the abbey enjoyed any formal privileges in this regard as early as 1327. Westminster Abbey no doubt aspired to become the English 'Saint-Denis' and it is interesting to note that it made unsuccessful attempts in the years after Edward II's death to secure a transfer of his remains from Gloucester.[27] However, it is less clear that the perspective of English kings between Henry III and Richard II matched the self-assured outlook of the Westminster monks. Only with the Will of Edward III, drawn up in 1376, does clear evidence emerge of any royal acknowledgement of Westminster's privileged status regarding royal burial, yet even Edward III had been happy to commit publicly to be buried overseas at Cologne Cathedral during the 1340s.[28]

Whichever way one interprets the timing and location of Edward II's funeral, the employment of a funeral effigy emerges as a clear-cut innovation within royal ritual practice. Royal funeral effigies were life-size representations of dead kings or queens that were manufactured specifically for purposes of display at a royal funeral celebration. They should not be confused

[25] Gransden, *Historical Writing II*, pp. 17–22.

[26] J. F. Burden, 'How Do You Bury a Deposed King? The Funeral of Richard II and the Establishment of Lancastrian Royal Authority in 1400', in *Henry IV: The Establishment of the Regime 1399–1406*, ed. G. Dodd and D. Biggs (York, 2003), pp. 35–53; Burden, 'Rituals of Royalty', pp. 137–63.

[27] Westminster Abbey Muniments 20344. I owe this reference to a personal correspondence from Professor J. R. S. Phillips.

[28] Ormrod, 'Personal Religion', p. 860, n. 68. P. Binski, *Westminster Abbey and the Plantagenets: Kingship and the Representation of Power, 1200–1400* (New Haven, 1995), p. 92.

with tomb effigies, though there were iconographical and stylistic similarities between the two forms of representation. Unlike tomb effigies, funeral effigies were not constructed as permanent monuments to the deceased. They were typically manufactured within a few days of a king or queen's death and seemingly their function ceased with the completion of the funeral celebrations.

Relying on the evidence of later royal funerals, it is probable that the effigy of Edward II would have been painted and adorned with royal robes and regalia and placed above the deposed king's coffin within his funeral hearse.[29] The great wardrobe accounts for 1327 make explicit the fact that the copper crown provided for the funeral was intended to adorn the funeral effigy.[30] Interestingly, the internal arrangement of the surviving administrative accounts for the funeral separate the four items not returned to the great wardrobe after the ceremony from other robes and regalia that were simply loaned by the great wardrobe for the occasion.[31] This division in the account suggests that the great wardrobe supplied robes and regalia for two quite distinct purposes. A small number of items were supplied on a permanent basis for use in adorning the embalmed corpse of the king. These items were unlikely to have been visible to mourners on the day of the funeral if, as seems probable, the corpse of the king was not publicly displayed.[32] By contrast, the larger number of items supplied by the great wardrobe on a loan basis would have been visible to mourners by virtue of their adorning the specially manufactured wooden funeral effigy of Edward II, which was publicly displayed in lieu of the deposed king's corpse.

The surviving funeral effigy of Edward III enables an impression to be obtained of how Edward II's funeral effigy might have appeared fifty years earlier. Analysis of Edward III's effigy head suggests that it articulated an impression of 'likeness' through the application of paint and hair. Indeed, the tell-tale sign of a stroke evident in the slight twisting of the king's mouth suggests that the effigy head incorporated a cast taken from Edward's death

---

[29] The earliest prescriptive reference to the use of a funeral effigy can only be dated to 1449. See *Liber regie capelle: A Manuscript in the Biblioteca Publica, Evora*, ed. W. Ullmann, Henry Bradshaw Series 92 (1959), 114. Evidence for the use of effigies at the funerals of Edward III and Henry V is summarized in Hope, 'Funeral Effigies', pp. 531–2; W. H. St John Hope, 'The Funeral, Monument and Chantry Chapel of King Henry the Fifth', *Archaeologia* 65 (1913–14), 129–86. Traces of paint and material fibres were revealed in conservation work on the surviving effigy of Edward III. See P. Lindley, 'Edward III', in *The Funeral Effigies of Westminster Abbey*, ed. A. Harvey and R. Mortimer (Woodbridge, 1994), pp. 31–4.

[30] PRO, E 101/383/3, m. 6.

[31] PRO, E 361/3, r. 8. See also Hope, 'Funeral Effigies', p. 531.

[32] Hope, 'Funeral Effigies', p. 531. Due to the rigidity of the corpse some of the vestments were slit open in order for them to be placed on the corpse before being sewn back together. On royal embalming and bodily decay, see E. A. R. Brown, 'Death and the Human Body in the Later Middle Ages: The Legislation of Boniface VIII on the Division of the Corpse', *Viator* 12 (1981), 221–70.

mask.[33] Clearly, it is impossible to assess the degree of likeness present in the lost effigy of Edward II, though the description that it was made *ad simili-tudinem* of the dead king is certainly intriguing.[34] The crudely carved trunk of Edward III's surviving funeral effigy would have been clothed with royal robes. Meanwhile, it is obvious from the frontally bent arms and the positioning of the missing hands on the effigy that items of regalia were intended to be held in a manner reminiscent of Edward III's gilt-copper tomb effigy. This stiff frontal posture is also reflected in contemporary manuscript illuminations of the funeral of a king, as seen for example in the Westminster Abbey-produced *Liber regalis*. The frontal representation of an enthroned or standing king holding items of regalia in either hand was the standard iconographical image of late medieval kingship. It is an image that appeared repeatedly on royal seals, in stained glass images and monumental sculpture, in manuscript illuminations and panel paintings of the period.

The aesthetic character of fully-robed royal funeral effigies not only drew parallels with the more permanent expression of royal iconography found in tomb effigies, it also placed funerary display firmly within the bounds of established royal representational tradition. However, more significant in the context of 1327 is the fact that the emergence of the royal funeral effigy tradition not only involved the utilization of familiar aesthetic motifs, but also explicitly emphasized continuity with traditions of the past. By examining the emergence of the funeral effigy in terms of its representational function, an impression emerges of Edward II's funeral as a surprisingly orthodox occasion which, notwithstanding its unusual aspects, strove to be in keeping with well-established traditions within English royal funeral practice. In particular, it is possible to identify two distinct but related representational dimensions of funerary arrangements in 1327, both of which were clearly informed by traditions that had emerged in royal funeral practice during the century and a half preceding Edward II's death.[35]

First, it had become established practice following the death of a king for his corpse to be placed on display dressed in royal robes and adorned with items of regalia. Due to the obvious problem of bodily decomposition, procedures for displaying royal corpses varied according to the individual circumstances in which different kings died and were buried. The bodies of Henry II (d. 1189), John (d. 1216) and Henry III (d. 1272) were all buried within a few days of their deaths. In each case, the corpse of the king was publicly

---

[33] Lindley, 'Ritual, Regicide and Representation', pp. 108–10.

[34] On the development of portraiture see A. Martindale, *Heroes, Ancestors, Relatives and the Birth of the Portrait* (The Hague, 1988).

[35] For more detailed discussion, see Hope, 'Funeral Effigies', pp. 523–30; E. M. Hallam, 'Royal Burial and The Cult of Kingship in France and England, 1060–1330', *Journal of Medieval History* 8 (1982), 359–80; A. Erlande-Brandenburg, *Le roi est mort: étude sur les funerailles, les sepultures et les tombeaux des rois de France jusqu'a la fin du XIIIeme siécle* (Geneva, 1975), pp. 15–17.

displayed dressed in royal robes as it was carried to the burial church.[36] Where a longer time lag separated the death and burial of a king, the royal corpse seems not to have been displayed as a prelude to burial. This appears to have been the case on the death of Richard I in 1199, though it is recorded that the king was still interred wearing coronation insignia.[37] Records do not describe the visual dimensions of the funeral of Edward I in 1307, but the three-month delay in the staging of the funeral meant that any display of the king's corpse was unlikely.

A second tradition, as witnessed in the burial of Richard I, was the interment of kings wearing robes associated with the day of their coronation.[38] Edward II was the first king since the Young King (d. 1183), to be described in contemporary sources as being buried in the linen consecration robes worn during the act of anointing at his coronation.[39] Whether or not interment in consecration robes was standard practice amongst twelfth- and thirteenth-century royalty, it clearly was established practice for royal corpses to be dressed and adorned for burial with the more splendid outer garments and regalia associated with coronation. *The Annals of Winchester* record that Richard I was interred in 1199 wearing the crown and other insignia worn at his second coronation in 1194.[40] Meanwhile, David Carpenter has argued persuasively that the rod, dalmatic, mantle, gold brooch, stockings and shoes which were provided on a permanent basis by the keeper of the wardrobe for the burial of Henry III in 1272 were similar if not identical to those used at the king's second coronation in 1220.[41] Significantly, a record of the appearance of the corpse of Edward I on the opening of the king's tomb in 1774 also demonstrates that he too was interred in robes and regalia associated with coronation. The king's

---

[36] For Henry II, see *Gesta regis Henrici secundi Benedicti abbatis*, ed. W. Stubbs, 2 vols., Rolls Series 49 (1867), II, 71. For John, see *Rogeri de Wendover liber qui dicitur flores historiarum*, ed. H. G. Hewlett, 3 vols., Rolls Series 84 (1886–9), II, 195. For Henry III, see 'Chronicon Thomae Wykes', in *Annales monastici*, ed. H. R. Luard, 5 vols., Rolls Series 36 (1864–9), IV, 252.

[37] 'Annales monasterii de Wintonia', in *Annales monastici*, ed. Luard, II, 71.

[38] See D. A. Carpenter, 'The Burial of King Henry III, the "Regalia" and Royal Ideology', in *The Reign of Henry III*, ed. D. A. Carpenter (London, 1996), pp. 427–61 (pp. 430–6).

[39] PRO, E 361/3, r. 8, '[. . .]fuit unctus die Coronacionis sue', printed in Hope, 'Funeral Effigies', p. 531. On the Young King, see 'Ymagines historiarium', in *Radulfi de Diceto decani Lundoniensis opera historica*, ed. W. Stubbs, 2 vols., Rolls Series 68 (1876), II, 20. See also *Matthaei Parisiensis, monachi Sancti Albani, chronica majora*, ed. H. R. Luard, 7 vols., Rolls Series 57 (1872–83), II, 319.

[40] 'Annales monasterii de Wintonia', II, 71.

[41] Carpenter, 'Burial of King Henry III', pp. 428–31, citing London, Public Record Office, E 372/116, m. 1d. At the opening of John's tomb in 1797 his corpse was described as being cloaked in a long robe of crimson damask with a 'monk's cowl' worn over the head and a sword placed in the king's hand. See V. Green, *An Account of the Discovery of the Body of King John, in the Cathedral Church of Worcester, July 17th 1797* (London, 1797), pp. 4–6. Carpenter, 'Burial of King Henry III', pp. 435–6, speculates that the monk's cowl might be interpreted as a coronation coif.

corpse is described as being bound tightly in waxed linen cloth overlaid with a dalmatic of red silk damask and wrapped around with a stole decorated with glass and beads. Within these outer layers it was revealed that the corpse was dressed in a royal mantle of crimson satin, fastened at the shoulder with a gilt-metal brooch. Edward's head was adorned with a light metal crown reckoned to be of 'inferior workmanship'. He held in his left hand a five-foot long rod surmounted with a white enamel rod, an object with clear stylistic resonances with the coronation rod associated with St Edward the Confessor, visually depicted in a lost thirteenth-century wall painting from the Painted Chamber of Westminster Palace. In the king's right hand he held a rod-like sceptre surmounted with a gilt-copper cross of 'most elegant workmanship'.[42]

The imaging of a king in death involved the juxtaposing of the physical body of the dead king with the insignia that symbolized the institution or office of kingship. This display of a dead king in the formal guise of his kingship dramatized a notion that the individual identity of a king was subsumed within the character of his kingly office. Clearly, the association connecting the individual king to the public persona of kingship was rooted in the act of anointment within coronation. Until 1272, this act of consecration was regarded as the formal moment of a king's accession, while the termination of a reign was reckoned to occur only with the actual burial of the deceased king.[43] The formal displaying of the king's corpse within funeral ritual articulated to a wider public audience the real political importance of the king's death. Equally, however, the unseen adornment of the royal corpse within its coffin testified on a deeper and more enduring level to the permanence of a king's institutional character. The re-utilization of actual coronation robes and regalia as fitting raiment for a dead king provided a tangible link between the sacral, status-altering nature of coronation within a king's lifetime and a sense of the abiding institutional identity of a king in the hereafter.[44] Only with the emergence of a new and more powerful sense of the inalienability of the coronation regalia in the later thirteenth century did it become the practice to manufacture facsimile regalia for royal burials and, later still, to cease using regalia in royal burials altogether.[45]

---

[42] J. Ayloffe, 'An Account of the Body of King Edward the First, as it Appeared on Opening his Tomb in the Year 1774', *Archaeologia* 3 (1775), 376–413.

[43] P. E. Schramm, *A History of the English Coronation*, trans. L. G. Wickham Legg (Oxford, 1937), pp. 166–7.

[44] The burial of kings in royal robes and regalia was not restricted to England in the thirteenth century. For surviving grave materials from the Castilian royal tombs at Las Huelgas, see C. Herrero Carretero, *Museo de Telas Medievales: Monasterio de Santa María la Real de Huelgas* (Madrid, 1988). The particular linkage of this practice to consecrated status is suggested by the burial of two thirteenth-century archbishops of York in their pontificals. See H. G. Ramm, 'The Tombs of Archbishop Walter de Gray (1216–55) and Godfrey de Ludham (1258–65) in York Minster, and their Contents', *Archaeologia* 103 (1971), 101–48.

[45] Carpenter, 'Burial of King Henry III', pp. 446–54.

How should the funeral of Edward II be interpreted? On the one hand, the evidence seems to suggest that the minority government of Edward III sought to pursue an orthodox path. This 'business as usual' approach was reflected in a number of aspects of the funeral arrangements. The scale and the costs of the funeral, the shouldering of administrative responsibility by the government, the status of the leading mourners and the liberal display of royal imagery around the funeral hearse, all amplified a sense of this being a distinctly royal occasion.[46] The decision to display publicly the formal insignia of kingship on a specially manufactured effigy image of Edward II clearly invited comparison with conventional, traditional practices for displaying the corpses of dead kings. Finally, the decision to inter the deposed king in his consecration robes seemed to emphasize to a perhaps surprising degree the irrevocability of anointed royal status and further suggested that the image of normality pervading the funeral arrangements was not simply restricted to public and visible aspects of the occasion.

On the other hand, if the ritual arrangements for the funeral of Edward II articulated an impression of ritual normality, manifested through the laying-on of a series of traditional practices and invented traditions, this impression of normality belied the fact that the funeral was staged within a highly irregular political context and, additionally, was removed entirely from the actual process of transferring royal authority from one king to another. In general, the burial of a king was the prelude to the coronation of a royal successor. In 1327 that chronology was reversed so that Edward III was already eleven months crowned at the time of his father's funeral. Furthermore, the fact of Edward II's deposition in January 1327 made it questionable whether he even ought to be afforded kingly status in death. Clearly, ritual practice had no established procedures for dealing with such an unusual scenario.

The funeral effigy used at the funeral of Edward II served as a surrogate corpse within the ritual, perhaps playing on an element of 'likeness' to verify the reality of Edward's death to a credulous public prepared to believe rumours of the king's escape from captivity and his survival in exile.[47] However, the key to understanding the effigy is to appreciate its function as a mannequin for displaying the institutional insignia of kingship. The visible presence of this royal insignia constituted a quite deliberate and very explicit visual statement on the nature of Edward II's royal identity within official political memory. Indeed, the unusual circumstances of Edward II's deposition

---

[46] PRO, E 101/383/2, records a total sum of £351 14s 10d received by the great wardrobe for the funeral arrangements. See Ormrod, 'Personal Religion', p. 870, n. 120.

[47] Lindley, 'Ritual, Regicide and Representation', p. 107; Haines, *Stratford*, pp. 210–11. See P. Strohm, 'Reburying Richard: Ceremony and Symbolic Relegitimation', in *England's Empty Throne: Usurpation and the Language of Legitimation, 1399–1422*, ed. P. Strohm (New Haven, CN, 1998), pp. 101–27, on the virulent rumour culture associated with Richard II's supposed survival after 1400.

and death actually created a pressure *for* the display of the dead king. This pressure was so strong that the unavailability of a corpse that could be shown constituted a major problem for the new royal government. The problem was not primarily the need to prove that Edward was truly dead. Instead, it was a problem of aesthetics linked to the key role the burying of an old king played in cementing the accession of a new king.

The most likely explanation for the prominent display of royal imagery at the funeral of Edward II was the existence of a conscious desire within the minority government of Edward III to represent the death and burial of Edward II as being part of a normal passage of royal succession. In this sense, the symbolic overtones of the funeral were entirely in keeping with the already well-established government policy of repackaging the deposition of Edward II as an act of voluntary abdication. Rather than viewing the funeral of Edward II as an embarrassing but necessary public event which ought to be banished to a remote locality, the minority government of Edward III utilized the occasion as an opportunity to buttress the position of the new king in a political environment in which there existed increasing evidence of hostility towards the ruling regime.[48] In essence, Edward II's funeral was conceived of as the occasion for a ritualized re-legitimization of the dead deposed king as a posthumous buttress to the dynastic legitimacy of his young, reigning son.

The rehabilitation of Edward II within official political memory only became possible with Edward's death, since this removed at a single stroke any residual constitutional improprieties concerning the position and authority of the new king. Although the manner of Edward III's accession was highly irregular and legally dubious, it did at least conform to a generally recognized order of succession.[49] Once Edward II was officially dead, it therefore became in the interests of Edward III to rehabilitate the political memory of his father, regardless of the inconvenient fact that Edward II's kingship had been artificially and publicly terminated. The death of Edward II liberated Edward III from the awkwardness of a situation in which the father was deemed unfit to rule, yet the rights of the son remained rooted in the principle of primogeniture.

Just as it served Edward III to emphasize retrospectively the legitimate authority of his deposed father, so also did it serve the interests of the widowed Queen Isabella. Isabella enjoyed an independent royal status as a princess of France and a natural personal influence in government as the mother of Edward III. Nevertheless, any claim that Isabella might have made to exercise real political authority within a regency government in England

---

[48] See McKisack, *Fourteenth Century*, p. 100; G. A. Holmes, 'The Rebellion of the Earl of Lancaster, 1328–9', *Bulletin of the Institute of Historical Research* 28 (1955), 84–9.

[49] Although Le Baker's unreliable assertion that Edward II was threatened with the disinheritance of his dynasty at the Kenilworth confrontation of 20 or 21 January 1327 does at least suggest that the succession rights of Edward III were not entirely beyond challenge. See *Chronicon Galfridi le Baker de Swynbroke*, ed. E. M. Thompson (Oxford, 1889), p. 28.

would have relied primarily upon her status as a widowed queen. The source of female royal authority in the later Middle Ages requires further investigation, but it is certainly intriguing, with regard to the later example of Joan of Kent, that royal motherhood alone seems not to have been a sufficient basis for gaining access to power within a minority royal government.[50] Judging by the character of Isabella's later piety and the details of her own funerary arrangements, the French queen clearly constructed her marital status as an absolutely central aspect of her self-identity. During her long years of privileged incarceration, Isabella celebrated the anniversary of Edward II's death in the same manner as she did those of other members of her immediate family. When she died in 1358, the dowager queen was dressed for burial in her wedding robes of 1308, articulating in this action a sense of the sacramental permanency of marriage, just as the burial of kings in coronation robes spoke of the permanency of anointed status. Meanwhile, Edward's heart casket was placed upon her chest.[51]

In the longer term, the political rehabilitation and re-legitimation of Edward II through his funeral celebrations set the tone for the attitude that Edward III adopted towards his father's memory over the subsequent course of his reign. Historians have sometimes been rather baffled by an apparent ambivalence in Edward III's attitude in this respect. On the one hand, Edward exhibited a noticeable degree of pious public devotion to his father's memory which was in keeping with his response to the deaths of other close members of his family.[52] In December 1328, for example, Edward III was at Gloucester to mark the first anniversary of his father's burial. Later, in September 1337, he visited the abbey once again, thereby giving tacit acknowledgement to the popular cult of the deposed king.[53] Edward also directed considerable royal

---

[50] On Joan, see W. M. Ormrod, 'In Bed with Joan of Kent: The King's Mother and the Peasants' Revolt', in *Medieval Women: Texts and Contexts in Late Medieval Britain. Essays for Felicity Riddy*, ed. J. Wogan-Browne, R. Voaden, A. Diamond, A. Hutchison, C. Meale and L. Johnson (Turnhout, 2000), pp. 277–92. Of course, the opportunities presented to Joan may have been inhibited by the fallout from Isabella's period of government.

[51] F. D. Blackley, 'Isabella of France, Queen of England 1308–1358, and the Late Medieval Cult of the Dead', *Canadian Journal of History* 14 (1980), 23–47; Blackley, 'The Tomb of Isabella', p. 161.

[52] Ormrod, 'Personal Religion', pp. 867–72.

[53] The implications of the timing of Edward III's visit of 1328 have not been remarked upon previously by historians. However, see D. Welander, *The History, Art and Architecture of Gloucester Cathedral* (Stroud, 1991), p. 144; Holmes, 'Rebellion of Lancaster', p. 84, citing *Calendar of Patent Rolls, 1327–30*, pp. 330–47 and 353–5 and *Calendar of Close Rolls, 1327–30*, pp. 336–56 and 420–5. For the 1337 visit, see Ormrod, 'Personal Religion', pp. 870–1. On the popular cult, see S. Walker, 'Political Saints in Later Medieval England', in *The McFarlane Legacy: Studies in Late Medieval Politics and Society*, ed. R. H. Britnell and A. J. Pollard (Stroud, 1995), pp. 77–106; J. M. Theilmann, 'Political Canonization and Political Symbolism in Medieval England', *Journal of British Studies* 29 (1990), 241–66.

patronage towards the monastic house at Gloucester, famously with his gift to the abbey in 1343 of a golden ship in fulfilment of a vow, but also in all likelihood as the patron of his father's magnificent and ostentatiously modern alabaster effigy and tomb constructed within the Abbey during the 1330s.[54] On the other hand, however, Edward III was considerably less than energetic when it came to investigating the circumstances of his father's death and he was notably lenient in his dealings with those accused of involvement in the king's murder.[55]

The rather ambivalent public attitude which Edward III exhibited towards the memory of his father underlines the peculiarity of the niche which Edward II occupied within the dynastic perspective of his son. The treatment of Edward II at his funeral responded to a pressing dynastic need on the part of Edward III and his advisors to rehabilitate the dangerously tarnished authority of an immediate progenitor. In essence, the ritualized rewriting of the political memory of Edward II was concerned with recovering and safeguarding the dignity and security of the office of kingship, which had been seriously eroded as a result of Edward's deposition. However, this ritualized, retrospective recognition of Edward II's honoured place within a succession of kings did not amount to an actual re-evaluation of the qualities or track record of his kingship. In this sense, the essentially pragmatic attitude taken by Edward III to the memory of his father was markedly different from the positively sympathetic attitude towards Edward II that was later exhibited by the deposed king's great-grandson, Richard II.[56]

Much historical debate on medieval royal ritual during the first part of the twentieth century centred around the argument over whether ritual should be characterized mostly in terms of continuity or mostly in terms of change. What the funeral of Edward II illustrates very effectively is that it was the interplay of continuity and change that gave political meaning and relevance to the performance of funeral rituals for the deposed king. Edward's funeral, like his deposition, was characterized by the fundamental paradox that it needed to employ innovation in order to seem ordinary.

By analysing medieval rituals in relation to their performative context it becomes possible to explore an important distinction between the 'purposes' and 'uses' of rites of passage.[57] Van Gennep's identification of the rite of passage as a process that effects and marks a changing of status in a ritual actor has encouraged anthropologists and subsequently historians to approach the study of rituals in typological terms. Accumulated observations of ritual practice are distilled to reveal the ritual in its basic or purest form, allowing the essential purpose served by the ritual within society to be better understood.

---

[54] *Historia monasterii Sancti Petri*, ed. Hart, I, 45–6. See also Ormrod, 'Personal Religion', pp. 870–1; Welander, *Gloucester Cathedral*, p. 147.

[55] Tout, 'Captivity and Death', pp. 98–100.

[56] Theilmann, 'Political Canonization', pp. 252–8.

[57] T. Gerholm, 'On Ritual: A Post-Modernist View', *Ethnos* 3–4 (1988), 190–203.

Yet, if historians seek to understand a ritual's purpose by analysing the common denominators in a mass of recorded ritual practice or, as is more commonly the case, through analysis of prescriptive injunctions on rituals preserved in liturgical texts and other surviving manuals, there is an inevitable danger that the contextual 'usefulness' that any particular ritual may have had for its participants will be lost from sight.

Since the study of medieval royal rituals has largely been undertaken with prescriptive texts providing the main source of evidence, there can be a tendency for research to reinforce an understanding of ritual as ordered and essentially unchanging. Additionally, such texts tend to point to the existence of canonical meanings lodged in the symbolism inherent within ritual practice, whether the prescribed symbols are objects, images, gestures or phrases. However, when ritual is examined in terms of performative practice rather then written prescription it is apparent that meanings were not only arbitrary, but ultimately were determined by the way in which individual participants and spectators experienced the ritual. Indeed, rites of passage will always be *experienced* more than they are *understood* by their participants. The contexts and juxtapositions in which familiar symbols were deployed within past rituals shaped the varied meanings and understandings of the ritual engendered in the participants. It is therefore only by examining the sensory environment in which a ritual was performed that it becomes possible to approach an understanding of how a participant's experience of the ritual was shaped and framed.

The great royal rites of passage of the fourteenth century were inherently purposeful in terms of legitimating the transference of sovereign authority from one ruler to another. However, what made the performance of ritual a political as well as a symbolic activity was the fact that it was useful as well as necessary. While prescription and tradition dictated that the basic formula of a ritual remain the same, it was the malleable nature of the performance that shaped each rite of passage as a unique opportunity for the organizer and experience for the participant. In this sense, the funeral of Edward II was only different from other royal rites of passage of the fourteenth century in that its invented tradition of deploying a funeral effigy of the dead king represented a more extreme example of the politicization of ritual performance.

Coming to Kingship:
Boy Kings and the Passage to Power
in Fourteenth-Century England

W. M. Ormrod

Rites of passage were a fundamental part of the repertoire of medieval (as they are of modern) monarchy, and played both a symbolic and a substantive role in the making and unmaking of kings.[1] There has been a good deal of work done especially on the religious aspects of these medieval rites, some of it informed by modern sociological and anthropological approaches, and all of it yielding interesting perspectives on the cultural significance of Christian doctrine and Catholic liturgy in the processes of ordered dynastic succession during the Middle Ages.[2] One need say little more in support of the argument that royal *inauguration* rituals in particular offer special insights into the way that medieval society negotiated the passage of power from one ruler to the next and invested the new regime with the constitutional and moral authority held to be inherent to the office of king.[3] In the present study, however, I want to consider the degree to which those rituals and other associated processes could be disturbed by, or adapted to fit, a particular and potentially anomalous situation: namely, the accession of a boy ruler to the English throne. My primary

---

[1]   I assume throughout the general definition of 'rites of passage' worked out by M. Rubin in the Introduction to this volume, and apply it to those ceremonies and events that marked changes in the personal or political lives of medieval monarchs. For the general role of ceremonial events in the life of a king, see the interesting range of case-studies covered in *Rituals of Royalty: Power and Ceremonial in Traditional Societies*, ed. D. Cannadine and S. Price (Cambridge, 1987), and in S. Bertelli, *The King's Body: Sacred Rituals of Power in Medieval and Early Modern Europe*, trans. R. B. Litchfield (University Park, PA, 2001), as well as the more detailed work on royal entries represented by G. Kipling, *Enter the King: Theatre, Liturgy, and Ritual in the Medieval Civic Triumph* (Oxford, 1998). It must be stressed throughout, however, that the present study is not about ritual in general but about those 'rites' that had some transformative effect on the status, role and/or public *persona* of the king.

[2]   For a general survey, see D. Cannadine, 'Introduction: Divine Rites of Kings', in *Rituals of Royalty*, ed. Cannadine and Price, pp. 1–19.

[3]   The literature is very large. Among recent work, the research of J. L. Nelson, *Politics and Ritual in Early Medieval Europe* (London, 1986), is fundamental. For a useful, succinct overview see R. A. Jackson, 'Kingship, Rituals of: Coronation', in *Dictionary of the Middle Ages*, ed. J. R. Strayer, 13 vols. (New York, 1982–9), VII, 256–9.

examples are the two that fall within the fourteenth century, Edward III and Richard II; although I shall be making comparisons with other examples between the thirteenth and sixteenth centuries, I should stress that my choice of focus is not merely dictated by the chronological confines of the present volume but reflects the fact that Edward III and Richard II represent a natural pairing, just as Henry III and Henry VI represent another, and that, although there was no formal observation of precedent in the arrangements made for the accession of boy kings, there are some interesting parallels (as well as some telling differences) to be observed in the manner and means by which Edward and Richard came into the plenitude of their royal power.

Since it will be necessary to trace, in order, the various steps by which kings too young to rule at the time of their accession achieved full authority later in their reigns, it may be helpful to set out here, very briefly, both the conceptual framework in which I am operating and the sequence of rituals through which I will argue that boy rulers had to pass before they could assert their full authority. This study represents a conscious attempt to move the focus of attention away from liturgical occasions and to suggest that there was a whole series of other rites of passage through which youthful rulers passed en route to earning the right to rule: these involved life-events (such as marriage and fatherhood), 'career firsts' (such as experience of leadership in war) and political initiatives (assertions of will in the exercise of government and more formal statements of the beginning of majority rule). As Joel Burden's work demonstrates, even the great set-piece liturgical moments in royal rites of passage – burial and coronation – were not straightforward and uncontested, and involved significant elements of secular ceremonial and political negotiation that tend too often to be ignored in preference for the better documented rituals of regalia.[4] It is my contention that where the youth of the new king compromised his ability to rule in his own right, a whole series of adjustments had to be made to the conventions of royal succession that fragmented and prolonged the process of inauguration and incorporated into it a series of significant events in the life and acts of the monarch.

We need to start this analysis with a clear statement that there was no formal prescription in medieval England either as to what arrangements ought to be made for the governance of the realm when the king was obviously too young to rule or, indeed, as to when such a king might be thought to be ready to assume the reins of power.[5] Although, as we shall see, certain significance

---

[4] J. F. Burden, 'Rituals of Royalty: Prescription, Politics and Practice in English Coronation and Royal Funeral Rituals, c. 1327 to c. 1485' (unpublished D.Phil. dissertation, University of York, 1999); and see J. Burden in this volume. For debate on the significance of the queen's coronation in later medieval England, see J. L. Laynesmith, 'Fertility Rite or Authority Ritual? The Queen's Coronation in England, 1445–87', in *Social Attitudes and Political Structures in the Fifteenth Century*, ed. T. Thornton (Stroud, 2000), pp. 52–68.

[5] C. T. Wood, *Joan of Arc and Richard III* (Oxford, 1988), pp. 29–44; F. L. Wiswall III, 'Royal Minorities and Protectorates in England, 1216–1549' (unpublished M.Litt. dissertation, University of St Andrews, 1989).

appears to have been attached to the notion of an age of majority at twenty-one in the cases of Henry III and Richard II, the parallel with the practice whereby the heir of a deceased tenant in chief could be kept in custody and only enter his estate at the attainment of that age did not bear directly on the circumstances of boy kings for the precise reason that (as was made clear in the arrangements for Henry VI's minority) the crown itself could not be considered a piece of real estate.[6] It is possible that some acknowledgement was made of the philosophical and canonical position whereby a child was deemed to pass from a stage of *infantia* (which lasted from birth to the age of seven) through *pueritia* (from seven to fourteen) into *adolescentia* (at fourteen):[7] this, with a little adjustment for precise ages and different political circumstances and cultures, might explain why Henry III had a regent and Henry VI, Edward V and Edward VI had protectors at the beginnings of their reigns, and why Edward III, at fourteen, was deemed old enough to function without such formal bestowal of substitute power onto another individual – though it also raises questions as to why Richard II, who was nine when he became king, had no regent for his first four or five years on the throne.[8] In certain respects, indeed, it is much easier to come to terms with the formal minority administrations of babies and infants – as with Henry III and Henry VI – than with the complicated and not wholly consistent positions adopted in 1327 and 1377.

The answer to the puzzle of what happened on those two latter occasions lies largely in the politics of the moment. In 1327, the fourteen-year-old Edward III might in a number of respects have been considered old enough to rule in his own right, and the arrangements made in his first parliament for an advisory council of senior political figures headed by Henry of Lancaster represented not so much a curb on his prerogative as the application of appropriate wisdom to his youthful regime.[9] But this was confounded by the competing claim of the new king's mother, Queen Isabella, the architect of the revolution that had brought about the downfall of Edward II and, as the daughter of Philip IV of France, a woman prepared to take herself seriously as a political figure in an otherwise masculine world. The *de facto* regency that

6 J. S. Roskell, 'The Office and Dignity of Protector of England with Special Reference to Its Origins', *English Historical Review* 68 (1953), 193–231; P. and F. Strong, 'The Last Will and Codicils of Henry V', *English Historical Review* 96 (1981), 78–102; R. A. Griffiths, *The Reign of King Henry VI: The Exercise of Royal Authority, 1422–1461* (London, 1981), p. 20.

7 N. Orme, *From Childhood to Chivalry: The Education of the English Kings and Aristocracy, 1066–1530* (London, 1984), p. 6.

8 See also discussion by A. Tuck, *Crown and Nobility, 1272–1461* (London, 1985), p. 175; R. Horrox, *Richard III: A Study of Service* (Cambridge, 1989), pp. 92–4; J. Watts, *Henry VI and the Politics of Kingship* (Cambridge, 1996), p. 120.

9 For this council, see J. F. Baldwin, 'The King's Council', in *The English Government at Work, 1327–1336*, ed. J. F. Willard, W. A. Morris, J. R. Strayer and W. H. Dunham, 3 vols. (Cambridge, MA, 1930–40), I, 129–61 (pp. 131–3). For what follows, see F. L. Wiswall III, 'Politics, Procedure and the "Non-Minority" of Edward III: Some Comparisons', in *The Age of Richard II*, ed. J. L. Gillespie (Stroud, 1997), pp. 7–25.

Isabella established for herself (and, through her, for her lover Roger Mortimer) was probably based on French precedent,[10] and the politically contentious nature of its work probably did much to discredit the practice of appointing women regents in later medieval England. It was the queen mother's ambition, then, and not necessarily the incapacity of her adolescent son, that caused the monarchy to be put into leading reins in 1327. Fifty years later, and in light of the precedent set by Edward III, it would have been much more difficult to argue that the nine-year-old Richard II had the capacity to rule alone, and the idea of a regency or protectorate may only have been abandoned because of the public distrust attaching to the only man fittingly placed to do the job, the new king's uncle, John of Gaunt.[11] And yet the compromise system devised to operate during Richard's nonage – that of a series of permanent or 'continual' councils to monitor and approve the dispensation of the royal grace – was itself abandoned (on grounds of cost) within three years,[12] suggesting that the political community was quite prepared (as it had been under the original scheme for Edward III's government in 1327) to tolerate a fairly liberal and informal system of checks upon the otherwise unfettered exercise of authority by young kings.

In coming to terms with what to us seems both an inconsistent and an astonishingly naive system for the transfer of effective power, it is necessary to point out that the king's right to rule was determined not by temporal age alone but also by his state of mind and quality of judgement. David Carpenter and John Watts have demonstrated, in their important studies of the minorities of Henry III and Henry VI, that the principal debate about coming to power centred on these kings' inclination, fitness and credibility to rule.[13] Thus, Watts has argued that the problem with establishing Henry VI's majority was not to do with the unscrupulous attempts of magnates to prolong their hold on power by artificially extending the fat years of minority corporate government, but simply because the vacuous Henry, who was fifteen when first prodded into action, could not be persuaded to undertake his responsibilities seriously and consistently.[14] Conversely, the papal permission granted to the fifteen-year-old Henry III to make personal use of his great seal

---

[10] A. Poulet, 'Capetian Women and the Regency: The Genesis of a Vocation', in *Medieval Queenship*, ed. J. C. Parsons (Stroud, 1993), pp. 93–116.

[11] A. Tuck, *Richard II and the English Nobility* (London, 1973), pp. 33–5; N. Saul, *Richard II* (London, 1997), pp. 27–30.

[12] N. B. Lewis, 'The "Continual Council" in the Early Years of Richard II, 1377–80', *English Historical Review* 41 (1926), 246–51; Tuck, *Richard II and the English Nobility*, pp. 35–49.

[13] D. A. Carpenter, *The Minority of Henry III* (London, 1990); Watts, *Henry VI*, pp. 102–204.

[14] See also J. L. Watts, 'The Counsels of King Henry VI, c. 1435–45', *English Historical Review* 106 (1991), 279–98; J. L. Watts, 'When did Henry VI's Minority End?', in *Trade, Devotion and Governance: Papers in Later Medieval History*, ed. D. J. Clayton, R. G. Davies and P. McNiven (Stroud, 1994), pp. 116–39.

indicated, as Carpenter puts it, 'that the maturity of the king's understanding made up for his immaturity in years'.[15] This emphasis on the capacity and inclinations of the boy king has important implications in our own case at least for Richard II, since the abandonment of the continual councils in 1380 is highly unlikely to have been requested and sanctioned by parliament had there not been a clear sign of the king's ability and willingness, though still only thirteen, to undertake at least some of the functions of an adult ruler. The high expectations that informed and accompanied such a transfer of power are, of course, evident slightly later in the chronicle accounts of the Peasants' Revolt, where the fourteen-year-old Richard is represented as the heroic and dynamic leader to whom all parties looked for effective action.[16] Clearly, then, age was both a relative and a slippery concept in the political culture of later medieval England.

All this is by way of prelude to a more systematic analysis of the stages through which both Edward III and Richard II passed between the moment of accession and the assumption of full control over their own regimes. To revert to that programme of events and rituals, I propose to divide the occasions in question into three categories: life events, initiations into the functions of monarchy and formal assertions of political authority. In order to stress their comparatively modest role in the story that I have to tell, I shall not say much about the rites that precipitated this longer process: namely, the death and burial of the old king and the formal succession and coronation of the new one. Not only was that order of events reversed in one of the cases that I examine, at the accession of Edward III,[17] but, more significantly, the role of the coronation in the process to which I refer here is much more symbolic than real. Since 1272, when it was determined that a new king's reign should date from his accession and not merely from his time of coronation,[18] the crowning ceremony had become, in effect, an occasion out of real time and could take place whenever was thought politically or logistically convenient. Thus, the coronations of Edward III and Richard II had nothing in themselves to demonstrate about the nature of the regimes that they confirmed: unlike Henry III's first coronation of 1216, which effectively constituted his position as king, the coronations of

---

[15] Carpenter, *Minority of Henry III*, p. 302. Similar signs of early fitness to take up the responsibilities of personal rule were later exhibited by the teenage Edward VI: J. Loach, *Edward VI* (London, 1999), pp. 97–102.

[16] Saul, *Richard II*, pp. 56–82; W. M. Ormrod, 'The Peasants' Revolt and the Government of England', *Journal of British Studies* 29 (1990), 1–30 (pp. 20–1); W. M. Ormrod, 'In Bed with Joan of Kent. The King's Mother and the Peasants' Revolt', in *Medieval Women: Texts and Contexts in Late Medieval Britain. Essays for Felicity Riddy*, ed. J. Wogan-Browne, R. Voaden, A. Diamond, A. Hutchinson, C. M. Meale and L. Johnson (Turnhout, 2000), pp. 277–92 (pp. 285–7).

[17] See the study by J. Burden in this volume.

[18] *Select Charters and Other Illustrations of English Constitutional History from the Earliest Times to the Reign of Edward I*, ed. W. Stubbs, 9th edn (Oxford, 1913), pp. 438–40; E. H. Kantorowicz, *The King's Two Bodies: A Study in Mediaeval Political Theology* (Princeton, 1957), pp. 328–9.

Edward III and Richard II were carried out soon after the dates of accession mainly in order to provide a sense of stability at moments of high political tension; and in fact none of these three coronations denoted in itself the unqualified inauguration into power of the relevant boy kings.[19] A parallel but distinct point can be made in terms of the timing of Henry VI's English and French coronations in 1429 and 1431. In this case the coronations were not carried out at the start of the reign, but delayed until the king had passed the age of seven: although the protectorate was formally concluded at this point on the grounds that the king had now personally undertaken the defence of the realm and the Church, the ceremonies were unconnected in themselves with the process of transfer from a minority to a majority regime.[20] One potentially important point to consider in this respect is the fact that, in spite of the divine sanction that coronation conferred, and the special mystical authority bestowed by the accompanying ritual of anointing, there is no direct evidence that any of the medieval kings discussed here systematically exercised the thaumaturgical powers associated with their office before formally asserting their right to rule (in the case of Edward III) or entering at least a transitional period from minority to majority (as in that of Henry VI).[21] My focus, therefore, is not on the formalized religious rites associated with royal inauguration but on the practical and political aspects of the transformation of boy kings into adult rulers.

The first category of rites of passage I have identified in the coming to power of such boy rulers are what I have called (according to the modern social science usage) 'life events'.[22] These are the occasions that mark out changes in the lifecycle and which, if they are repeatable, are held to be of special significance in their first manifestation: I am referring to the changes of

[19] Henry III was held to have acceded on the date of his coronation, 28 October 1216 (his predecessor having died on 18/19 October); Edward III acceded on 25 January 1327 (the day after his predecessor's death) and was crowned on 1 February; Richard II acceded on 22 June 1377 (the day after his predecessor's death) and was crowned on 16 July. By comparison, Edward I was held to have acceded on the day of his predecessor's funeral (20 November 1272, four days after Henry III's death) and was crowned on 19 August 1274; Edward II acceded on 8 July 1307 and was crowned on 25 February 1308.

[20] Griffiths, *Reign of King Henry VI*, pp. 189–94; Watts, *Henry VI*, pp. 117–18 and 120.

[21] The material relating both to the royal touch and to the provision of cramp rings is problematic for reasons set out by Marc Bloch, *The Royal Touch: Sacred Monarchy and Scrofula in England and France*, trans. J. E. Anderson (London, 1973), pp. 246–52. In particular, we have no direct evidence of practice under Richard II. However, the absence of any references to either practice in the surviving household accounts for Edward III's reign before 1330 seems instructive (see the further details of such accounts missed by Bloch, discussed by W. M. Ormrod, 'The Personal Religion of Edward III', *Speculum* 64 [1989], 849–77 [pp. 862–3]), as may be the fact that the earliest references to the provision of cramp rings in the accounts for Henry VI comes only from 1442 (Bloch, *Royal Touch*, p. 251).

[22] E.g., L. H. Cohen, *Life Events and Psychological Functioning: Theoretical and Methodological Issues* (Newbury Park, CA, 1988).

status associated with marriage and the production of children. These can be considered important in the lifecycle of any medieval king (and, indeed, of anyone else), but they did not play a dynamic part in the ruler's coming to power if the wife and at least some of the children were already, as it were, in place at the time of accession: the weddings and births of members of the wider royal family beyond the direct line of succession did not necessarily create the public excitement in medieval England that they were later accustomed to generate in the media-minded twentieth century.[23] Such events could take on a much greater significance in the case of rulers who succeeded to the throne at sufficiently young an age to have their adult life events take place within the span of their own reigns. This point applies to some degree to those who succeeded when fully of age to rule: witness in our period the case of Edward II, twenty-three at the time of his accession, whose coronation was delayed in order to allow it to be a double ceremony following his nuptials with Isabella of France, and whose first offspring, the future Edward III, was therefore born in the purple in 1312.[24] There are particular reasons, however, to assume that life events took on an even greater resonance in the reigns of kings who acceded as boys. Marriage marked an important stage in the assertion of a male's personal independence, and the birth of a first son proved the father's maturity and potency as well as securing him a supporter and successor in the next generation.[25] Marriage and the production of children therefore represented the transition from adolescence to adulthood that was a necessary precondition to the transfer of full power into the hands of a king who had been reigning, in a technical sense, since boyhood.

The stories of the marriages of Edward III and Richard II confirm this hypothesis, if only, ironically, in the first case by demonstrating how the principle was temporarily confounded by those who wished to keep the young king in the confines of unofficial regency. Edward III's marriage to Philippa of Hainault took place in York Minster on 26 January 1328.[26] Contemporary commentators had comparatively little to say about the match,

---

23 Thus see, e.g., the problems surrounding the identification of Edward I's children by his first wife: J. C. Parsons, 'The Year of Eleanor of Castile's Birth and her Children by Edward I', *Mediaeval Studies* 46 (1984), 249–65.

24 E. A. R. Brown, *Customary Aids and Royal Finance in Capetian France: The Marriage Aid of Philip the Fair* (Cambridge, MA, 1992), pp. 12–22.

25 This point can be traced in detail both through the 'ages of man' *topos* and through a gendered approach that sees masculinity as assumed and defined by the transition of males, via marriage, from youth to maturity. See, amongst much else, E. Sears, *The Ages of Man: Medieval Interpretations of the Life Cycle* (Princeton, 1986), pp. 98–9; S. Mosher Stuard, 'Burdens of Matrimony: Husbanding and Gender in Medieval Italy', in *Medieval Masculinities: Regarding Men in the Middle Ages*, ed. C. A. Lees (Minneapolis, 1994), pp. 61–71.

26 The date has been established by C. Shenton, 'The English Court and the Restoration of Royal Prestige, 1327–1345' (unpublished D.Phil. dissertation, University of Oxford, 1995), p. 149.

or the ceremony,[27] partly perhaps because they were probably unimpressed with the daughter of a mere Netherlandish duke when they had been used, in recent generations, to attracting high-status French and Spanish princesses as their queens. We may suggest, however, that there was another reason for the muted response: namely, the fact that England already had a queen, Isabella, who was now in effect running the realm, had negotiated the alliance with Hainault more or less independently, and had clearly determined to create for herself a form of regency that allowed her to exercise a significant part of the royal prerogative power.[28] The only way that court ritual, and the political culture that surrounded it, could accommodate the (not infrequent) phenom-enon of two queens was to have the widow of the old king give precedence to the wife of the new one: this is what indeed had happened in Isabella's favour after her own arrival in England in 1308, when Edward I's second wife (and Isabella's aunt), Margaret of France, had gradually distanced herself from the functions of consort and taken to a quiet retirement.[29] Isabella's strat-egy was the very opposite: significantly, she was accused of depriving her new daughter-in-law of coronation until February 1330,[30] thus compromising the functioning of the latter's queenship and belittling her status: it was Isabella, not Philippa, who performed the symbolic functions of intercessor for the king's grace (sometimes in effect interceding with *herself*) during 1328 and 1329.[31] Richard II's marriage to Anne of Bohemia on 20 January 1382,[32] by contrast, was a much more obvious turning point in his own coming to kingship. Richard's mother, Joan of Kent, princess of Wales, had acted in some respects as a kind of queenly substitute during his boyhood years, but lacked (as Philippa had originally lacked) the validation of coronation to establish her formally in this role. Anne of Bohemia therefore provided England with

---

[27] 'Gesta Edwardi de Carnarvan auctore canonico Bridlingtoniensis cum continua-tione ad A.D. 1377', in *Chronicles of the Reigns of Edward I and Edward II*, ed. W. Stubbs, 2 vols., Rolls Series 76 (London, 1882–3), II, 99; 'Annales Paulini', in *Chronicles of the Reigns of Edward I and Edward II*, ed. Stubbs, I, 338–9. By contrast, modern scholarship has invested the marriage with considerable significance, mainly because of its role in the transmission of cultural forms from the courtly traditions of Northern France and the Low Countries: see J. Vale, *Edward III and Chivalry: Chivalric Society and its Contexts, 1270–1350* (Woodbridge, 1982), pp. 43–7.

[28] The fullest account of Isabella's role is P. C. Doherty, 'Isabella, Queen of England 1308–1330' (unpublished D.Phil. dissertation, University of Oxford, 1977). See also N. M. Fryde, *The Tyranny and Fall of Edward II, 1321–1326* (Cambridge, 1979), pp. 207–27.

[29] J. C. Parsons, 'The Intercessionary Patronage of Queens Margaret and Isabella of France', in *Thirteenth Century England VI*, ed. M. Prestwich, R. H. Britnell and R. Frame (Woodbridge, 1997), pp. 145–56.

[30] *Rotuli parliamentorum*, 6 vols. (London, 1783), II, 7, 11. For Philippa's coronation, see Shenton, 'English Court', pp. 145–8.

[31] Parsons, 'Intercessionary Patronage', p. 156.

[32] Saul, *Richard II*, p. 90.

the prospect of its first genuine queen since Philippa's own death in 1369, and, despite the ambivalence of some of the chroniclers with regard to the diplomatic context of the marriage,[33] the wedding – and the coronation that followed hard upon, on 22 January – were given enormous significance by the political community in parliament: Anne's newly acquired role as peace-maker was exploited in order to justify the otherwise rather sensitive decision to resolve the issues arising from the recent Peasants' Revolt by abandoning the policy of repression and adopting the politics of pardon.[34] Anne in 1382 therefore represented a much more obvious 'new' stage in the career of her husband than had Philippa in 1328, though both weddings arguably marked an important rite of passage in personal terms for kings whose office relied to some degree on the existence of a consort to fulfil the full range of functions associated with monarchy in later medieval England.[35]

I have intimated above that marriage alone, however, had only limited potential as a political or constitutional rite of passage. As John Carmi Parsons has shown, it was often only with her first pregnancy, and her first son, that the queen herself really reached political maturity.[36] It is suggested here that something of the same issue also attaches to the office of king when held by juveniles. The failure of a royal couple to bear children had something of an infantilizing effect on *both* parties: we know from the example of Henry VI that the king's political credibility was compromised by the long period between his marriage to Margaret of Anjou in 1445 and the birth of their only son in 1453.[37] Something of the same point might be applied to Richard II, whose twelve-year marriage to Anne of Bohemia was, for whatever reason, childless.[38] It is now very difficult for us to appreciate how his subjects articulated their speculations on Richard's lack of offspring and its future

---

[33] Ibid., pp. 90–1.
[34] Ormrod, 'In Bed with Joan of Kent', pp. 287–91. See also Anne's role as *mediatrix* for the Londoners in 1381–2: P. Strohm, *Hochon's Arrow* (Princeton, 1992), pp. 105–6.
[35] Laynesmith, 'Fertility Rite or Authority Ritual?', p. 68, argues that the coronation of a queen following her marriage 'made the king's kingship complete'.
[36] J. C. Parsons, 'Family, Sex, and Power: The Rhythms of Medieval Queenship', in *Medieval Queenship*, ed. Parsons, pp. 1–11 (pp. 4–5). The point is developed more generally in relation to the queen's fecundity in J. C. Parsons, 'The Pregnant Queen as Counsellor and the Medieval Construction of Motherhood', in *Medieval Mothering*, ed. J. C. Parsons and B. Wheeler (New York, 1996), pp. 39–61. Parsons, 'Intercessionary Patronage', pp. 149 and 152–3, shows how Anne of Bohemia assumed a political role as a kind of substitute for fecundity, and explores the unusual case of Queen Isabella, who assumed the role of *mediatrix* as soon as she arrived in England, rather than (as would normally be expected) after the withdrawal/death of the dowager queen (and/or the new queen's first pregnancy).
[37] Griffiths, *Reign of King Henry VI*, pp. 231–74.
[38] C. M. Barron, 'Richard II: Image and Reality', in *Making and Meaning: The Wilton Diptych*, ed. D. Gordon (London, 1993), pp. 3–19 (p. 15) suggests that Richard and Anne may have observed the medieval convention of chastity within marriage; but see also Saul, *Richard II*, pp. 456–7.

consequences.[39] But if we match the basic anthropological model of an adolescent becoming a man by fathering a male child with the special dynastic imperative inherent in medieval monarchy, it may not be too hazardous to suggest that those issues found some coded expression in the debate at the time of Richard's deposition concerning the king's so-called 'youth'.[40] One of the things that Henry IV had was a quiverful of sturdy sons. Youth and age thus become defined partly in terms of generational shift: to become 'mature' (in every sense of the word) demanded the achievement of progeny. And this, of course, is what Edward III and Queen Philippa had done – ultimately, indeed, spectacularly so.[41] Their case emphasizes most particularly the point I am making about the birth of children in the coming to power of youthful kings, for it was precisely the public disclosure of Philippa's first pregnancy in 1330 that created an effective fracture in Queen Isabella's assumed powers of regency. It was held imperative that Philippa be crowned before she gave birth (an interesting perspective worthy of discussion in its own right); and her elevation to the full rank of crowned and anointed royal consort inevitably raised issues about the basis on which Isabella herself continued to exercise royal power.[42] The birth of the new Prince Edward in June – like his father, born in the purple – had a galvanizing effect at least upon the king, himself now approaching his eighteenth birthday: while the specific timing of the coup carried out by Edward III and his close friends against Roger Mortimer and Queen Isabella at Nottingham in October 1330 must be accounted for principally in terms of pragmatism, there remains a strong sense in which this strike for power was itself driven by the special frustration felt by a husband and new father at the humiliating infantilization he had suffered at the hands of his mother and her lover.

My second category of events in the transformation of boy kings into fully-fledged rulers consists of what I earlier called 'career firsts': the initiations into a particular range of activities that were especially valorized in kings and were therefore performed in a ritualistic manner and invested with special symbolic significance. Prior to the fourteenth century, there was a whole range of administrative and judicial functions that might be included in this category: the first time the king personally authorized the use of the great seal, presided over his council or sat in judgment in the exchequer or the superior courts. By the fourteenth century, however, the inexorable development of bureaucratic monarchy had reached a stage in which the king's presence in these contexts and on these

---

[39] The only reasonably clear evidence relates to the debate on the succession, for which see Saul, *Richard II*, pp. 396–7. The wider question of Richard's attitude towards the extended royal family has not been systematically addressed, but useful frameworks in which to consider this matter are provided by R. A. Griffiths, *King and Country: England and Wales in the Fifteenth Century* (London, 1991), pp. 1–10 and 83–101.

[40] M. Bennett, *Richard II and the Revolution of 1399* (Stroud, 1999), pp. 197–8. For the tradition that youthful kings took no counsel or bad counsel, see below at nn. 72–3.

[41] W. M. Ormrod, 'Edward III and his Family', *Journal of British Studies* 26 (1987), 398–422 (p. 398).

[42] Shenton, 'English Court', p. 146.

occasions had become token or even fictional. A good example is provided by the practices of the chancery, the office of the king's great seal. The great seal was fundamental to the exercise of royal prerogative since it was in instruments authorized by it that the crown dispensed all major patronage. The transition from minority to majority under Henry III can to some degree, indeed, be traced principally in terms of the king's relations to the great seal.[43] For the first two years of the reign there was no great seal at all; from 1218 Henry had a seal, but no personal control over it; from 1223 he had personal custody of the seal but was restricted in his use of it; and finally, in 1227, he assumed the right to issue charters under the great seal, thus, in effect, declaring himself to be in full control of the government conducted in his name. What made the existence, control and functioning of the great seal such a live issue during Henry III's early years was the understanding that the regency and minority ought not to issue any acts that permanently alienated the king's landed and jurisdictional rights: such, indeed, was the sensitivity of the matter that a number of benefi-ciaries felt that the charters issued to them after Henry's assumption of major-ity (at the age of nineteen) were still not fully valid and sought to renew them after he reached twenty-one – an unassailable age of majority which had the weighty sanction of feudal law.[44] By contrast, there was no gradual 'working in' of the great seal during the minorities of Edward III, Richard II and Henry VI: in each case, the young king was assumed to have taken control of the seal from the outset of his reign.[45] Convention demanded that the exercise of patronage be limited until the king was in a position to assert his own will,[46] but this was interpreted merely in terms of the sort of discretion that came with the ability to reason and discriminate, *not* with the formal assumption of a majority: this explains why it was possible, if still contentious, for Richard II and Henry VI to use their personal seal, the signet, as a means of authorizing major grants under the great seal in advance of their technical and formal assumptions of full power.[47] And even in the case of Edward III, where there is clear evidence that the royal will was flouted in the appropriation of patronage by Queen Isabella and Roger Mortimer, it remains striking that neither the king nor his subjects, in the manner of the previous century, thought to question the validity of the new charters issued between 1327 and 1330.[48] The achievement of majority by

---

[43] For what follows, see Carpenter, *Minority of Henry III*, pp. 94, 301–2, 321–3 and 389.

[44] Ibid., pp. 123–4.

[45] Wiswall, '"Non-Minority" of Edward III', pp. 8–12.

[46] W. M. Ormrod, *The Reign of Edward III: Crown and Political Society in England, 1327–1377* (London, 1990), p. 43.

[47] Tuck, *Richard II and the English Nobility*, pp. 33, 53–4 and 65–9; B. Wolffe, *Henry VI* (London, 1981), p. 25. Watts, *Henry VI*, p. 147 and n. 99, indicates the problem of asso-ciating signet letters with the personal will of Henry VI.

[48] That is, there was no rush after 1330, as there had been in 1327 (and was to be again in 1377), to secure confirmations of existing charters: see *Calendar of the Charter Rolls Preserved in the Public Record Office, Henry III–Henry VIII, 1216–1516*, 6 vols. (London, 1903–27), 1327–41, *passim*.

the kings of the fourteenth and fifteenth centuries could not, therefore, be effected by the assumption of control over the great seal: the new emphasis on the continuity of government between one reign and the next had helped to create a series of administrative fictions that accommodated many of the problems arising from the absence of the king's real presence in government, and had rendered royal assumptions of authority within the central bureaucracy and political agencies of state somewhat less potent as ritualized statements of the passage of power.

The one symbolically and substantively significant activity associated with kingship that was not apparently affected by the processes of bureaucratization and depersonalization during the fourteenth and fifteenth centuries was the enterprise of war. Leadership in war – by which I mean actually heading up and managing military campaigns – was of enormous significance to the vision of successful kingship perpetuated both by the crown and by the political community of later medieval England. The rites of passage associated with the entry into knighthood were still of significance in the later Middle Ages insofar as they were restricted to a privileged sector of society and denoted membership of the military elite;[49] but the growing distinction between the formal assumption of knighthood and the performance of service in war means that the two processes as they applied to kings might, for present purposes, be divided, with dubbing being considered in my earlier category of 'life events' and the debut on campaign being regarded in the current category of 'career firsts'. Kings tended, for obvious reasons, to be knighted at a young age: the future Richard II was ten when, as a prelude to his introduction to the Order of the Garter, he was knighted by his grandfather in April 1377.[50] Although princes and kings might be introduced to the realities of war at a very early stage, they would not normally participate actively in campaigns until they were in their teens: Henry III was fifteen when he undertook formal leadership of the Welsh war in 1223; Edward III was fourteen when he accompanied Mortimer on the Stanhope Park campaign of 1327; the Black Prince was sixteen when he won his spurs at Crecy; and the future Henry V was also sixteen at the time of his first military engagement at Shrewsbury. In the latter two cases just cited, those of the Black Prince and Henry V, the debuts were achieved in battles at which the princes' fathers took formal command. Edward III's own first outing is rather more ambiguous, but perhaps (for him) usefully so: although he technically stood at the head of the army mounted against the Scots in 1327, and was thus understood to have received his military 'blooding' in the engagement at Stanhope Park, it was widely accepted that the strategy of the campaign was determined by the Queen and Mortimer, and that the young king was therefore not personally responsible for the military and diplomatic fiasco that ensued: in this, as in other respects, it was convenient for Edward III later to

---

[49] R. Barber, *The Knight and Chivalry*, rev. edn (Woodbridge, 1995), pp. 29–35.
[50] Saul, *Richard II*, p. 22.

place responsibility for the mistakes of his minority on his mother's lover, and to make a very public statement both of his refutation of those policies and of his personal commitment to war in launching his second – and this time triumphant – campaign against the Scots in 1332–3.[51] The image of the strenuous young knight frustrated by the military mismanagement of Mortimer was certainly current a generation or so later in chronicle accounts of the Stanhope Park campaign and its aftermath,[52] and it may be that this episode had an impact not merely upon the young king and his followers but also upon the wider political community's sense of Edward III's potential, if thwarted, qualities of military leadership even before they were proved unequivocally in the 1330s and 1340s. What all this suggests is that a military debut, even if problematic in its outcomes, was a substantive statement of a young king's commitment to honour the traditions of his ancestors and to lead his people in war against the enemy.

If we read them in this context, then the debates about Richard II's responsibilities for military leadership during the 1380s begin to take on a cultural, as well as political, significance in the history of his coming to power. It is well known that the negotiations for taxation in the parliaments of 1384 and 1386 involved statements – both by the commons and by the crown – of the need for the king to undertake the personal leadership of campaigns in France.[53] In the meantime, in 1385, Richard actually undertook his first formal military expedition at the head of an English army mounted against the Scots.[54] The fact that this campaign failed in its attempt to draw the Scots into battle might not in itself be regarded as negating its significance as a royal rite of passage: witness the remarks above about Edward III and the Stanhope Park campaign. The political problem, however, was that the Scottish expedition of 1385 was a distraction from the need and preference declared in parliament for the royal presence at the head of an army in France. As had happened with Edward III, some *post facto* rationalization helped to deflect responsibility for such ventures away from the king himself: the parliament of 1386 sought, both in the general sense of political mismanagement and in the more specific terms of diplomatic, military and fiscal policy, to make a scapegoat of the dismissed and discredited chancellor, Michael de la Pole.[55] But whereas Edward III had sought consciously after 1330 to reinforce his own nascent credibility as a war leader, Richard II did nothing, preferring a contentious policy of peace towards France and taking up arms again only in order to lead

[51] C. J. Rogers, *War Cruel and Sharp. English Strategy under Edward III, 1327–1360* (Woodbridge, 2000), pp. 10–76.

[52] Ibid., p. 22 and n. 69.

[53] *Rotuli parliamentorum*, III, 184–5 and 203–4; M. Jurkowski, C. L. Smith and D. Crook, *Lay Taxes in England and Wales, 1188–1688* (London, 1998), pp. 64–5.

[54] C. J. Neville, *Violence, Custom and Law: The Anglo-Scottish Border Lands in the Later Middle Ages* (Edinburgh, 1998), pp. 66–7.

[55] J. S. Roskell, *The Impeachment of Michael de la Pole, Earl of Suffolk, in the Context of the Reign of Richard II* (Manchester, 1984).

his two expeditions to Ireland in the 1390s. The important thing to note in the present context is the manner in which the political community recognized it both as an obligation and as a rite of passage that a king growing to manhood should affirm himself as standing in the tradition of martial monarchy. Edward III was still only twenty when he won his great victory over the Scots at Halidon Hill in 1333; Richard II may have suggested his capacity for military leadership during the suppression of the Peasants' Revolt (when he was only fourteen) and, in a symbolic way at least, during the Scottish expedition of 1385 (when he was eighteen); but the fact that he reached the age of twenty-one and more without experiencing a single battle against an external enemy may have had a formative influence on the polity's attitude towards his political maturity.

This leads me to the final category of events in what I have defined as the passage to power by boy rulers in later medieval England: namely, the formal assertion of personal will in the exercise of government. To a degree, this act is an extension of the 'career firsts' discussed above. But the declaration of achievement of full power by a fourteenth- and fifteenth-century king was qualitatively different from the assertion of his right to control certain administrative processes, for the reasons already set out: namely, that the bureaucratization of government processes during the later Middle Ages made fictions of the king's real presence, so that taking formal charge of the great seal, for example, was not in itself a sufficiently transformative action when it came to asserting the majorities of Edward III, Richard II and Henry VI. The statements of majority rule made by (or in the name of) those kings were therefore different in kind, as well merely of degree, from that which established Henry III in control of his regime.[56] In Henry VI's case, indeed, as Watts has demonstrated, it was the very absence of such a public assumption of the exercise of royal will that fatally compromised the regime in the late

---

[56] For Henry III's declaration of his majority in 1227, see Carpenter, *Minority of Henry III*, p. 389. The regulations of the council meeting in November 1437 have often been taken to represent the formal statement of Henry VI's assumption of majority: see, e.g., B. P. Wolffe, 'The Personal Rule of Henry VI', in *Fifteenth Century England, 1399–1509*, ed. S. B. Chrimes, C. D. Ross and R. A. Griffiths (Stroud, 1995), pp. 29–48 (pp. 35–6); Wolffe, *Henry VI*, pp. 87–92; Griffiths, *Reign of King Henry VI*, pp. 275–8. But as Watts points out (*Henry VI*, p. 133 and n. 41), the recognition of Henry VI's right to rule came not from the king himself but from those who were exercising his rights in minority, and this statement of 'majority' therefore lacked the personal assertion of the royal will that had been present in the cases of Henry III (1227), Edward III (1330) and Richard II (1389). It might be added – and this is a point that has not previously been discussed – that the settlement of 1437 is recorded entirely in the minutes of the king's council, whereas the majority statements of 1227, 1330 and 1389 were all publicly announced by letters under the great seal. For 1227 and 1437, see *Rotuli litterarum clausarum in Turri Londiniensi asservati*, ed. T. Duffus Hardy, 2 vols. (London, 1862–6), II, 207; *Proceedings and Ordinances of the Privy Council*, ed. N. H. Nicolas, 7 vols. (London, 1834–7), V, 312–15. For 1330 and 1389 see below at nn. 58 and 61.

1430s and 1440s.[57] What, then, of the records of Edward III and Richard II in this respect?

For the first of our fourteenth-century examples, the position is clear and unambiguous. Edward III asserted his independent control of the government carried out in his name by ambushing and arresting Roger Mortimer at Nottingham on the night of 19 October 1330 and – very significantly – issuing a proclamation on the following day to advertise the change in the structure of power within his regime and his own declared intent to rule well and wisely. To quote the writ of proclamation:

> [. . .] the king's affairs and the affairs of his realm have been directed until now to the damage and dishonour of him and his realm and to the impoverishment of his people [. . .] ; wherefore he has, of his own knowledge and will, caused certain persons to be arrested, to wit the earl of March [etc], and he wills that all men shall know that he will henceforth govern his people according to right and reason, as befits his royal dignity, and that the affairs that concern him and the estate of his realm shall be directed by the common counsel of the magnates of his realm and in no other wise [. . .][58]

This declaration of intent, issued a month short of the king's eighteenth birthday, might in some senses seem trite and conventional: but it was also a statement of the fundamental truths understood by contemporary political society to underpin the performance of good governance. Without it, furthermore, Edward III would have lost a useful opportunity not only for a statement of honourable intent, but also, much more importantly, to declare himself in full possession of his own prerogatives. So far as I am aware, no uncertainties were expressed about the king's age at the time in the way that they had been on Henry III's assumption, at nineteen, of control over royal rights of patronage.[59] In one sense it is enough to say that this silence represents a collective statement of relief on the part of the polity that the unofficial minority of 1327–30 was over: anything would be better than rule by Isabella and Mortimer. But in any case the statement was, in a sense, unassailable. As a decisive and dramatic assertion of personal will by the young king, it represented precisely what the political community sought in the problematic environment of royal adolescence: that is, a symbolic demonstration of the king's resolve to take control of the regime conducted in his name. The foregoing discussion suggests that such a public statement could not exist in isolation but needed to be preceded and complemented by a series of other public representations of that ruler's fitness to undertake such responsibilities: and, for all that he was still not quite eighteen, Edward III had already notched up a sufficient number of life events (marriage, fatherhood) and career firsts (military experience) to

---

[57] Watts, *Henry VI*, pp. 107–11, 252–4 and 261–2.
[58] *Calendar of the Close Rolls Preserved in the Public Record Office, Edward I–Richard III, 1272–1485*, 45 vols. (London, 1892–1954), *1330–3*, pp. 158–9.
[59] For Henry III, see above at n. 44.

mark his passage from adolescence to maturity and thus to prove his credibility as a king. The fact that Edward had not actually been allowed to exercise personal discretion in his own government before October 1330 – and, indeed, had been positively thwarted in the attempt to do so – indicates that, in this case, it was the king's accumulated rites of passage, much more than any proven ability to undertake the specific details of his job specification, that made politically plausible his bid for full power.

In the case of Richard II, the public assumption of personal rule is a rather more anomalous and problematic matter. As is well known, Richard's only formal statement of his assumption of majority occurred in May 1389, when he was already twenty-two. Such attention as has been accorded the event has tended to concentrate on the king's actions in council, where the chroniclers report him as having claimed freedom from constraint and the right (immediately exercised) to dismiss and appoint ministers of state.[60] But it is worth pointing out here that the matter was also duly proclaimed, in the same manner as Edward III's assumption of full power in 1330. The writ of proclamation announced that:

> We, desirous of good rule, and the prosperous and happy governance of our kingdom of England and all the people and lieges of our said realm, both to conserve peace and tranquillity in our said realm and firmly to observe the laws and customs of the said realm [. . .], with the advice, assent and counsel of the prelates, lords and great men of our said realm, have taken upon our own person the governance of the realm, purposing to rule [. . .] the kingdom and our said people in our own person, with the deliberation of our council, more prosperously than heretofore, to the greater peace of our said people and the fuller exhibition of justice [. . .][61]

The usual interpretation of this assertion of will places it in the context of the attempts of 1386–8 to put the crown into commission and rule through a series of representative councils: in other words, the historiography sees the assumption of personal rule as a reaction to a particular set of political problems encountered in the middle of the reign.[62] There is no doubt that the statement of May 1389 heralded – and was perhaps the necessary precursor to – a series of governmental initiatives that sought to publicize Richard's personal authority and establish his political credibility.[63] But in linking the public declaration of his majority only with the constitutional experiments

---

[60] Thus, e.g., R. H. Jones, *The Royal Policy of Richard II: Absolutism in the Middle Ages* (Oxford, 1968), pp. 64–5; Tuck, *Richard II and the English Nobility*, pp. 137–8. For the chronicle account, see below at n. 70.

[61] *Calendar of Close Rolls, 1385–9*, p. 671.

[62] Thus, e.g., M. McKisack, *The Fourteenth Century* (Oxford, 1959), pp. 463–4. The other possible prompt to Richard's decision was the action of Charles VI of France in taking personal control of his government in 1388.

[63] Saul, *Richard II*, pp. 203–4 and 235–6; Bennett, *Richard II and the Revolution of 1399*, pp. 36–9.

of 1386–8, it may be that historians may have lost sight of an important issue that coloured the politics of the entirety of the reign down to 1389: namely, the degree to which the king was, or was not, capable of governing himself and therefore also his regime.

I should like to argue that the very establishment of the continual council of 1386 – which was otherwise, as Richard himself never tired of pointing out towards the end of his reign, a flagrant usurpation of the royal prerogative – had been justified in the eyes of most of the political community precisely because the king had not yet formally asserted his majority.[64] Since the abandonment of the last of the continual councils of the minority in 1380 and the king's achievement of adolescence in 1381, there had been no shortage of private and public debate over the manifestations of a form of personal rule: but these manifestations had all been in terms of challenges to bureaucratic convention (using the signet as a means of unilaterally authorizing grants of patronage) and to fiscal probity (the squandering of war subsidies and over-extravagance, so far as parliament was concerned, in the expenditure of the royal household).[65] The debates of the mid-1380s that culminated in the revival of the notion of a council in 1386 were predicated on the notion that the king could not be trusted to regulate himself and needed to have good counsel imposed upon him: or, to put it another way, that his increasing bids for the *right* to rule were themselves a marker of his unsuitability to *exercise* that rule. It is especially significant in this respect that the continual council of 1386 was appointed for one year only,[66] and was therefore scheduled, originally, to be disbanded a matter of weeks before Richard's twenty-first birthday in January 1388.[67] It may be suggested that it was Richard's suspicion of the efforts of the baronial opposition artificially to *prolong* the life of that commission that therefore particularly provoked his wrath and caused him, during August 1387, to seek formal statements from his legal advisers on the unconstitutionality – indeed, the *treachery* – of the setting up of the extraordinary council in 1386.[68] It is therefore suggested here that Richard's formal

---

[64] This analysis pursues ideas developed in W. M. Ormrod, 'Government by Commission: The Continual Council of 1386 and English Royal Administration', *Peritia* 10 (1996), 303–21.

[65] Tuck, *Richard II and the English Nobility*, pp. 67–8, 130 and 139; J. J. N. Palmer, 'The Impeachment of Michael de la Pole in 1386', *Bulletin of the Institute of Historical Research* 42 (1969), 96–101; J. J. N. Palmer, 'The Parliament of 1385 and the Constitutional Crisis of 1386', *Speculum* 46 (1971), 477–90; C. Given-Wilson, *The Royal Household and the King's Affinity: Service, Politics and Finance in England, 1360–1413* (London, 1986), pp. 113, 115 and 117–18.

[66] *Rotuli parliamentorum*, III, 220; *Statutes of the Realm*, 11 vols. (London, 1810–28), II, 40–3; *Calendar of the Patent Rolls Preserved in the Public Record Office, Henry III–Henry VII, 1232–1509*, 52 vols. (London, 1910–59), *1385–9*, p. 244.

[67] McKisack, *Fourteenth Century*, p. 446.

[68] Tuck, *Richard II and the English Nobility*, p. 109, and Ormrod, 'Government by Commission', pp. 306–7, argue that Richard co-operated with the commission

pronouncement of his majority in May 1389 needs to be taken seriously by historians as an uncompromising and unassailable statement of the power that the king had sought to assume throughout the early 1380s but in which his rights had been contested by a polity that regarded him as too 'young' (that is, in this case, too much lacking in counsel)[69] to do the job in a trustworthy manner.

Richard II's inability to assert himself formally before he was already past the age of twenty-one was, then, not simply a matter of negligence or forgetfuless, but a measure of the suspicion with which the whole of his regime up to 1388–9 had been regarded by the polity. Certainly, the report of the assertion of the king's will found in the Westminster chronicle refers to Richard's exasperation at the constraints placed upon him not just during 1386–8 but throughout the first twelve years of his reign;[70] and in another proclamation issued shortly after the one announcing the assumption of personal rule, the king alluded to the many taxes borne by the realm 'since, in his tender years, [he] took upon himself the government thereof' – a statement that artfully absolved Richard of personal responsibility for the actions of his regime right from the beginning of the reign.[71] The king's belated statement of his majority in May 1389 was therefore more than a mere reaction to the events of the previous two or three years: it was an attempt, constitutionally constructed and politically driven, to scotch once and for all the arguments that his tendency towards the undesirable traits of youth entitled the polity to place any further constraints on his exercise of personal will.

* * *

The process of transforming boy rulers into adult kings is well understood to have been problematic in late medieval England, and the solutions established to deal with such difficulties were essentially driven by pragmatism rather than any prescriptive formula. This study has argued that 'coming to kingship' was not only a gradual process but also one that needed, in order to

at least until mid-1387. For the king's attempt to declare the setting up of the commission an act of treason, see S. B. Chrimes, 'Richard II's Questions to the Judges, 1387', *Law Quarterly Review* 72 (1956), 365–90.

[69] For the tradition of the young king being led astray by bad counsel, see, amongst much else, the story of the Old Testament King Rehoboam, who 'rejected the advice of his elders and consulted the young men who had grown up with him' (I Kings 12. 8), cited in John Stratford's letter to Edward III (1341) and in 'The III Consideracions right necesserye to the good governaunce of a Prince' (mid-fifteenth century). *English Historical Documents, 1327–1485*, ed. A. R. Myers (London, 1969), no. 23; *Four English Political Tracts of the Later Middle Ages*, ed. J.-P. Genet, Camden Society 4th series 18 (London, 1977), 192.

[70] *The Westminster Chronicle, 1381–1394*, ed. L. C. Hector and B. F. Harvey (Oxford, 1982), pp. 390–2.

[71] *Calendar of Close Rolls, 1385–9*, p. 679.

effect a smooth transition, to be marked by a series of acts and public statements which, both symbolically and substantively, marked the king's
progress from youth to maturity and convinced a polity deeply troubled by
the potential disruption of a royal minority that the king was able, inclined
and suitable to undertake personal control over the governance of the realm.
It has tried to shift the focus away from a traditional emphasis on the sacral
elements of king-making and on the bureaucratic processes whereby the royal
will was articulated, and instead has paid attention to the secular performance of kingship and its engagement with the expectations and norms of
contemporary political society. It might be said that acceding to the throne
before the age of discretion or maturity marked such a fundamental problem
for the polity that no such king could ever entirely escape the legacy of his
nonage: in all the principal cases discussed here – those of Henry III, Edward III,
Richard II and Henry VI – there is evidence of discourses continuing into, or
revived during, majority rule that sought to represent and rationalize the
king's inadequacies through the characteristics of youth. This was a potent
challenge: it was deeply wounding, both personally and politically, for an
adult king to be called a 'boy'.[72] The most striking instance and evidence of
this discourse occurs with Richard II, whose youthful promise, epitomized in
his assumption of political leadership during the Peasants' Revolt, not only
gave way to the political perception during the mid-1380s of his personal
immaturity and unsuitability to rule, but also, at the very end of his reign and
after the deposition of 1399, precipitated a further criticism of his volatility,
untrustworthiness and neglect of good counsel that was articulated explicitly
in the contrast between Richard's 'youth' and his usurper Bolingbroke's
maturity.[73] That Richard II and Henry IV were in fact of roughly the same
temporal age is but further evidence both of the relativity of time as it
applied to medieval rulers and of the subtle and contested significance
attaching to the rites whereby Plantagenet boys made their passage to power
as kings.[74]

[72] Louise VIII of France ridiculed Henry III as 'a boy and a pauper' in 1224: Carpenter,
Minority of Henry III, p. 372. For criticisms of Edward III's naivety and lack of coun-
sel during the 1330s and early 1340s, see Shenton, 'The English Court', pp. 217–21.
For Richard II, see below at n. 73. Henry VI's lack of political acumen was characterized by some contemporary commentators of the 1450s in terms of inexperience
and naivety: Griffiths, *Reign of King Henry VI*, pp. 242 and 254. K. B. McFalarne, *The
Nobility of Later Medieval England* (Oxford, 1973), p. 284, famously commented that,
'In Henry VI second childhood succeeded first without the usual interval and under
him the medieval kingship was in abeyance.'
[73] Above at n. 40. For specific representations of Richard II as Rehoboam during and
after his reign, see Bennett, *Richard II and the Revolution of 1399*, pp. 34 and 197;
S. Walker, 'Richard II's Reputation', in *The Reign of Richard II*, ed. G. Dodd (Stroud,
2000), pp. 119–28 (p. 120).
[74] Richard was born in January 1367; Bolingbroke's date of birth is uncertain, but was
probably April 1366.

Boy/Man into Clerk/Priest:
The Making of the Late Medieval Clergy

P. H. Cullum

In principle, in fourteenth-century England the process of moving between the status of lay child and that of adult priest was long, and involved submission to a series of rites of passage or initiations. The process, however, was clear and each stage was tied to an age requirement so that the boy progressed from child to adult and lay to priest in a parallel development.[1] The orders had been developed in the early Church and remained accepted through the Middle Ages.[2] In the journey between boy or man and priest, there were seven orders divided between four minor and three major orders, and only once one embarked upon the latter was celibacy a requirement. The minor orders were doorkeeper, exorcist, lector and acolyte; the major orders were generally regarded as sub-deacon, deacon and priest, though some thought deacon, priest and bishop more appropriate. The sub-deacon was somewhat ambivalent as to grade, for until the thirteenth century it had been regarded as a minor order, and there is some evidence to suggest that that was still how it was perceived.[3] The lowest of the minor orders could be received at any time after the age of seven, but none could become an acolyte before the age of fourteen. Entry to the major orders, and hence to the vows of celibacy, took place rather later: eighteen to become a sub-deacon, nineteen for deacon, twenty-four to be a priest.[4] In practice, there were by the end of the fourteenth century significant variations from the theory.

The transformation which turned a young layman into that (by the later Middle Ages) fuzzily defined creature a 'clerk' or into the conceptually much

---

[1] Rites of passages which both admit children into adulthood and the uninitiated into 'groups defined by powerful secrets' are to be found widely in many parts of the world. J. S. La Fontaine, *Initiation: Ritual Drama and Secret Knowledge across the World* (Harmondsworth, 1985), p. 102.

[2] K. W. T. Carleton, 'The *Traditio Instrumentorum* in the Reform of Ordination Rites in the Sixteenth Century', in *Continuity and Change in Christian Worship*, ed. R. N. Swanson, Studies in Church History 35 (1999), 172–84 (pp. 173–5).

[3] *The Concise Oxford Dictionary of the Christian Church*, ed. E. A. Livingstone (Oxford, 1980), p. 370.

[4] Some, such as John de Burgh in his *Pupilla Oculi*, accepted a candidate who was more than twenty-three (i.e. in his twenty-fourth year), quoted in J. Shinners and W. J. Dohar, *Pastors and the Care of Souls in Medieval England* (Notre Dame, 1998), p. 58.

sharper 'priest' was a long and complex one. A 'clerk' was a male person who was in principle literate, and usually (but by the later fourteenth century not necessarily), in at least minor orders. He could be a boy helping the parish priest who was considering a clerical career, a married schoolmaster, a major royal administrator or a priest with several benefices; by contrast a priest was an adult male who fulfilled all the necessary preconditions of status and knowledge, had been ordained, and was thus able to perform the sacramental functions confined to the priesthood. In theory that transition began when a boy entered into the lowest of the minor orders and was completed when he finally achieved the status of priest, but in practice by the end of the fourteenth century this process was becoming chronologically compressed. Indeed in the years after the Black Death, it would appear that it was quite common to delay entry to the major orders, as progression through the major orders came in successive ordination ceremonies. As the priesthood could not (except with a dispensation) be granted before the age of twenty-four, it seems likely that commitment to the clerical life came only a year or so before this.[5] What is more, men were waiting past the minimum age for admission to the various orders and not making a final decision until they had secured some benefice. Thus an older tradition of seeing advancement through the orders as essentially age-related, and in part a mapping of increasing maturity reflected in a series of age-specific rites of passage, was increasingly being replaced, at least for a clerical elite, with a shift from one kind of adulthood, that of the layman, to another, that of the priest. This shift was marked partly by the acquisition of sacerdotal powers, but also by the move from marriageable to celibate. It was essentially oppositional rather than developmental, though older understandings remained important.

The other shift which is characteristic of this period is that the successful outcome of entry into minor orders was no longer necessarily, or only, as a priest. The later Middle Ages saw a considerable expansion of an occupational group called clerks, not all of whom were priests, and not all of whom made their living within the church. The spread of literacy, and the need for access to the written word even by many who were themselves illiterate or semi-literate, produced a range of means by which those who had had some clerical training could make a living. These might range from singing for souls to schoolmastering, from estate administration to legal practice. Not all of those who had embarked on the priestly training but found aspects of the life, such as celibacy, uncongenial needed simply to grit their teeth and get on with it. There were respectable alternatives for men who wished to progress no further than the minor orders and who were thus still eligible to marry. There were also roles available within the Church for men who could not or would not advance to the priesthood. It was increasingly common for ecclesiastical lawyers from the fourteenth century to be married laymen, albeit often in

---

[5] R. N. Swanson, *Church and Society in Late Medieval England* (Oxford, 1989), p. 42.

minor orders.[6] At the parochial level it was also possible to remain as a parish clerk, and for increasing numbers, particularly in larger towns, this did become a lifelong career for some men. There were thus an increasing number of professions allied to ministry.[7] However it also meant that the distinctiveness of the clerical estate was becoming eroded. A rite of passage which had been designed to separate the clergy from the laity no longer clearly did so, or perhaps only did so at the final hurdle of that progress, the ordination as priest, and even then less clearly than in the past. Only the sacerdotal powers were now distinctive and unique. One of the consequences of this was that there was increasing concern during the later Middle Ages about those who had acquired a sufficiency of clerisy to claim benefit of clergy if they ever came before the secular courts. My title refers to some of these complexities: entry into the church might come in youth or adulthood; taking of the minor orders did not necessarily lead to priesthood; boy or man might become clerk or priest.

Arnold van Gennep has seen rites of passage as consisting of three elements: separation, liminality, reincorporation.[8] We may see each individual rite in this way or, by contrast, see the whole process in this way. Marking with the tonsure was a sign of separation from lay life, but the period between this and entry into the priesthood represented a liminal space, neither wholly lay nor wholly clerical, partaking of both and neither. Those who did not make it past acolyte could be reincorporated into the lay world if they so chose, simply by letting the tonsure grow out. Those who succeeded in completing the major orders would be fully incorporated or initiated into the priesthood and would have a new identity that firmly demarcated them from lay life.

If we are to consider entry into the clergy as a rite of passage and think about it anthropologically, then we must be aware that it was not a single rite but a series of rites, which took place (in theory) over a considerable number of years. According to Peter Marshall '[t]o move from being a mere layman to becoming a priest was to undergo a radical ontological change'.[9] It was a process, rather than a single event, which was designed both to convey necessary ritual knowledge but also to inculcate particular values and personal and collective identity. Because they did take place over a number of years they can also be thought of as, in principle, life-stage rituals, marking attainment of particular stages of development, knowledge and maturity.

The intensity and duration of each of these rituals also increased over time. The relatively brief ceremonial involved in the conferment of the lower minor

---

[6] P. H. Cullum, 'Learning to be a Man, Learning to be a Priest in Late Medieval England', in *Learning and Literacy in Medieval England and Abroad*, ed. S. Rees-Jones (Turnhout, 2003), pp. 135–53 (pp. 144–7).

[7] Just as modern medicine employs an increasing number of professionals who are not qualified doctors but have specific medical skills. These professions allied to medicine are increasingly taught in universities, in part alongside medical students.

[8] V. Turner, 'Variations on a Theme of Liminality', in *Secular Ritual*, ed. S. F. Moore and B. G. Myerhoff (Amsterdam, 1977), p. 36.

[9] P. Marshall, *The Catholic Priesthood and the English Reformation* (Oxford, 1994), p. 109.

orders often took place in the familiar space of the candidate's own parish church, and with relatively small numbers of other candidates present, though in the awe-inspiring presence of the bishop. The induction into major orders was a more demanding ritual which might involve the candidate being away from home for a week,[10] and segregated with other candidates for initiation, undergoing the ordeal of demonstrating their mastery of the skills and ritual knowledge necessary to their desired new status, knowing that some at least would be found wanting.[11]

The extent and difficulty of the questioning to which candidates to the major orders were subjected is unknown, as is the frequency with which candidates were turned down. Nevertheless it is clear that bishops and their officials did sometimes limit progression where they were concerned about the knowledge of candidates. Henry Wakefield, bishop of Worcester, in 1383 required three men he ordained as deacons to attend grammar school for two years before he would consider them for the priesthood. Others he admitted to the diaconate or priesthood but banned from celebrating for a year until they had remedied educational deficiencies.[12] This difficult and anxiety-provoking experience, culminated for the successful in the ordination ceremony, itself probably something of an ordeal, lasting several hours as often a hundred or more young men were initiated into their new orders by the most senior clerics of the diocese. Here the younger men were welcomed into the clerical body and finally left the church bearing or wearing the symbols of their new status.

It may be no accident that the minor orders had been established to commence no earlier than age seven, around the time at which children were thought capable of having a moral sense and a sense of the holy, and culminated not earlier than age fourteen, a period of young adulthood. However the high Middle Ages appear to represent a period of change in attitude to children by the Church.[13] Whereas before the Fourth Lateran Council of 1215 it had not been uncommon for children to receive Communion (e.g. at Baptism)

---

[10] Candidates were expected to present themselves on the Wednesday before the Saturday on which ordinations were to take place; allowing a day or two of travel in each direction would mean candidates could be away from home for six to eight days.

[11] '[H]umbling and submission to ordeal [. . .] goes with preparation for elitehood', Turner, 'Variations', p. 39. This ordeal however does not compare in intensity with those often found in tribal societies, which frequently involve humiliation, endurance and physical marking such as scarring.

[12] *A Calendar of the Register of Henry Wakefield, Bishop of Worcester 1375–95*, ed. W. P. Marett, Worcestershire Historical Society New Series 7 (1972), pp. 187, 189 and 193. As Marett points out '[t]he fact that these entries come in groups in the ordination lists of certain dates suggests that on other dates similar conditions might have been exacted but another clerk did not record them', p. xxv.

[13] '[T]here seems to have been a large shift of opinion about children among the clergy during the twelfth century. After 1200, childhood was more likely to be regarded as a distinct sub-adult condition, requiring separate treatment', N. Orme, *Medieval Children* (London, 2001), p. 216.

or to go to Confession, by the fourteenth century these were confined to those who had reached the 'age of discernment', usually twelve or fourteen.[14] The minor orders were all intended to shape a vocation but, as was appropriate to children, were non-binding. It was not until the child was old enough to make a formal vow, around fourteen, that he could become an acolyte.[15] Changing clerical attitudes might suggest a reluctance to impose even non-binding orders on those considered definitely 'sub-adult'. This development may also parallel the disappearance of child oblates in the monastic life to be replaced by voluntary entry during the teens.[16]

Ordinations to ranks lower than acolyte were very rarely recorded in bishops' registers by the fourteenth century and so we know very little about them, and it is not clear how far they continued to exist.[17] The minor orders which no longer had much official notice were doorkeeper, exorcist and lector. The doorkeeper was the lowest of the orders and the post involved tasks similar to those of a modern verger: keeping the church tidy and secure, opening up for Mass, and ringing the bell.[18] Lectors or readers read from both Old and New Testaments during the Mass and also sang the lessons. They also performed minor blessings of bread and first fruits.[19] Early Church exorcists were particularly engaged in the laying on of hands to those possessed and also to catechumens, but by the Middle Ages assisted with blessings, pouring water for the celebrant at Mass and organizing the lay communicants.[20] The acolyte's main function was in relation to lights in the church, holding a torch at the elevation or carrying a candle before the Sacrament when it was carried to the dying.[21] In the Communion he provided the water and the wine.

It was possible for a young man to receive admission to all the minor orders in one day.[22] These conferments of minor orders could take place on days other than the four Ember Days and at Easter, when ordinations to the priesthood took place, but these were expected to be restricted in number and held on feasts or solemn occasions. It is likely that bishops carried out conferments of minor orders as they moved around the diocese, ordaining small numbers of young men in their localities, rather than bringing together large numbers as was the case with major ordinations. This seems to be what Pope Alexander III envisaged in a letter to Robert de Bethune, bishop of Hereford,

---

[14] Ibid., pp. 213–16.

[15] Ibid., p. 216.

[16] See below for the movement of secular acolytes into the monastic life.

[17] John de Burgh made reference to the different orders in his *Pupilla Oculi* of 1384 but it is not clear whether they were actually regarded as separate and distinct grades.

[18] Shinners and Dohar, *Pastors and the Care of Souls*, p. 50; P. Heath, *English Parish Clergy on the Eve of the Reformation* (London, 1969), p. 14.

[19] Ibid.

[20] Ibid.

[21] Shinners and Dohar, *Pastors and the Care of Souls*, p. 50.

[22] Ibid., p. 57.

in the second quarter of the twelfth century: 'bishops are permitted to ordain one or two men to minor orders on Sundays and other feast days'.[23] When Wolstan de Bransford, bishop of Worcester 1339–49, carried out his only ordination at his chapel at Withington on the second Sunday in Lent 1342, it was of two acolytes, by contrast with the Embertide ordination a month earlier at Cheltenham when he had ordained thirty-three acolytes, twenty-two subdeacons, twenty deacons and twenty-nine priests.[24] Bishop Wakefield, in the same diocese, nearly half a century later conducted conferments of acolyte's orders at major ordinations, but did confer the first tonsure on other occasions, in his own chapel and as he moved around the diocese. This suggests that the first tonsure effectively subsumed the lower minor orders and was taken only shortly before admission to acolyte's orders: that is, nearer to the age of twelve or thirteen than seven, and thus around the age of discernment. Of the twelve youths who received the first tonsure at Bishop Wakefield's September 1377 ordination ceremony and whose later careers can be traced, eight must have been at least twelve and two at least ten years of age, given those later careers.

The first tonsure was a significant event. It does not seem to have been tied to the taking of any particular order and could be given before any of the other orders, but not to a child, and had to be imposed at the very latest at the same time as taking acolyte's orders.[25] Bishop Wakefield regularly recorded the imposition of the first tonsure in his register, and it seems generally to have preceded the taking of acolyte's orders.[26] By the early sixteenth century the registers of the bishops of Exeter regularly listed ordinations of *tonsurati et acoliti* as a single group, suggesting a conflation of these two.[27]

The tonsure was popularly called 'benett' or blessing. When Margaret Paston sought in 1479 to have her son Walter, then a student at Oxford, appointed to the family benefice of Oxnead, William Pykenhyam, archdeacon of Suffolk and a family friend, pointed out why it was not possible.

I have reseyved yowr letter, and undrestonde yowr desyre, whyche ys ageyns the lawe for three causys. Oon ys, for that yowr son Watre ys not tonsewryd, in modre tunge callyd Benett, a nodre cause, that he is not xxiiij

[23] Ibid., p. 55.

[24] *A Calendar of the Register of Wolstan de Bransford, Bishop of Worcester 1339–49*, ed. R. M. Haines, Worcestershire Historical Society 4 and Historical Manuscripts Commission Joint Publication 9 (1966), 442.

[25] '[T]he one who receives first tonsure in order to be ordained an acolyte should be more than fourteen years old.' John de Burgh, writing in 1384, here elides the first tonsure with acolyte's orders. This was clearly not widespread contemporary practice, but does suggest that there was an argument for making first tonsure a late rather than early experience. Shinners and Dohar, *Pastors and the Care of Souls*, p. 58.

[26] Of the twenty-four who received the first tonsure on 19 Sept. 1377, only one received acolyte's orders at the same time; twelve are subsequently recorded as receiving acolyte's or higher orders. *Wakefield Register*, pp. 170–2.

[27] J. A. F. Thompson, *The Early Tudor Church and Society* (Harlow, 1993), p. 141.

yeer of aghe, whyche is requiryd complete; the thryde ye owte of ryzt to be preste within dwelmonthe after that he is parson, with owte so were he hadd a dyspensacion fro Rome be owre Holy Fadre the Pope, the whyche I am certen can not be hadde.[28]

The Pastons were never ones to let minor matters like canon law stand in the way of advantage, if they could help it, but Margaret had perhaps realized that there might be problems, and may have attempted to smooth Walter's path. Pykenham signed off 'I send yow yowre presente agen in the boxe.' Pykenham does however seem to have been taking a fairly strict line, suggesting that Walter could not manage to become a priest within a year. We know from other evidence that this was in fact possible, unless of course Walter was significantly below the canonical age. The emphasis on having achieved a complete twenty-four years of age, rather than simply being in his twenty-fourth year, which a number of historians have argued was in fact usual practice, was also unusually strict. It is of course possible that Pykenham thought Walter an unsuitable candidate, despite his study, and this was his way of dissuading the family from pursuing this path.

Several ordinals with a ceremony for the conferment of each order survive. The two used here are the Magdalen College pontifical and the pontifical of Christopher Bainbridge.[29] These two largely agree in form and words, indicating the conservatism of the ceremony. The elements for the conferment of the minor orders are much briefer and less elaborate than those for the conferment of major orders. In the ceremony for the minor orders the archdeacon vouched for the candidate's character, knowledge and morals (*natura, scientia et moribus*) and presented him to the bishop, and the bishop instructed him in his office, laid hands on him, gave him the symbol of his office, and an appropriate blessing.[30] Doorkeepers received a key.[31] The lector received a lectionary, and a blessing which emphasized the care with which his office should be carried out; he should read 'assiduously and distinctly'.[32] The exorcists received a book containing exorcisms and a blessing, which emphasized their power over demons.[33] The acolyte received from the bishop a candlestick with a candle, and from the archdeacon an empty ewer or holy water bowl, with emphasis on its use at the Eucharist.[34] The blessing and prayers

[28] *The Paston Letters*, ed. J. Gairdner (Gloucester, 1983), no. 941.
[29] *The Pontifical of Magdalen College*, ed. H. A.Wilson, Henry Bradshaw Society 39 (1910), dating from the fourteenth century; *Liber pontificalis Chr. Bainbridge Archiepiscopi Eboracensis*, ed. W. G. Henderson, Surtees Society 61 (1875), dating from the early sixteenth century. The texts are very similar, though the latter is more detailed, including the use of music, and has thus been preferred here.
[30] *Liber pontificalis*, pp. 6–7.
[31] Ibid.
[32] Ibid., p. 9: 'assiduitate lectionum distincte'.
[33] Ibid., p. 10: 'ut per impositionem manuum et oris officium, potestatem et imperium habeant spiritus immundos coercendi'.
[34] Ibid., pp. 11–13.

for the acolyte are significantly longer than for the more junior orders. They emphasize Christ as the light and the offering of water and wine, reflecting the water and blood of Christ's side wound. The bishop exhorted them to do well, and to pray for him, and the acolytes were allowed to kiss his hand.[35]

The ordinal makes it clear that the competence of young men to take on the office which they sought had been tested, though how carefully we do not know. We do know that for an Embertide ordination all candidates were expected to assemble on the Wednesday before the Saturday ordination so that they could be examined by the archdeacon. As there were often more than a hundred candidates, the bishop would often assign other diocesan officials to assist the archdeacon in his task.[36] There was clearly more concern to check the abilities and credentials of applicants for major orders than those for minor orders.[37] This aspect of the rite can be seen to partake of the character of an ordeal, and only those who survived the test would progress on to the initiation ceremony itself. Not everyone had to go through this aspect of the ritual, or not at this point. Some appeared bearing letters dimissory, testimonial letters from archdeacon or religious superior that they were competent to proceed.[38]

The major orders, taken in the late teens, and priesthood, well into the twenties, were more serious and binding, and the late age of entry compared to those for most ways of life was designed to establish a sense of the extraordinary and responsible nature of the priestly vocation by confining it to those who were clearly mature. Arguably, from the twelfth century on, the admission to the higher orders, because it also brought with it a commitment to celibacy which clearly differentiated the cleric from the layperson, also acted as an equivalent to marriage in its signal that the individual was not merely an adult but a full member of the community. For laypeople, marriage and the setting up of their own households saw them moving out from their parents' authority to establish themselves as independent householders. Admission into the major orders could be regarded as equivalent, as marriage to the Church, although the liturgies do not seem to use this imagery. The new priest would receive the courtesy title *dominus* to signal his superiority to the lay estate.

We have little sense of the wastage rate, of how many did not progress from minor to major orders or into the priesthood. Dohar, in his study of the diocese of Hereford, suggests that just before the Black Death (1345–8) the bishop was ordaining around 130 acolytes and seventy priests per year, which suggests that little more than half of those who made it to acolyte would

---

[35] Ibid., p. 13.

[36] John de Burgh quoted in Shinners and Dohar, *Pastors and the Care of Souls*, p. 57.

[37] Thomson, *Early Tudor Church*, p. 11.

[38] E.g. in 1378 Thomas Russel appeared for imposition of acolyte's orders at Kidderminster, bearing letters dimissory from the abbot of Evesham. *Wakefield Register*, p. 172.

eventually win through to the priesthood.[39] Presumably the levels of non-survival between first commitment to the clerical life and acolyte were even higher. Even between deacon and priest in the last two ordinations of 1348, there was a drop-out rate of nearly twenty per cent, although tracking deacons for a longer period might have produced a higher level of completion.[40] However this may have been very sensitive to change. Ordination levels were high in the late thirteenth century, after the Black Death, and in the late fifteenth and first two decades of the sixteenth centuries. In the first and last of these the supply of ordained men outweighed the number of benefices available. In the early sixteenth century between fifty-five and eighty per cent of a diocese's clergy might be unbeneficed, and dependent on insecure employment. Knowledge of this situation might discourage the less earnest. On the other hand the shortage of priests after the Black Death and the expanding opportunities as chantry priests and household chaplains may have encouraged some, who might otherwise have looked elsewhere for employment, to hang on.

Examination of Bishop Wakefield's register suggests that in Worcester in the 1370s and 80s wastage was still quite high. Of forty-seven who became secular acolytes on 19 September 1377, subsequent careers of any kind can be traced for twenty-two, of whom thirteen can probably be traced as priests.[41] It is particularly difficult to follow men through to service in a benefice, as although in institutions clerics' full names are usually given, once instituted the register habitually refers to beneficed clergy as 'n, vicar of x', which may be similar to the custom observed in a number of medieval monasteries of substituting a monk's place of origin for his family surname.[42] Of twenty-four young men who received the first tonsure at that ceremony, twelve had a subsequent clerical career; six made it no further than acolyte; four are known to have become priests, including two who became monks. Of sixty first tonsures performed outside ordination ceremonies in 1377–9, sixteen appear to have had some further ecclesiastical career; five definitely became priests (one as a monk); and another four may have done.

This would suggest only just over a quarter of acolytes became priests and perhaps ten to fifteen per cent of first tonsures did so, but this is almost certainly an under-enumeration. The numbers of those presenting for orders gives a rather different picture. During 1377–8, ninety-six received first tonsure;

---

[39] W. J. Dohar, *The Black Death and Pastoral Leadership: The Diocese of Hereford in the Fourteenth Century* (Philadelphia, 1995), p. 50.

[40] Ibid., p. 51. And, of course, some deacons who would otherwise have become priests probably died in the Black Death.

[41] More may be traceable but the names are too common to be certain whether one or two individuals are being referred to. There is also some instability of surnames, men sometimes appearing with a family name, sometimes a toponym (e.g. John Matheme, who is almost certainly also John Jouet of Matheme).

[42] E.g.'Dns. John, V. of Childs Wickham. Dns. John, R. of Postlip [. . .] Dns. John, R. of Hatherop', *Wakefield Register*, 835, p. 153.

eighty-seven secular and fifteen religious (total 102) became acolytes; thirty-four secular and twenty-three religious (total fifty-seven) became priests. During 1378–9 seventy-eight received first tonsure; eighty secular and fourteen religious (total ninety-four) became acolytes; thirty-two secular and eleven religious (total forty-three) became priests. The number receiving first tonsure did not massively outnumber those who became acolytes: indeed, in both years acolytes outnumbered first tonsures. This indicates that, at least in the 1370s and 80s, acquisition of first tonsure was not a general precaution taken by many parents to give their sons the benefit of clerical status. Rather, it marked a serious intention to pursue a clerical career. It suggests that in those years around half of the youths who took the first tonsure or became acolytes could reasonably expect to become priests. It may be of course that aspirants to clerical status were fewer in the 1370s and 1380s at a time when other economic opportunities were more open than they had previously been, or would be again a century later.

One of the things that this demonstrates is that it was fairly common for young men to embark on a clerical career within the ranks of the secular clergy, and only subsequently to decide on the monastic life. We can observe some individuals who followed this route, such as John Parton of Painswick who became a secular acolyte in 1377, but within four years became a deacon as a monk of Tewkesbury Abbey, or John Swelle who received the first tonsure at the same ceremony, and again at the identical ceremony a few years later also became a deacon, while now a monk of Hailes.[43] As the figures below indicate, the supply of religious acolytes was often insufficient to provide an adequate number of monastic priests. The shortfall must have been made up by recruits who had already embarked on minor orders as seculars. This would again support arguments that entry into the monastic life was something embarked upon in the mid- to later teens.

The reason for the delay in moving from acolyte to sub-deacon is not clear. Swanson has argued that men, particularly the better educated, were delaying final commitment to celibacy until they knew whether they would get a benefice. Cooper, by contrast, sees this as being imposed by the clerical authorities as a test of vocation and perhaps also for remedying of educational defects.[44] In some cases, particularly during the later fourteenth century, the issue may not have been 'delay' but that there was an increased number of men who met the age requirements because they were entering the clergy as adults. Henry Knighton commented on the widowers entering the Church

---

[43] Ibid., 873, pp. 170–1 and 885, p. 179. Some young men appear to have been an 'age set' progressing through ordination ceremonies together, an experience which may have helped to consolidate their sense of belonging to a special group, whether or not this reflected potential 'out of ceremony' experiences as fellow-students.

[44] T. Cooper, *The Last Generation of English Catholic Clergy: Parish Priests in the Diocese of Coventry and Lichfield in the Early Sixteenth Century*, Studies in the History of Medieval Religion 15 (Woodbridge, 1999), p. 18.

after the Black Death.[45] As opportunities opened up within the Church, men who had lost families, or who might have rejected a clerical career earlier for its lack of prospects, might well change their minds. For these men, there was no reason to delay ordination, other than to remedy educational defects, and for them the rites of passage were about transformation of lay into clerical estate, not about age-related issues at all.

By the time a young man received acolyte's orders, if not earlier, he must have been looking for a parish in which he could pursue the studies to take him safely through the next orders. In theory he could train 'on the job' with a parish priest, and no doubt a significant number did so. The boys who came to receive the first tonsure from Bishop Wakefield as he travelled around the diocese were no doubt in this position, either still living at home or lodging with the priest. But a much higher proportion of those boys who would make successful clerical careers came to the formal Embertide ordinations. Some came because they lived nearby, but it is likely that the majority were there because their clerical teachers and even schools were sufficiently professionally aware to ensure their attendance. Some boys would have been attending either the song or grammar schools often associated with cathedrals and larger religious houses; others would have lived in the households of senior clergy.[46] Masters at schools associated with churches such as Tewkesbury, Kidderminster and Worcester were well placed to have their charges ordained at ceremonies at their respective churches, where many of Wakefield's early ordinations took place, or at Hartlebury, near Kidderminster, the bishop's principal residence, which became a favourite venue.

Boys trained in the households of the senior clergy could, if able, expect rapid promotion, but most young men would need to look for an occupation to support their studies during or after their grammar school education. A boy might then be thought as ready for on-the-job training as a holy water clerk in a parish.[47] Exactly what a holy water clerk meant in terms of orders is not clear, but it was presumably equivalent at least to an exorcist, given that this post was particularly concerned with blessings, for which holy water was generally required. As we have seen above, it was probably effectively associated with the reception of the first tonsure and a formal intention to enter the church. The post could however be performed by an acolyte, and Heath suggests acolyte or sub-deacon. In 1287 the Statutes of Exeter required that in every church within ten miles of a town or city of the diocese (implicitly with a suitable school) the post of holy water clerk should be reserved to a student, and this was probably more widely observed than just in the south-west. The fact that the Exeter Statutes reserved this post to a student and anticipated some opposition from parishioners suggests that in practice this post often

---

[45] *Chronicon Henrici Knighton, vel Cnitthon, monachi Leycestrensis*, ed. J. R. Lumby Rolls Series 92, 2 vols. (London, 1889–95) I, 63.
[46] Cullum, 'Learning to be a Man', pp. 139–40.
[47] Heath, *English Parish Clergy*, p. 19.

went to a boy with no more than a song school education or who was being educated privately by one of the parish clergy.

There is some more definite evidence that young men with a serious intention and real prospect of entering the clerical profession tended to cluster near the schools. In both 1377 and 1381, the collectors of the clerical poll taxes in the diocese of Lincoln listed separately the clerks of the Minster close and also of the Deanery of Christianity, that is the sub-division of the archdeaconry which covered the parishes of the city of Lincoln and its immediate hinterland. The clerks here were neither beneficed clergy nor choristers, both of whom are listed separately. In the Minster close, poor clerks were listed together, as were unbeneficed chaplains without habits and clerks. It therefore seems likely that here clerks were those who were at least in acolyte's orders, but might also be in major orders but not yet priested.[48] The population density of clerks in the Deanery seems to be significantly higher than elsewhere in the diocese. In 1377 there were sixteen clerks among thirty parishes and in 1381 fifteen among thirty-two parishes.[49] They were not, however, evenly divided, for in 1377 three parishes had two clerks each and in 1381 two parishes had two clerks and one had three. Mostly these were middling parishes: St Martin in Dernstall had two priests and two clerks in 1377, St Peter at Arches had the same, as did St Augustine beyond the walls in 1381. Also in 1381, St Mark had three priests and three clerks. Of the fifteen parishes which had clerks on one or other occasion, only six had them at both dates, and only the wealthy parish of St Benedict, with eleven clergy in both years (in 1381 six of them paid at 6s 8d, the rate for beneficed clergy, and the others at 3s 4d), had two on both occasions. St Peter at Pleas, with six clergy, had one clerk on each occasion. It is not very surprising to find wealthier parishes needing and being able to afford clerks, but perhaps more surprisingly the other parishes which had clerks in both years were one-man operations: St Paul in the Bail, St John in Newport and Holy Trinity, Wigford. Such parishes must have had some kind of assistance provided at Mass but presumably by boys too young to pay the poll tax or who had not yet received the first tonsure and were therefore not counted among the clergy. These poor parishes presumably could not afford to support two priests; a young man in training provided the necessary support at Mass that could not be done by boys and was cheaper to employ than a priest. He may also have supplemented the priest's income, either by paying for his training or by providing free labour.

Helpfully the draft of the 1381 return gives us not only full names (as opposed to just first names in 1377) but also their order.[50] Of these, ten were

[48] *Clerical Poll-Taxes of the Diocese of Lincoln, 1377–81*, ed. A. K. McHardy, Lincoln Record Society 81 (1992), p. 2.
[49] Ibid., pp. 3–5 and 98–100. By comparison in the next listed deanery, of Wraggoe, in 1377 there were twenty-nine parishes with three clerks in total.
[50] Ibid., p. 141.

acolytes, two were deacons and one was a sub-deacon; two were simply described as clerks. Moreover, although the general pattern is of a fairly shifting population, there is some stability. In two parishes, there is good reason to think that the names for 1377 were the same as those for 1381. At St Benedict's it is probably not safe to assume that the John of 1377 is the same as John Gardiner in 1381, given the commonness of the name; on the other hand, in the same parish there is a good chance that Vincent Barbour remained in situ. Similarly, although William had been replaced by John de Halsham at St Martin in Dernstall, Peter fitzNicholas de Welton was presumably the same as Peter de Welton. Vincent, Peter and John were all described as acolytes in 1381, and must have been at least tonsured and over the age of fourteen in 1377 to fall within the terms of the tax. They would have spent four years in a single parish, with at least two priests providing teaching and mentoring, and in close proximity to the Lincoln cathedral school. They were presumably eligible to move fairly soon into the sub-diaconate. Indeed, there is a good chance that they were already old enough to become sub-deacons, and were delaying the move into major orders as Swanson argues. While the numbers here look very small, it is because we are looking at two snapshots rather than a continuous process. Men might spend relatively little time as sub-deacons, or even as deacons, and so they are difficult to spot in this kind of situation. We also do not know whether it was usual for a young man to move on from his acolyte's parish to another when he received his next promotion. Unfortunately, none of the clerks, deacons or sub-deacons can be traced in 1377 or 1379. What we cannot see are the boys who were too young and/or not tonsured in 1377 but who may be among the acolytes or clerks in 1381, some of who might still have been in their original parish. The relatively high proportion of clerks in the Deanery of Christianity, most of them acolytes, suggests that in Lincoln many parishes in and around the city did have posts for young men who would spend part of their time in the schools.

The relative paucity of these posts, or at least indications of clerks in them, in adjoining deaneries does suggest that there was an attempt to bring these young men together for training and inculcation of a clerical identity. Clerks, some of them presumably young, can be found in other deaneries. It was clearly not impossible to train away from Lincoln, not surprising given the size of the diocese. Where they can be found, the impression is that they tend to be in clusters, several to a church, often associated with religious houses or with larger parishes with a more substantial staff. For example, in 1377 Friskney, with six priests, also had a deacon and an acolyte.[51]

Among the major orders it was the sub-deacon's job to read the Epistle during the Mass, to prepare the Mass vessels and to assist the priest at the altar. The deacon's job was to join with the priest in the singing of the Mass, and Bishop Charlton of Hereford refused to advance a group of sub-deacons because he did not feel the quality of their chant was good enough. He gave

[51] Ibid., p. 8.

them six months to improve before they could apply again for ordination. Deacons could also administer some of the sacraments such as baptism and marriage, and could also preside at a funeral, although not perform the funeral Mass.

The ceremony for the ordination of a sub-deacon marked a major shift in seriousness that was marked by the presentation of vestments appropriate to the office. The sub-deacon was instructed that his job was to prepare the necessaries of the altar and to serve the deacon humbly. He then received an empty paten and chalice from the bishop, and from the archdeacon a full ewer, a hand basin and towel, so that the priest could wash his hands before the Mass. He was then enjoined 'if until now you have been slow to church, now you must be quick, if sleepy, now wakeful, if drunk, now sober, if until now incontinent, now you must become chaste'. After a further blessing he received the maniple and tunic.[52]

Deacons and priests enjoyed a far more elaborate liturgy than had been the case for the other orders. Again the archdeacon testified that they were worthy of the honour, and the bishop asked all present if there were any reasons if any should not be ordained. After the Litany and instruction, each deacon would come forward individually; the bishop placed a hand upon his head and whispered 'receive the Holy Spirit'. He then received a stole, which was placed over his left shoulder and under his right arm, and a Gospel book. After a further prayer he received the dalmatic. This was followed by a reading from Luke.[53]

The priest was instructed that his duties were to offer the Mass, to bless, lead in prayer, to preach, consecrate and baptize. The priest then received the imposition of hands, not just by the bishop but by all concelebrants. He then had his stole moved to fall over both shoulders, and was adjured to accept the yoke of God. He then received the chasuble, after which he was consecrated with the anointing of his hands with holy oil. This was followed by presentation of a paten with bread and a chalice containing wine. The service concluded with a communion.[54]

* * *

By the end of the fourteenth century it is increasingly clear that the canon law on the process of becoming a priest was becoming distanced from actual practice. The mapping of the orders as age-specific rituals was more and more a fiction, as was the significance of the lower orders. Indeed, the liturgy for

---

[52] *Liber pontificalis*, pp. 14–15. 'si usque nunc fuistis tardi ad ecclesiam, amodo debetis esse assidui; si usque nunc somnolenti, amodo vigiles; si usque nunc ebriosi, amodo sobrii; si usque nunc inhonesti, amodo casti'.
[53] Ibid., pp. 16–33.
[54] Ibid., pp. 34–42.

these may have appeared very archaic. That the liturgy should remain an ancient, timeless receptacle of tradition may have been in part its function, but there seems to have been no attempt to move it from the archaic to the timeless. More and more often, entry to the clerical estate was a process embarked upon after a boy had reached the age of discretion, and even in adulthood. The minor orders below acolyte were rolled up in the first tonsure, and the procession through the orders was less a mapping of age than one of competence and seniority. It could also be a means by which a young man navigated his way not only into the secular clergy but also the monastic life, as significant (though small) numbers began as secular acolytes but took major orders as monks, indicating that this preference for adult candidates also extended to the monastic life. What some of the records of these rituals do help to tell us about, however, is the way that increasingly it was those young men in the right place to get a good education who were most likely to progress.

Even for those who did make that final transition into priest, the journey was not yet over. On leaving the church, the newly made priest was not yet in a position to take up a benefice with cure of souls. He had to wait until he was twenty-five before he could do that, and even during the late fourteenth century there was not always a permanent benefice for every would-be parish priest. The lucky ones would achieve that final rite of passage, induction into a cure.

Manners Maketh Man:
Living, Dining and Becoming a Man
in the Later Middle Ages

Sharon Wells

Man must consume food in order to live. About this simple fact even most academics would not choose to argue. One might even care to suggest that if food carries any absolute value it is its nutritional value. In fact, however, even this can be seen as a culturally-constructed value. Take the example of sugar. In the Middle Ages, cane sugar was imported into England in vast quantities from its place of production, the 'leyes and pondes faste by þe ryuer Nilus'.[1] As an imported good, sugar carried with it the exoticism of its foreign place of production. It was an expensive item associated with the luxury of the court.[2] It was valued, however, not only for its ability to render foods more palatable through its sweetness, but also as a powerful medicine. John Trevisa attributed sugar with the ability to

> druye and to clense, and to dissolue and tempre, and to make þynne and cliere, and to moist þe wombe wiþouten eny fretyng or gnawynge, and to clense þe stomak, and to plane and smeþy row3nesse of þe breste and of þe longen, and to clere þe voys and to don away hosnesse and cowhe, and to restore humour and moisture þat is yspend and ywasted[. . .][3]

He concluded that it was 'þerfore most profitable in medicynes and in electuaries, in poudres and suripes'.[4] This perceived health-giving aspect of sugar has been lost today. For example, whereas 'triacle', sugar (or honey) mixed with wine and herbs, in the medieval period was a highly valued medicine, considered to have almost miraculous curative properties, today it is an inexpensive product, thought more likely to cause dental caries and obesity

---

[1] John Trevisa, *On the Properties of Things: John Trevisa's Translation of Bartholomaeus Anglicus' De proprietatibus rerum*, ed. M. C. Seymour, 3 vols. (London, 1975), II, 1090.

[2] For a discussion of the status of sugar in the Middle Ages see C. Rawcliffe, *Medicine and Society in Later Medieval England* (London, 1999), pp. 150–1.

[3] Trevisa, *On the Properties of Things*, II, 1091.

[4] Ibid.

than to cure illness.[5] Sugar has been reduced in stature to an 'everyday' consumable; its place of origin is no longer exotic and it is affordable to all.[6] It is seen rather as a potential health-hazard, empty calories lacking any true nutritional benefit. Yet, even this status as health-inhibitor means that sugar continues to occupy a somewhat ambiguous position in the ordering of foods, somewhere between 'food' and 'non-food'. It functions as gift material (for example, the box of chocolates given to a hostess) or on the margins of the 'proper' meal (the dessert).[7]

In every age, man's attitude towards this basic fact of life is complicated by the ideas which shape his own society. Foods exist laden with symbolic meanings which are specific to the social and cultural environment in which that food is produced and consumed. It is not my intention, however, in this chapter to look at the symbolic meanings of food itself, but rather to examine the rituals surrounding the consumption of food within the high-status medieval household. Through an examination of both historical and literary sources I will consider the ways in which these rituals might be involved in the construction of a concept of adulthood and manliness. Clifford Geertz, in considering the role of ritual in society, suggests that at the political centre of any complexly ordered society there is both a governing élite and a set of symbolic forms expressing the fact that it is in truth governing. This élite justify their existence and order their actions in terms of a collection of ceremonies, insignia, formalities, etc. that they have either inherited or, in more revolutionary situations, invented.[8] Geertz suggests that it is these that mark the centre and give what goes on there its aura of not merely being important, but in some odd fashion connected with the way that the world is built.[9] It is my intention to look at the rituals of dining in order to consider the ways in which heads of households justified their positions of leadership and conferred upon

---

[5] See, G. Watson, *Theriac and Mithridatum: A Study in Therapeutics* (London, 1976). London apothecaries obviously did a thriving trade in treacle, as Margaret Paston begged her husband to send her from London 'a potte with triacle in hast, for I have ben ryght evyll att ese, and yowr dowtghtere bothe', cited in Rawcliffe, *Medicine and Society*, p. 153. For examples of treacle being cited as a cure for the plague see London, British Library, MS Egerton 2572, fol. 67v; '*De pestilencia*', ed. R. H. Bowers, *Southern Folklore Quarterly* 20 (1956), 120; P. Pickett, 'A Translation of the "Canutus" Plague Treatise', in *Popular and Practical Science in Medieval England*, ed. L. M. Matheson (East Lansing, 1994), p. 276.

[6] For a study of the changing face of sugar see S. W. Mintz, *Sweetness and Power: The Place of Sugar in Modern History* (New York, 1985).

[7] There is an unspoken sense of propriety in the structuring of meals which prohibits the presentation of a sweet dish as the main course: A. Beardsworth and T. Keil, *Sociology on the Menu: An Invitation to the Study of Food and Society* (London, 1977), pp. 242–53.

[8] C. Geertz, 'Centres, Kings and Charisma: Reflections on the Symbolics of Power', in *Culture and its Creators: Essays in Honour of Edward Shils*, ed. J. Ben-David and T. N. Clark (Chicago, 1977), pp. 152–3.

[9] Ibid.

themselves the mantle of manhood. Edward Shils puts forward the idea that it is the involvement of leaders of societies in arenas of 'serious acts' that confers charisma.[10] It is my contention that the great hall is just such an arena and that the rituals of dining constitute those 'serious acts' which confer charisma.

In recent years scholars have become increasingly interested in the ways in which the architectural environment is related to the ordering of human relationships.[11] Links have been drawn between the amorphous concept of culture (and its reflection in human behaviour patterns) and the architectural settings in which human beings live out their lives. Amos Rapoport, in his study of architecture and behaviour in modern societies, proposes a reciprocal relationship between human activities and the built environment. Not only are environments constructed specifically to contain human activities, they also manipulate those activities by providing appropriate props and 'codes'. The architectural setting which defines any given situation reminds the occupants of rules and established hierarchies, thus shaping their behaviour.[12] Rapoport suggests that cues to behaviour are provided by fixed-feature elements (e.g. walls and floors), semi-fixed-feature elements (e.g. furnishings) and non-fixed-feature elements (e.g. people and their actions).[13]

In the medieval hall the fixed and semi-fixed-feature elements cohered to reinforce the status of the head of the household. In physical terms the hall occupied the central place in the 'typical' tri-partite manor-house plan. Attached to one end were the service rooms (the kitchen, pantry and buttery) and at the other the private apartments of the lord.[14] Thus, as in the medieval parish church, there was a distinct gradation as one moved from the low service end to the high, exclusive end occupied by the lord.[15] The hall itself was a large open space, often with a central open hearth. Fireplaces and chimneys had come into use on the continent in the eleventh century and were common in town houses in England by the twelfth century.[16] Thus, the fact that central open hearths were common in halls can be seen only as a deliberate archaism, perhaps indicative of a mythology which was drawn upon in the Middle Ages in order to link the medieval hall with the illustrious halls found in literary texts.

---

[10] E. Shils, 'Charisma, Order, and Status', *American Sociological Review* 30 (1965), 199–213.

[11] See, for example, B. Hillier and J. Hanson, *The Social Logic of Space* (Cambridge, 1984); S. Kent, 'Activity Areas and Architecture: An Interdisciplinary Study of the Relationship Between the Use of Space and Domestic Built Environments', in *Domestic Architecture and the Use of Space*, ed. S. Kent (Cambridge, 1990), pp. 1 8.

[12] A. Rappaport, 'Systems of Activities and Systems of Settings', in *Domestic Architecture and the Use of Space*, ed. Kent, pp. 9–20.

[13] Ibid., p. 13.

[14] J. Grenville, *Medieval Housing* (London, 1997), pp. 89–90.

[15] Ibid., p. 90; E. Sandon, *Suffolk Houses: A Study of Domestic Architecture* (Woodbridge, 1977), p. 41.

[16] M. Thompson, *The Medieval Hall: The Basis of Secular Domestic Life, 600–1600 AD* (Aldershot, 1995), p. 101.

The hall was a multifunctional space and as a result possessed little fixed furniture.[17] At mealtimes trestle tables were moved into the hall. At the end of the hall furthest from the service area the lord's table was set up. Other tables were arranged longitudinally. The lord's table was often placed upon a raised dais, becoming quite literally a high table, the importance of the lord's position at the table being emphasized by the presence of a canopy above where he sat.[18] Placed near the high table was the cupboard which contained a display of fine plate. By the fifteenth century at least, the number of shelves the cupboard had was directly related to the status of the lord.[19] In addition to the gleaming array of plate, the cupboard was sometimes draped with silks or cloth-of-gold, or might have a carved canopy to draw the eye of the observer.[20] In the later Middle Ages further attention was sometimes drawn to the high table by the addition of an oriel window at the high end of the hall.[21] The high table functioned both to ensure the visibility of the head of the household and to allow the observation of all the guests in the hall. The fifteenth-century adaptation of Bishop Grosseteste's *Household Statutes* states that the whole household should eat together in the hall and instructs the lord to 'sytte 3e euer in the myddul of the hye borde, that youre fysegge and chere be schewyd to alle men of bothe partyes, and that 3e may see ly3htly the seruicis and defawtis'.[22] The visible presence of the lord thus acted on two levels to ensure control over the household.

In the public arena between the service rooms and the lord's private chamber both fixed and semi-fixed features acted as indicators of social gradations, focusing attention on the most prestigious figure in the hall, the lord. Non-fixed-feature elements, the rituals of dining, also had their role to play. In courtesy texts of the period, rituals are prescribed which acknowledge the superior status of the lord and give instructions for the ordering of all others in the hall according to a fixed hierarchy. On entering the hall, an individual was subject to rules dictating issues such as seating and quality and quantity of food. The *Boke of Nurture* recommends that the marshal of the hall should before any feast 'demeene what estates shall sitte in the hall' so as to be sure to seat them correctly according to social status, also giving instructions regarding with how many people an individual of given rank should share a mess of food.[23] All guests in the hall were seated strictly according to rank.

[17] M. Wood, *The English Medieval House* (London, 1965), p. 49.
[18] Grenville, *Medieval Housing*, p. 89.
[19] C. M. Woolgar, *The Great Household in Late Medieval England* (New Haven, 1999), p. 149.
[20] C. A. Wilson, 'From Medieval Great Hall to Country-House Dining Room: The Furniture and Setting of the Social Meal', in *The Appetite and the Eye*, ed. C. A. Wilson (Edinburgh, 1987), pp. 31–2.
[21] As can be seen in the medieval Old Hall at Gainsborough: J. Vernon, *Gainsborough Old Hall: A Guide* (London, 1989), p. 5.
[22] Bishop Grosseteste, 'Household Statutes', in *The Babees Book*, ed. F. J. Furnivall, EETS OS 32 (London, 1868), p. 329.
[23] John Russell, *Boke of Nurture*, in *The Babees Book*, ed. Furnivall, pp. 188–94.

The position in which an individual was placed at the table was of great importance, even to the point of dictating the behaviour of that individual. When the group with Margery Kempe decide to humiliate her, so that 'þe pepyl xuld not makyn of hir ne han hir in reputation', they make her sit in a lowly position at the table with the result that 'sche durst ful euyl spekyn a word'.[24] Likewise, an example in a fifteenth-century school-book records the lament of a schoolboy: 'I sytt often tymes emongest them at melys tyme the which be of more dignite and worshipe then I, wher I may not speke except they appose me, but I hade lever fare hardely and sytt emongest my companyons wher I may be mery and speke what I wyll.'[25]

The architectural setting and the ritual of the hall combined to ensure the position of the lord: he had his hands washed before all others, was served the most select dishes and had to share his mess of food with no one. Even the location of the hall's entrances allowed the lord to process to the high table in full view of the household. In very prestigious households, his food would have made a ceremonial entrance, perhaps accompanied by music from the musicians' gallery located above the service doorways. It then made its way to the high end of the hall to be expertly carved in front of the lord.[26] Thus, although communal dining in the hall, the centre of the secular house, undoubtedly contributed to a sense of common household identity, it also served to redefine social boundaries. Not only was the superiority of the lord guaranteed, the status of every single member of the household (and also that of guests) was reflected in what was eaten, who served whom and the number of people with whom an individual was expected to share a mess. Household unity existed through the emphasis on hierarchy.

There is nothing surprising to us about this notion of a medieval feast serving as an ideal image of the society in which it took place. We readily accept the fact that the sharing together of food, the congregation at set times and the rules and rituals that govern any feast, medieval or otherwise, are as important (and probably more so) than the sustenance derived from the food provided. Here, therefore, I wish to focus more particularly on how the medieval feast might be seen as an arena for the demonstration of manhood. This I will do by first considering the medieval theory of gesture.

The modern definition of gesture includes any kind of bodily movement or posture, including facial expression, which transmits a message to the observer. The message might be deliberately intended and expressed in some acceptable code, or might be inadvertent and expressed symptomatically.[27]

---

[24] Margery Kempe, *The Book of Margery Kempe*, ed. S. B. Meech and H. E. Allen, EETS OS 212 (London, 1940), p. 62.

[25] *A Fifteenth-Century School Book from a Manuscript in the British Library (MS Arundel 249)*, ed. W. Nelson (Oxford, 1956), p. 12.

[26] Wynkyn de Worde, *The Boke of Keruynge*, in *The Babees Book*, ed. Furnivall, pp. 260–86.

[27] K. Thomas, 'Introduction', in *A Cultural History of Gesture: From Antiquity to the Present Day*, ed. J. Bremmer and H. Roodenburg (Cambridge, 1991), p. 1.

Gesture is, therefore, a language, and as a language it can serve either to separate or unite individuals. In the Middle Ages gesture was used to perform precisely both of these functions. Jean-Claude Schmitt has referred to the culture of the Middle Ages as a 'gestural culture'.[28] By this he means both that the movements and attitudes of the human body played a crucial role in social relationships in the medieval period, and also that medieval culture thought about its own gestures and indeed constructed a medieval theory of gesture. The most elaborate theory of gestures of the entire Middle Ages was provided by Hugh of Saint Victor's *De institutio novitiorum*, written in the first half of the twelfth century.[29] Hugh, writing this text within the monastic context, aimed to integrate novices into the monastic environment through a prescribed catalogue of gestures. By describing gestures to be performed in both religious ritual and everyday monastic life, Hugh anticipated the incorporation of novices into the specific gestural community which was the medieval monastery.

At work behind Hugh's prescriptions was the medieval belief that gestures were expressions of the inner movements of the soul, of feelings and of the moral values of individuals.[30] Gestures were thought to be expressions of both vice and virtue, and thus gestures could be classified as either good or bad. Just as gestures might demonstrate the moving of an individual's soul, so, conversely, through the manipulation of one's gestures one might improve one's spiritual state. In other words, through the disciplining of one's external gestures it was possible to mould one's internal soul. Thus, through prescribing gestures for novices to perform, specifically religious gestures which moved the novice away from the gestures of the secular world, Hugh hoped to ensure the cultivation of a higher spiritual state.

The importance of gestures in the moulding of the inner life of the individual was not restricted to the monastic context. Jonathan Nicholls has suggested that secular courtesy texts, which dictated courteous behaviour and gesture, derived from monastic rules and customaries.[31] Thus, just as Hugh of Saint Victor wrote a text giving instructions as to the gestures appropriate for the religious life, so secular writers produced texts, such as the *Mirrors for Princes*, which informed the members of high-status households of the gestures appropriate for individuals of distinction. In the secular context, the external gestures which expressed one's inner nature revealed not only the state of one's soul, but also one's social status. For example, Giles of Rome's *De regimine principum*, translated into Middle English by John Trevisa, gives instructions to young nobles in the matter of

---

[28] J.-C. Schmitt, 'The Rationale of Gestures in the West: Third to Thirteenth Centuries', in *A Cultural History of Gesture*, ed. Bremmer and Roodenburg, pp. 59–70 (p. 59).

[29] Ibid., p. 67.

[30] Ibid., pp. 60–4.

[31] J. Nicholls, *The Matter of Courtesy: Medieval Courtesy Books and the Gawain Poet* (Cambridge, 1985), pp. 22–3.

'beryng'.[32] It suggests that even the smallest of gestures are of great significance as they reveal the true nature of the individual, and through them the 'meuyng disposicion of the soule may be know'.[33] In this text, Giles states that the noble child must learn not to exhibit inappropriate gestures, as such gestures will transmit the wrong message about the noble status of the youth. For example, wandering glances are to be discouraged for 'þerby þei scholde be holde liyt hedede and lowe and feynt herted for it wold seme þat he wondrede of alle thinges'.[34] In other words, the uncontrolled gaze is enough to suggest a 'lowe' social status.

At the root of both religious and secular conduct literature is the belief that youth is a time of a lack of control. According to Trevisa's Middle-English translation of Bartholomaeus Anglicus' *De proprietatibus rerum*, the transition from infant to youth is marked very much in food terms:

> þe childe is properliche clepid *puer* when he is iwanied from melk and departid from þe brest and þe tete, and knoweþ good and euel [. . .] þanne he is iput and sette to lore vndir tutours and compelled to fonge lore and chastisinge.[35]

At this point of nutritional separation from the nurse or mother, the youth enters the phase of intensive instruction designed to discipline the body and mind. To such discipline the child is inherently deeply resistant. Bartholomaeus goes on to state that such children 'haþ nou3t gret maistre or þei come to þe 3ere of puberte', that is, that they are at the mercy of forces other than reason. They

> holde no counsaile but þey wreyen and tellen oute alle þat þey see and here. Sodeynnly þey lau3e and sodeynly þey wepe. Alwey þey crie and iangle and ape and make mowes; vnneþe þey ben stille while þey slepe. Whanne þey ben iwassche of filthe and hore anon þey defoulen hemself eft.[36]

This lack of control is, unsurprisingly, strongly manifested at the table, the arena in which a given society receives its social definition. It is almost with a tone of despair, recognizable to every modern mother of a teenage son who has come home to find a ransacked refrigerator, that he concludes his section on the male youth: they 'thinkiþ onlich in wombe ioye, and knowiþ nou3t þe mesure of here owne wombe. Thei coueiten and desiren to ete and drinke alwey. Vnneþe þey risen out of here bed and axen mete anon.'[37] The table

---

[32] John Trevisa, *The Governance of Kings and Princes: John Trevisa's Middle English Translation of the* De regimine principum *of Aegidius of Rome*, ed. D. C. Fowler *et al.* (New York, 1997), p. 234.

[33] Ibid.

[34] Ibid., p. 230.

[35] Trevisa, *On the Properties of Things*, I, 300.

[36] Ibid., pp. 300–1.

[37] Ibid., p. 301.

manners of the medieval youth leave much to be desired. Sometimes the youth was so unsocialized as to fail even to drag himself as far as the table in order to satisfy his appetite. An example from an Oxford school-book charts the fond memories of a schoolboy regarding his old childhood life of 'slouthe', when 'My brekefast was brought to my beddys side as ofte as me liste to call therfor, and so many tymes I was first fedde or I were cledde.' In his new regime of study and instruction, the schoolboy laments that 'Brekfastes that were sumtyme brought at my biddynge is dryven oute of countery and never shall cum agayne.'[38] Such lack of control over the youthful appetite was not always regarded in later life with such affection. For example, Thomas Hoccleve's 'La male regle' complains that the narrator's health in later life has been ruined by uncontrolled eating in youth, against the advice of 'Reson'.[39] Likewise, when the narrator of John Lydgate's 'Testament' recalls the ill-advised actions of his youth to the woman called 'remembraunce of myspent tyme', neglect of the correct table manners are amongst those actions he regrets: 'With vnwasshe hondes' he went 'to dyner'.[40] Lydgate's failure in table manners is given equal weight to other 'sins' such as lying, being angry with his friends and preferring to play games rather than go to church, as all equally reveal his moral and spiritual failings.[41]

It is unsurprising, therefore, to find that Middle English courtesy literature engages directly with many of these conceptions of the youth as the uncontrolled individual in need of tuition and instruction in order to bridle his headstrong nature. In such literature, it is possible to perceive a clear link between the control of gesture and behaviour and the ideas of both adulthood and high social status. Such texts usually set up a hierarchical relationship between the tutor-figure and the youth to be instructed (usually modelled on that of father and son) in which the tutor-figure is the epitome of knowledge and control (and, therefore, I would argue, masculinity).[42] Most courtesy texts contain some rules on table etiquette and a number are entirely devoted to the subject. Generally, they consider the meal as the most important event in social life and concentrate their precepts on or around it. The instruction offered by the tutor-figure falls into two categories: information on how to behave as a diner at table (for example, not to put meat from one's plate into the communal dish, not to spit whilst at the table or not to throw bones on the floor) or how to serve at table those of a higher status (for example, how to cut the bread). The degree to which control and table etiquette had been

[38] *A Fifteenth-Century School Book*, ed. Nelson, pp. 1–2.

[39] Thomas Hoccleve, 'La male regle', in *Hoccleve's Work's: The Minor Poems*, ed. F. J. Furnivall EETS ES 61 and 73 (London, 1970), pp. 28–9.

[40] John Lydgate, 'The Testament of Dan John Lydgate', in *The Minor Poems of John Lydgate: Part 1*, ed. H. MacCracken, EETS ES 107 (London, 1911), pp. 339 and 353.

[41] Ibid., pp. 352–3.

[42] There are several examples of this kind of hierarchical instructional relationship to be found in *The Babees Book*, ed. Furnivall.

absorbed into medieval society is evidenced by the poem *Cleanness*, where the traditional image of Christ breaking the bread at the Last Supper has to be modified to fit in with medieval table rules which stated that bread must never be broken but cut. Hence, Christ is described as breaking the bread more cleanly than all the knives 'of Tolowse moght tyght hit to kerve'.[43]

It is easy to see how a society which placed such a high regard on the controlled gesture as the embodiment of a pure soul and high social status would see getting to grips with specific techniques, such as the art of carving or the washing of a lord's hands, as a particularly efficient apprenticeship in becoming a man. As in the tale of *Kyng Alisaunder*, first a youth is instructed in the art of 'curtessye', of how to comport himself at table, and then 'the chasse and chevalrye/ To weld in armes gaye'.[44] Having mastered the many intricacies of table etiquette, the youth is ready to move on to more obviously manly pursuits such as hunting and fighting. In *The Canterbury Tales* we can see the distinction of maturity between the Knight and his son the Squire through the descriptions in 'The General Prologue'. While the Knight, who loves 'curteisie', is described as taking the position of honour at the head of the 'bord', above other foreign knights in Prussia, his 'Curteis' son 'carf biforn his fader at the table'.[45] In Chaucer's description of the Knight, the image of the Knight at the head of the table elides silently with that of the brave and victorious Knight at battle. The Knight's ability to comport himself both at the table and on the battlefield are both presented as evidence of his manhood and high status. By contrast, the Squire is linked by Chaucer with the spring, the season associated by Lydgate and others with misspent youth. Thus Chaucer suggests his lack of self-control and immaturity. The implication is that the Squire has yet to reach the end of his training in table etiquette and therefore manhood. This supposition is confirmed by the tale told by the Squire in which feasting plays a large part.[46] In fact, feasting plays such a large part that it actually impedes the progress of the narrative. If one looks carefully at 'The Squire's Tale' one notices that the narrative is so weighed down by feasting and gourmandizing that it fails to take off. The Squire's youthful lack of control is betrayed in his inability to get a feast to behave in a controlled fashion within his attempt at creating a romance.[47]

---

[43] *Cleanness*, in *Sir Gawain and the Green Knight, Pearl, Cleanness, Patience*, ed. J. J. Anderson (London, 1996), p. 102, ll. 105–8. This incident is discussed in E. B. Keiser, 'The Festive Decorum of *Cleanness*', in *Chivalric Literature: Essays on the Relations Between Literature and Life in the Later Middle Ages*, ed. L. D. Benson and J. Leyerle (Kalamazoo, 1980), p. 71.

[44] Cited in Nicholls, *The Matter of Courtesy*, p. 49.

[45] Geoffrey Chaucer, *The Riverside Chaucer*, ed. L. D. Benson *et al.*, 3rd edn (Oxford, 1987), pp. 24–5, ll. 46, 52 and 99–100.

[46] Ibid., pp. 169–77.

[47] In fact, the whole of 'The Squire's Tale' betrays immaturity. It is as though the Squire has an idea of the components of a romance (magical items, feasts, etc.) but is not yet man enough to realize how they should fit into the text, or that there is some sense of

As such, therefore, it is possible to imagine that at some point within a young man's life the transition is made from the apprentice carver to the self-assured, self-controlled lord at the head of the table. If this transition was marked by a specific ceremonial occasion we cannot tell; the sources are silent on this matter. However, I think that a clear link can be drawn between being a man and being able to behave correctly at the dining table, and I intend, in the style of a true literature student, to demonstrate this fact by showing where it doesn't happen, by looking at *Sir Gawain and the Green Knight*. This is, to some extent, an unusual text to choose as *Sir Gawain* has been examined almost to the point of exhaustion from the point of view of feasting by both food historians and literary scholars such as Derek Brewer and Jonathan Nicholls.[48] However, I think that new light can be shed on the poem if it is viewed from the perspective of medieval theories of gesture.

Literary critics, such as Brewer and Nicholls, have often remarked how the feast at Camelot in *Sir Gawain* is the model of perfect courtesy and etiquette. Indeed, I would suggest that it is constructed precisely as a perfect model of the medieval feast in order to make that which is wrong take much sharper focus. Trevisa's translation of Bartholomaeus' *De proprietatibus rerum* contains a description of those things which 'hiʒtiþ and worshipiþ' a feast.[49] He suggests that a feast should be held at an appropriate time and place, that the company should be good, the service honest and courteous, that there should be musical entertainment and that the food should be plenteous and various. Indeed, these features combined with the above mentioned architectural elements can be seen at work in the idealized New Year's feast at Camelot. The feast takes place in the great hall after the mass in the chapel has come to an end and following the exchange of 'yeres yiftes' (l. 67).[50] The position of honour at the high table on the raised dais is marked by the presence of

> a selure [. . .] over
> Of tryed Tolouse, of Tars tapites innoghe,
> That were embrawded and beten wyth the best gemmes.
>
> (ll. 76–8)

moderation or decorum regarding their presence. Hence, we end up with a text which is deformed by disproportionate quantities of romance ingredients and is spiralling out of the control of its narrator, until the merciful interruption by the Franklin.

[48] Virtually every account concerning food in the Middle Ages makes reference to *Sir Gawain*. D. S. Brewer, 'Courtesy and the Gawain Poet', in *Patterns of Love and Courtesy: Essays in Memory of C. S. Lewis*, ed. J. Lawler (London, 1966), pp. 54–85; D. Brewer, 'Feasts in England and English Literature in the Fourteenth Century', in *Feste und feiern im mittelalter: Paderborner symposion de mediävistenverbandes*, ed. D. Altenburg, J. Jarnut and H.-H. Steinhoff (Sigmaringen, 1991), pp. 13–26; D. S. Brewer, 'Feasts', in *A Companion to the Gawain Poet*, ed. D. S. Brewer and J. Gibson (Cambridge, 1997), pp. 131–42; Nicholls, *The Matter of Courtesy*.

[49] Trevisa, *On the Properties of Things*, I, 330–1.

[50] All line references for this text are taken from *Sir Gawain and the Green Knight*, ed. Anderson.

All the guests in the hall are seated strictly according to their rank: 'The best burne ay abof, as hit best semed' (l. 73). Each of the persons on the high dais has their seating position dictated by their relationship to King Arthur, the elevated social status of these individuals being further emphasized by their being given 'doubble' (l. 61) quantities of food.[51] The food is brought promptly to the table to the accompaniment of 'crakkyng of trumpes' (l. 116) and 'nakryn noyse with the noble pipes' (l. 118). The food itself is lavish both in quality and quantity, with 'Dayntes [. . .] of dere metes', 'Foysoun of the fresche', 'sere sewes' and 'Good ber and bryght wyn bothe' (ll. 121–9).

Not all of Bartholomaeus' constituents, however, are present at this feast, and these constituents tend to be ignored by scholars applying Bartholomaeus' outlines to the Camelot feast. I would argue, however, that taking note of these missing constituents allows a more informed reading of this feasting scene. Bartholomaeus also suggests that the host should be of 'glad chere' and that the guests should have a feeling of safety and be able to enjoy the feast free from 'harm and damage'.[52] It is precisely the lack of these constituents that causes the ensuing chaos at this feast. At the feast, Arthur is in a distracted state of mind. According to the rules of etiquette, Arthur should be in the position of honour, at the head of table under the embroidered canopy. In fact, this place is occupied by a woman, by Guinevere. Arthur refuses to take his proper place at the table until he has either heard 'an uncouthe tale' of 'aldres, of armes, of other adventures', or has heard a request for one of his knights to joust and 'Lede lif for lyf' (ll. 91–9). By refusing to take his proper place in the feast, Arthur fails to provide the necessary central stability to the occasion. In other words, Arthur fails to be the perfect host, that which ensures the feeling of security at a feast. Moreover, I would argue that Arthur's fractious state is a demonstration of his lack of self-control and thus his failure to show himself as a man. The entertainment which Arthur craves was a routine part of a grand feast and would have occurred later in proceedings. By failing to take his proper place at the proper time, Arthur reveals himself as the equivalent of a modern child who whines for his pudding whilst failing to eat his plate of broccoli and spinach.

Indeed, the poet is at pains to stress the youth, or more precisely the imma-turity, of the Camelot court. The court is described as being in its 'first age' (l. 54), while the feast is described as taking place on a New Year which was so youthful it was only just newly arrived ('Whyl Nw Yer was so yep that hit was nwe cummen'(l. 60)). As for Arthur himself, he is described as 'sumquat childgered' (l. 86). While a great deal of ink has been spilt over the years argu-ing over whether or not this epithet contains an implicit criticism of Arthur, I think, if it is read in combination with the other descriptions bestowed upon Arthur and in the light of medieval gestural theory, we cannot fail to see it in

---

[51] Brewer, 'Feasts', p. 133.
[52] Trevisa, *On the Properties of Things*, I, 330–1.

a pejorative light.[53] The lines following the attribution of 'childgered' to
Arthur read:

> His lif liked hym lyght, he lovied the lasse
> Auther to lenge lye or to longe sitte,
> So bisied him his yonge blod and his brayn wylde.   (ll. 87–9)

To take first the comment that his life pleased him best when it was light:
Bartholomaeus says of youths, that they

> þinken onliche on þinges þat beþ and recchiþ nouȝt of thingis þat schl be,
> hy loueþ playes and game and venytes and forsake most þinges worth, and
> aȝenward, for most worth þey holde lest worth or nouȝt worth. Þey . . .
> wepiþ more for þe losse of an appil þanne for þe losse of þeire heritage.[54]

Thus, Arthur is revealed as typically immature in his outlook. His inability to
sit or stand for any length of time also echoes Bartholomaeus' earlier-
mentioned criticism that adolescents can hardly keep 'stille' even 'while þey
slepe'. Moreover, his restlessness betrays a rejection of the medieval idea of
controlled gestures which demonstrate inner worth, status and maturity. The
further statement, that Arthur's behaviour is at the whim of his 'yonge blod
and his brayn wylde', is likewise hardly indicative of maturity. The instability of the young was traditionally attributed to their failure to be ruled by
Reason; instead they were thought to be ruled by their sanguine tempera-
ment, their 'yonge blod'. Thus Arthur's behaviour at the feast, rather than
demonstrating his status as perfect host (and therefore protector of his
guests), in fact, reveals him to be immature and not a man (and therefore not
fitted to being the head of the feast).

This fact is compounded by the arrival of the Green Knight. As a result of
Arthur's failure to act as the secure, centralizing force at the feast, the arrival
of the Green Knight throws the feast into chaos and inspires fear in the guests.
Arthur has failed to make his guests feel secure as to his own control of the
feast. Scholars tend to see the ensuing disorder as a result of the Green
Knight's failure to fit in with feast etiquette. In contrast, I would argue that the
Green Knight can be seen as a perfectly regulated part of the feast, while it is
Arthur's behaviour prior to and after his arrival that is the cause of disorder.
The Green Knight arrives when the 'fyrst cource' has been 'kyndely served'
(l. 135) and his arrival is marked by 'An other noyse ful newe' (l. 132). The
Green Knight's arrival, therefore, sounds suspiciously like the arrival of a
complex 'soteltie' or 'entremet', which would be brought out at the end of
each course at great banquets to the accompaniment of music.

---

[53] For the various critical responses to the word 'childgered' see, for example,
P. A. Moody, 'The *Childgered* Arthur of *Sir Gawain and the Green Knight*', *Studies in
Medieval Culture* 8–9 (1976), 173–80.

[54] Trevisa, *On the Properties of Things*, I, 301.

In the later medieval period these 'sotelties' had reached fantastical proportions. For example, a cookery book from the fifteenth century, compiled by the chief cook of Duke Amadeus of Savoy, gives instructions for the making of a castle to be brought in as an 'entremet'.[55] The base of this castle was to be formed by a four-man litter, while the castle itself was to have four towers defended by archers. Each of the towers was to have at its base either a fire-breathing boar's head, a large stuffed pike, a fire-breathing glazed piglet, or a fire-breathing redressed swan, all of which were to be eaten by the guests. In addition there was to be a fountain gushing wine in the courtyard, with a redressed peacock beside it. Inside the castle was to be a group of musicians – a truly magnificent piece of culinary handiwork.

It was not uncommon in the later medieval period to have interactive 'sotelties', with which the head of the feast would have to interact, and which were usually designed to ratify the host's social position. For example, the herald's menu for the 1479 feast marking the installation of John Morton as bishop of Ely records a 'sotelte' at the end of each course.[56] The 'sotelte' at the end of the second course was a representation of God as a shepherd. The menu also records a poem of two stanzas which accompanied the 'sotelte'. The first stanza, which was spoken by God, gave the bishop instructions on how to rule his church, while the second, which was spoken by the bishop, contains a promise from the bishop to both rule and guide his church according to God and also 'to expel al rebel'. The 'sotelte' at the end of the first course had been a white lion, the emblem of Edward IV, while its accompanying verse reminded the gathering of diners of the king's role in the bishop's appointment. Thus the entire elaborate feast served to celebrate the trustworthiness of the new bishop and ratified his position on both a regal and divine level.

I think it is the poet's deliberate intention that we identify the Green Knight's entrance with that of a 'soteltie'. Even Arthur himself refers to the Green Knight as an 'enterlude', one of the musical entertainments or revels that would take place between courses, often accompanying a 'soteltie'.[57] Certainly it is possible to read him allegorically in the way in which many 'sotelties' were read. After all, the description of the Green Knight carries distinct resonances of the figure of 'Youth' in *The Parlement of the Thre*

---

[55] See *Chiquart's On Cookery: A Fifteenth-Century Savoyard Culinary Treatise*, ed. and trans. T. Scully (New York, 1985), pp. 30–6.

[56] See C. Nighman, 'Intricate Subtleties: Entertainment at Bishop Morton's Installation Feast', *Records of Early English Drama Newsletter* 22 (1997), 6–9.

[57] Brewer notes the attribution of this description to the Green Knight but continues to see him as the cause of disruption and the subversive element of the feast: Brewer, 'Feasts', p. 133. The relationship between the Green Knight and plays which were performed during medieval feasts is discussed in V. L. Weiss, '*Sir Gawain and the Green Knight* and the Fourteenth-Century Interlude', in *Text and Matter: New Critical Perspectives of the Pearl-Poet*, ed. R. J. Blanch, M. Y. Miller and J. N. Wasserman (New York, 1991), pp. 229–39.

Ages.[58] Youth in this poem is a particularly interesting figure as he seems to embody neither immaturity nor maturity in entirety, existing rather as a kind of liminal figure. At the age of thirty, Youth in this text is on the cusp of manhood. In a sense, therefore, in confronting the Green Knight, Arthur can be seen as symbolically confronting his own transitional state between youth and maturity. Unfortunately, he fails successfully to complete this particular rite of passage.

Arthur's reaction to the Green Knight's taunting is telling, as it reveals the ultimate in lack of control. He is described thus by the poet:

> The blod schot for scam into his schyre face and lere.
> He wex as wroth as wynde.   (ll. 317–18)

As we saw earlier, being moved to anger was one of those things Lydgate associated with immaturity and a wasted youth. Likewise, according to the Middle English translation of Christine de Pisan's *Livre du corps de policie*, anger was a vice which ill fitted a prince: 'ther is no thyng more to be repreued in a prynce than ire and hate'.[59] This is explained to be as a result of the lack of control that it reveals: if 'he can not be lorde and mastir [. . .] and ouercome it [anger], it is a sign that he is not vertuous. And a man withoute vertue is not worthy for to be worschipful'.[60] That is, a lord who cannot control his anger is not worthy of respect. It is because Arthur is immature enough to be unnecessarily moved to anger that he does not command the respect of his court. Thus, he is not initially championed by one of his knights in the challenge from the Green Knight. Significantly, not only is the description of the Green Knight reminiscent of a 'soteltie', it also brings to mind the official horseman who would ride round at a new monarch's coronation.[61] The role of such a horseman was to take up the challenge of anyone who thought the new monarch not fit to be king. Here, of course, his role has been inverted; he takes the role of the challenger rather than the defender. The overall effect is to question Arthur's validity as king.

Through such identifications, the poet succeeds in drawing attention to Arthur's lack of control (and hence lack of manliness). Arthur is shown not to have mastered the self-control entailed in table etiquette; he has not mastered the self-control that marks him out as being a man. Arthur has revealed himself to be socially out of his depth; in effect, Arthur is found lacking in the social skills which would have told him which cutlery to use to deal with a Green Knight. Gawain's intervention is an attempt to remedy the situation and save Arthur's

---

[58] *The Parlement of the Thre Ages: An Alliterative Poem on the Nine Worthies and the Heroes of Romance*, ed. I. Gollancz (London, 1915), ll. 169–264.

[59] *The Middle English Translation of Christine de Pisan's* Livre du corps de policie, ed. D. Bornstein (Heidelberg, 1977), p. 112.

[60] Ibid.

[61] See, for example, the description of the coronation of Bolingbroke: Jean Froissart, *Chronicles*, ed. and trans. G. Bereton (London, 1978), p. 466.

dignity (which Arthur himself should have been man enough not to lose). In fact, Gawain shows himself to be an inefficient carver of Green Knights, but one with potential. Gawain's quest takes him to Bercilak's castle where he is given a crash course in courtesy and table etiquette. It cannot be insignificant that the residence of that mature paragon of courtesy, Bercilak, is a castle that is described as looking as though it were 'pared out of paper' (l. 802).[62] This description, like that of the Green Knight, brings to mind a 'soteltie', such as that referred to by Chaucer's Parson, which is 'peynted and castelled with papir'.[63]

In this environment Gawain is to learn what is true courtesy. When he arrives at the castle he possesses a courtesy which allows the alliteratively linked 'clannes' and 'cortaysye' (l. 653), two points of the pentangle, to be put in opposition. He allows himself to be manoeuvred into a position in which it seems to become a matter of politeness to sleep with one's host's wife, surely the absolute pinnacle of bad manners. The courtesy with which Gawain arrives at the castle is verbal courtesy, the art of 'luf-talkyng' (l. 927). Through the highly ritualized gesture of the kiss of fealty which Gawain exchanges with Bercilak at the end of each day's hunting, Gawain learns, at the cost of a physical scar, the fundamental inseparability of the external gesture and inner intention.[64] When Gawain falsely exchanges winnings with Bercilak on the third occasion, the kiss of fealty is transformed into something resembling Judas' kiss of betrayal, in which the physical gesture does not match internal emotions.[65] His stay with Bercilak teaches him the importance of behaviour and the power of gesture to shape the inner state of the soul. Gawain returns to Camelot older, wiser and a man.

It seems strange to us to think of table manners being an indication of manhood, and that table etiquette might function as a rite of passage. Yet, even today we have interactive food experiences which can mark an effective transition from one stage of life to another. The wedding cake must be neatly cut by the bride and groom to mark the move into a happy married life (a feat which is considered important enough to require the cake-maker to surreptitiously pre-slice the cake).[66] Likewise, the birthday cake marks the transition from one year into the next, with the successful blowing out of the candles in one go ensuring the granting of a wish. Even the young sportsman in the bar is required to drink the entire yard of ale in a single draught without spilling it to show he is a man. Perhaps the idea of food as a rite of passage is not such an alien idea after all.

---

[62] For a discussion of this line see R. W. Ackerman, ' "Pared Out of Paper": *Gawain* 802 and *Purity* 1408', *Journal of English and Romance Philology* 56 (1957), 410–17.

[63] Chaucer, *The Riverside Chaucer*, p. 301, l. 445.

[64] For a discussion of the kiss of fealty see J. R. Major, ' "Bastard Feudalism" and the Kiss: Changing Mores in Late Medieval and Early Modern France', *Journal of Interdisciplinary History* 17 (1987), 509–35.

[65] On the kiss of betrayal see N. J. Perella, *The Kiss Sacred and Profane: An Interpretative History of Kiss Symbolism and Related Religio-Erotic Themes* (Berkeley, 1969), pp. 28–9.

[66] S. R. Charsley, *Wedding Cakes and Cultural History* (London, 1992), p. 14.

Rites of Passage in French and English Romances

Helen Phillips

Many romances are concerned with the processes of growing up, and contain references to real-life 'rites of passage' for medieval boys and men, particularly of the landowning class, and also fictional and fantastic variants on these. Others trace a hero's progress through formative experiences of lonely testing, hardship or humiliation, which have affinities with rites of passage, experiences through which the hero is changed, matured and ends in more satisfactory, even triumphant, conformity with the ideals of upper-class masculine adult identity. This paper examines all three categories: historically accurate rites; fictional or fantastic variants; and times of trial. Other themes often accompanying this focus on youthful development and times of trial include families lost and found, the hero's eventual creation of a new family and – especially – exploration of the nature of true knighthood and of how far lineage or nurture create a knight. Kennedy points to an 'identity theme': a hero discovers who he is, gains a name (sometimes literally) through prowess or reclaims lost reputations.[1] Love is often involved in romances' rites of passage: the hero's wedding frequently forms part of his career's triumphant finale; initiation into heterosexual love may represent perilous testing or another step towards knightly identity; some romances represent youths as learning to negotiate competition between the claims of the male and female spheres.[2] Rites of passage are inevitably prominent in romances and are the focus for both celebration and problematization of medieval chivalry and masculinity. Female characters may be depicted at the culturally defined key stages of their own life-journey, overwhelmingly three (all focused on relationships with men): falling in love, wedding and giving birth to sons. But their lives and rites of passage usually figure only as part of a masculine life-story, as mothers, heiresses, brides or hostile temptresses.[3] 'That romance treats

[1] E. Kennedy, *Lancelot and the Grail* (Oxford, 1980), p. 10. I would like to thank Glyn Burgess and Ian Buckley for their help on various aspects of this article.
[2] See S. Gaunt, 'From Epic to Romance: Gender and Sexuality in the *Roman d'Éneas*', *Romanic Review* 83 (1992), 1–27; S. Crane, *Gender and Romance in Chaucer's* Canterbury Tales (Princeton, 1994), pp. 39–54.
[3] S. Gaunt, *Gender and Genre in Medieval French Literature* (Cambridge, 1995); S. Fisher, 'Women and Men in Late Medieval English Romance', in *The Cambridge Companion*

masculine experience as universal', writes Crane, 'does not free masculinity from constraints and contradictions.'[4] Recent criticism sees not only love but also debate about gender as central preoccupations in romance.[5] We might add debate about power, violence, class and identity. Women and family households formed an important element in romance readership. Romance reading had an educative role. Given the culturally formative ideological importance of chivalric fiction, and the directly didactic and exemplary force of many romances, how did female readers view their representation? Did it mould negatively their own self-images and development?[6]

To explore what romances fourteenth-century readers read we cannot just consider fourteenth-century compositions. Older romances continued to be read, copied, rewritten and translated over several centuries. Fourteenth- and fifteenth-century English aristocrats and princes who owned libraries often had a preponderance of French books, many of them romances. Fourteenth-century readers were familiar, in a variety of ways, with heroes and romance stories, many of them originally French, that often went back to the twelfth century. The depiction of rites of passage shows both changes over time and also continuities. Late-medieval romance readers received richly mixed images of knighthood and rites of passage, including the archaic and the somewhat fanciful.

Why were heroes' *enfances* and development from childhood to maturity so important in romance, compared, for example, with classical epic? Celtic influence has been suggested.[7] The phenomenon prompted writers to explore the nature of chivalric values, especially problematic areas like the co-existence of a military élite with Christian culture; the ethical evaluation of aggression, luxury and pride; the issue of whether birth predestines the highborn to superior virtue, prowess and honour; and, finally, the two conflicting medieval models of masculine 'life-journey': monasticism and chivalry.

In the first category above – descriptions of rites of passage as historically experienced by medieval upper-class young men – dubbing is the most common.[8] Details vary. In French romances ages range between fifteen (*Cligés,*

to *Medieval Romance*, ed. R. L. Krueger (Cambridge, 2001), pp. 150–64; F. Riddy, 'Middle English Romance: Family, Marriage, Intimacy', in *Cambridge Companion*, ed. Krueger, pp. 235–52.

4 Crane, *Gender and Romance*, p. 26.
5 See R. L. Krueger, 'Questions of Gender in Old French Courtly Romance', in *Cambridge Companion*, ed. Krueger, pp. 132–49.
6 R. L. Krueger, *Women Readers and the Ideology of Gender in Old French Romance*, Cambridge Studies in Old French (Cambridge, 1993); C. M. Meale, ' "gode men / Wiues maydnes & alle men": Romance and its Audiences', in *Readings in Medieval English Romance*, ed. C. M. Meale (Cambridge, 1994), pp. 209–26. P. Coss, *The Lady in Medieval England 1000–1500* (Stroud, 1998), pp. 174–81; Crane, *Gender and Romance*, pp. 194–203.
7 M. P. Cosman, *The Education of the Hero in Arthurian Romance* (Chapel Hill, 1965).
8 M.-L. Chênerie, *Le Chevalier errant dans les romans arthuriens en vers des XIIe et XIIIe siècles*, Publications romanes et francaises 172 (Geneva, 1986); J. Flori, 'Sémantique

l. 2725) and twenty-four (*Yder*, l. 914). As in other respects, later medieval romances may depict the practices of an earlier era. The cost of armour made youthful dubbing wish fulfilment rather than reality by the thirteenth century.[9] The occasion is often an important festival, especially Pentecost (symbolizing spiritual transformation). Lancelot's is St John's Day, a midsummer holiday, and possibly associates his new identity with the saint.[10] One or more of the following ritual elements may be mentioned: a bath (particularly in French romances), vigil, mass, the girding with the sword, strapping on of the right or both spurs, the accolade and a statement about the duties of knighthood.[11] One man may be knighted or a group; often companions were knighted by the newly dubbed hero. Flori traced the changing meaning of 'dubbing', from a simple provision of arms in the eleventh century, towards more ritual and a sense of conferring membership of an elite, during the twelfth century.[12] In the twelfth-century *chanson de geste, Garin le Loherain*, men may become excellent mounted warriors without being *chevaliers*: already that involved a ceremony by the king.[13] Kay shows the two authors of *Raoul de Cambrai*, also twelfth century, using *chevalier* differently, the first in the earlier, technical and military sense, the second more frequently and with additional amorous and romantic associations.[14] Some writers imbue dubbing with a religious aura, as in the integration of secular and mystical ideals in the Lady of the Lake's exposition of knights' duties in the early thirteenth century *Lancelot du Lac* (ll. 142–6). Usually, if dubbing receives detailed description, the main function seems secular, to mark the hero's rising success, typically after a time of trial. Where a serious religious perspective on the human life-journey appears, it more commonly takes the form of an entirely alternative way of life to that of secular knighthood, as in the *Queste del saint graal* or *Pèlerinage de vie humaine*.

In its first section, *Lancelot* gives dubbing climactic importance, fictionally, spiritually and emotionally: from the boy's intense desire to become a knight,

et société médiévale: Le verbe *adouber* et son évolution au XIIe siècle', *Annales ESC: économies, sociétés, civilisations* 31 (1976), 915–40; J. Flori, *L'essor de la chevalerie: XIe–XIIe*, Travaux d'histoire éthico-politique 46 (Geneva, 1986); J. Flori, 'Pour une histoire de la chevalerie: l'addoubement dans les romans de Chrétien de Troyes', *Romania* 100 (1986), 21–53; R. W. Ackerman, 'The Knighting Ceremonies in the Middle English Romances', *Speculum* 35 (1960), 285–313.

[9] Chênerie, *Chevalier errant*, pp. 43–4.

[10] *Lancelot du Lac: The Non-Cycle Old French Romance*, ed. E. Kennedy, 2 vols. (Oxford, 1980), pp. 146–7.

[11] Chênerie, *Chevalier errant*, pp. 40–1; M. Keen, *Chivalry* (New Haven, 1984), pp. 64–82; R. Barber, *The Knight and Chivalry* (Woodbridge, 1974), pp. 38–9 and 292–3.

[12] Flori, 'Sémantique'; See M. Bloch, *Feudal Society*, trans. L. A. Manyon (London, 1962), pp. 311–13 and 435–44; Barber, *Knight and Chivalry*, pp. 24 and 35; J. Le Goff, 'Le rituel symbolique de la vassalité', in *Pour un autre Moyen Age* (Paris, 1977), pp. 349–415.

[13] Flori, 'Sémantique'; Keen, *Chivalry*, pp. 66–7.

[14] *Raoul de Cambrai*, ed. S. Kay (Oxford, 1992), pp. xliii–xlv.

a sequence of youthful experiences illustrating his innately chivalric nature, the Lady's exposition of knightly duties and an elaborate description of the sumptuous arms she provides. Further significance accrues from stringent conditions: it must be on St John's Day and use of the Lady's equipment. The ceremony reveals lost kindred. Lancelot wears a knight's robe; there is vigil, Mass and accolade. Surrounding events increase its emotional resonance: it coincides with his first encounter with Guenevere, throwing him into a love reverie; after it he heals the wounded knight (healing remains associated with Lancelot in romance), undertakes his cause and vows to defend the Lady of Nohaut.

English texts which describe dubbing in detail include *King Horn* (c. 1250), *Havelok* (c. 1275), *Libeaus Desconus* (c. 1325–50?), *King Alisaunder* (c. 1330) and Lovelich's *Merlin* (c. 1425).[15] *Merlin*, written by a London merchant for a fellow-merchant, relishes realistic detail. It describes several knights' dubbing: Arthur girding on the sword and right spur, another knight the left, Arthur dubbing the knight, smiting him 'Riht in the Nekke', bidding him be a good knight, vigil in the chapel and Mass next day, followed by the feast, sports (quintain) and costly gifts (ll. 25733–824). *Kyng Alisaunder* describes the dubbing after the twelve-year-old prince is deemed precociously to have completed intellectual and practical training. King Philip girds on the sword, gives the accolade, bids him be a good knight; he receives his spurs, and at the feast a hundred new knights are dubbed. Alysaunder sits by the king and is given treasure to distribute. Unusually, he is crowned during his father's lifetime. In *Libeaus Desconnus* Arthur gives the aspirant a name, 'Fair Unknown', gives fine arms, sword, hangs the shield on him and tells Gawain (his unrecognized father) to teach him knightly skills. The young man then swears to fight Arthur's enemies, asking to be granted the next challenge (ll. 31–96). This martial trial after dubbing, confirming fitness for knighthood, occurs elsewhere, including *Horn*.

Contrasting with *Merlin*'s straightforward *vraisemblance*, Horn's knighting forms the hub of a complex drama, by which he regains the status rightly his by lineage, escaping from the lowlier career track of apprenticeship as a royal servant to that of knighthood through initiation into a sexual union. Initially, the king decrees the fifteen-year-old foundling will learn the 'mestere' of a royal steward: hunting and falconry, riding with a shield (one manuscript), harping, singing and serving the cup at table (ll. 190 and 240–54). Dubbing and initiation into love redirect this career trajectory, and are linked: as often, a young hero's capacity to attract a well-placed heiress functions virtually as an indicator of genetic superiority. When the impassioned princess Rymenhild asks Horn to return her love, he makes it a condition that she ask

---

[15] *King Horn*, ed. J. R. Lumby, EETS OS 14 (London, 1866), pp. 495–504; *Lybeaus Desconus*, ed. M. Mills, EETS OS 261 (London, 1969), pp. 41–177; *Kyng Alisaunder*, ed. G. V. Smithers, 2 vols., EETS OS 227 and 237 (London, 1952, 1957), II, 786–833; *Lovelich's Merlin*, ed. E. A. Kock, 3 vols., EETS ES 93, 112 and OS 185 (London, 1899, 1910, 1932), III.

her father to dub him (ll. 264–496).[16] Horn comes before the king with twelve companions, is girded with a sword and spurs, set on a steed, dubbed with a sword and told to be a good knight. He dismounts and knights his companions. A feast, apparently all-male, follows; Rymenhild frets at the delay before her next meeting with Horn. He says he will marry her only after performing some knightly battle: progress through the stages of knighthood represents a higher priority than proceeding towards sexual union. Implicitly success will qualify him to marry her. She gives him a ring. This marks the occasion of his dubbing: at this stage Rymenhild's love is Horn's opening to improve his standing in the masculine hierarchy and attain the first crucial step in changing his rank, dubbing. Her ring, with power to help in his first battle, signifies assistance in his upward career path, exactly like the princess's love so far. A parallel is the Lady's girdle in *Gawain*, figuring more in the drama of the hero's contracts and status among other men – Bertilak, Arthur and the Round Table – than as symbol of heterosexual exchange; such breaking of modern readers' expectations foregrounds the importance of knightly masculine bonds. Horn's first battle after dubbing is the archetypal knightly battle against Christendom's enemies, Saracens, that justified the role of a warrior class in Christian society.

His credentials thus established, Horn's love-story proper, his adventures and the convoluted plot can proceed. *Horn* is no crude narrative: it presents with lively emotional sophistication the – in its cultural paradigm – linked joys of the hero's military advancement and advantageous union. That prioritization that makes love await and serve key-moves in career-advancement appears graphically in *Gamelyn* where a woman only appears (two lines) in the final summary of the hero's successes: he acquires a rich unnamed wife. Later episodes show Horn and Rymenhild as devoted, but these early scenes illustrate how readily marriage is equated with advancement. Bélanger found this masculine wish-fulfilment equation prominent in *chansons de geste*; a father's declaration in *Garin* is typical: 'Take my daughter: you have deserved her well, and herewith I give you my land and people' (ll. 2108–9).[17]

Havelok's dubbing, placed late in the plot, also sees him become king: the climactic vindication of the hero's rightful status after trials and long exile from his heritage. He receives subjects' homage and oath, is dubbed and then

---

16 Each Horn romance links these elements differently. In the *Roman de Horn*, he says he is too lowborn to return her love before proving his prowess. After fighting Saracens he accepts her ring. These are typical twelfth-century emphases – less entanglement between success in love and military career, less concern with knightly ceremony, more with fighting to defend Christendom. *Horn Child* (c. 1330) is simple macho progression through fighting, adventure and success, with love providing the motivation for exploits. *Ponthus* rewrites the Horn story to teach gentle conduct and knightly ideals to young men.

17 *Garin le Loherain*, ed. J. E. Vallerie (New York, 1947), also see ll. 3247–8, 7053–6 and 11567–71; J.-L. Roland Bélanger, *Damedieus: The Religious Context of the French Epic* (Geneva, 1975), pp. 98–100.

invested with power over the kingdom. There follow spear fights, sword and buckler play, wrestling, music, board games, reading of romances, songs, bull-baiting, boar-baiting and a feast at which knights and barons are made.[18] The elaborately described ceremony balances a less satisfactory ritual earlier in Havelok's career: his wedding, where, as a bondman imposed on a high-born heiress, he is uncomfortably ill-matched to the ceremony in which he is chief actor.

Early medieval aristocrats' status might depend on the standing of the lord they served as well as their lineage. Romance continues to mirror this: youths seek, or are sent by guardians to receive, dubbing from great lords, especially Arthur.[19] As chivalric ceremonies developed, it was frequently the king who dubbed. In the late medieval period particularly, fictional and real-life cere-monies of knighthood, whether dubbing, chivalric orders or tournaments, were twin images of the same cultural myth; real-life rituals and literature reinforced each other.

Some romances reflect the transitions by which children passed from one developmental environment and tutelage to another. Early education was in women's hands but boys then moved to masculine training, often in another household. The Lady of the Lake, fostering Lancelot, provides a male tutor from the age of three. *Sir Degare's* (c. 1320) foundling hero is reared by a woman until ten and then educated by her brother, a hermit, till twenty. Some fictional female educators are fantastic: the Lady of the Lake; Morgan, rearing Floriant in *Floriant and Florete*. Romance often devalues human female educa-tors: a culturally coercive masculine mockery may depict maternal attempts to rear a boy away from the perils of warrior culture as doomed to failure, because of the inborn proclivity of knightly-born boys to become knights. Maternal tutelage can create a *dümmling* role for the young hero, something to be corrected by masculine guidance. The motif of a wilderness-educated boy ruthlessly abandoning his mother to join knights, after seeing knights for the first time, perhaps fictionalizes the historical transition of boys from a world of female educators to that of men. The Perceval romances are the classic example.[20] *Generides* (c. 1380) mingles parents and sexual partners, suggesting a fictional confrontation of real-life anxiety over the need for boys to break away from the female in order to achieve adult masculine identity and marry. Generides is reared in the forest by a fairy single mother. He leaves his mother

---

[18] *The Lay of Havelok the Dane*, ed. W. W. Skeat, EETS ES 4 (London, 1868), ll. 2312–53.

[19] Keen, *Chivalry*, pp. 68–9.

[20] *Sir Perceval of Galles* (c. 1300–50) shows a mother's well-founded fear of losing her son, her husband having died through a vengeance-feud, yet this romance depicts her pacific woodland education as particularly idiotic, though the child-mother relationship is tenderly presented; female intervention is ridiculed when it enters the public sphere of masculine development and control. Cosman, *Education*, pp. 52 and 103–13, comments that Perceval romances show religious instruction from his mother, chivalric from the uncle, and maternal precepts lead him to be regarded as a fool.

to join his father Aufreus's court, is propositioned by his father's adulterous wife, falsely accused of seeking sex with her, flees and finds true love of his own. Aufreus marries Generides' mother, the first wife tries to part Generides from his sweetheart, but all ends happily with his biological parents properly married, his own wedding and eventual kingship. The social vision romances depict frequently conflates the family group, lost and found, and a high-prestige masculine community in which a youth may achieve adult conformity and success, often gravitating to lost uncles and royal fathers who rule chivalric courts.

William of Palerne (c. 1350–61) and its source *Guillaume de Palerne* (c. 1200), tell the story of a boy moving from female educators who turn murderous, to masculine tutelage of a caring if bizarre kind.[21] This romance shows a strong interest in pedagogy and ambivalent attitudes to the question of whether knightly skills are inherited or learned, using the common plot of the displaced highborn child to expose ambiguities surrounding this issue. William is sent at four to be educated by two ladies, but having survived their plot to poison him, is seized by a friendly werewolf (enchanted by his stepmother) and looked after in a forest cave. He is discovered by a kind cowherd, whose wife rears him until he is old enough for the cowherd to teach him his professional skills: herding, archery and hunting. He is next discovered by the emperor and returned to the court, where his interrupted knightly education continues. The emperor entrusts the boy to his daughter. She initiates him into love. After three years he is knighted and demonstrates military prowess. Already in the cowherd's world he won attention for his handsomeness, generosity, wisdom and courtesy, and attracted a band of young followers. This shows him a natural leader, innately possessing those attributes justifying his class's social leadership. Before he leaves, the cowherd, for whom the youth feels exemplary respect and affection, instructs him about behaviour at court: he should be obedient, pleasant, modest, moderate, no tale-teller, loyal to his lord, generous to the poor, and treat rich and poor alike (implausibly, the cowherd's own father was at court, which is why he can provide this instruction). This motif endorses the concept of training (nurture), but William's natural charms and leadership, and the fact that at court he acquires the skills of a courtier without teaching, endorse the concept of inborn chivalry (nature). When an enemy threatens, he begs the emperor to dub him. Simultaneously eighty princes' sons are knighted to fight under him.

This romance moves its hero in and out of conventional upbringing, neither denying him the privileged education to which birth entitles him, despite a period of temporary displacement and disadvantage, nor showing his acquisition of knightly qualities as wholly dependent on training. Conventional steps in a hero's maturation, like dubbing, courtly education and a princess's love, do appear, but figure more as rewards for a chivalric

---

[21] *William of Palerne*, ed. W. W. Skeat, EETS ES 1 (London, 1987).

identity he already possesses, than stages in its acquisition.[22] *Lancelot du Lac's* hero is taught knightly skills by his tutor (hunting, riding, chess and backgammon, especially), but naturally possesses generosity, leadership of other boys, modesty, handsomeness, moderation and respect for noble men. We are also told that his joy and anger (especially against cruelty) are extreme; he is confident and succeeds in exploits, causing some to find him arrogant, because of a certain inner 'joie' (prefiguring his future passion for his mistress); he follows his own will when he considers himself right, regardless of the tutor's attempts to curb him. This profile, asserting a model of knightly personality that includes the quality of being self-willed but innately right, is not derived from education, a point demonstrated when the tutor, a mean-spirited man, criticizes behaviour that is actually noble and Lancelot beats him up. The romance's handling of Lancelot's *enfances* is an encomium of the knight as a superior being called on to behave in a superior way, centring on the Lady's speech about knights' obligations as defenders of the Church (ll. 141–8). A developmental dynamic runs through the narrative, with Lancelot's name changing at crucial points. Romances that directly teach knightly behaviour (like *William of Palerne* and *Lancelot*) doubtless formed part of upper-class education. *Ponthus* (French 1390, English c. 1400–50), exemplifies the increasingly moral or pedagogic trend, shows its young hero learning hawking, hunting, chess, dancing, singing and piety: every morning, before eating, he washed his hands, said his prayers and attended Mass; never swore great oaths, gave to the poor (unostentatiously), was as glad to lose as win, never mocked or listened to detractors. Though passionately in love he renounces pre-marital sex.[23]

Many writers are clearly less concerned simply to reflect historical rites than, through them, to probe what knighthood – the ideal socialization as an adult upper-class male which rites of passage serve – involves. They may use fantastic or symbolic variations on rites of passage to validate or examine the concept of a privileged caste. The Northern *Octavian* (c. 1350) illustrates this and explores the relationship of the knight to the tradesman and aspects of the economic structure which produces class privileges.[24] It tells of two high-born boys. One, Octavian, after being stolen by a lioness obtains a conventional upper-class upbringing: christening, riding, fighting and dubbing. His brother, stolen by an ape, saved by a knight, captured by outlaws, then sold, offers the opportunity for examining the different expectations and rites of

---

[22] Besides the nature-nurture issue, Arlyn Diamond sees a distinction 'between nobility (as a social practice based on inherited rank and power) and chivalry (as a social ideology based on virtue and personal morality)'; through relationships between nobles and animals, and nobles and the lower classes, the romance projects an ideal of kind-heartedness as true nobility, integrated with a conservative social vision: a benevolent patriarchy, 'Loving Beasts: *William of Palerne*', in *The Spirit of Popular Romance*, ed. A. Putter and J. Gilbert (Harlow, 2000), pp. 142–56 (pp. 146 and 155).

[23] *King Ponthus and the Fair Sidonie*, ed. F. J. Mather (Baltimore, 1897), pp. 11–12 and 17.

[24] *Octavian*, ed. F. McSparran, EETS OS 289 (London, 1986).

passage of a bourgeois and an aristocrat. He is brought up by a Paris trades-man. He is baptized as Florent, the first of three names given him in the narrative. At seven he is apprenticed to learn the trade of *chaungere* (ll. 640–4); specifically, he begins to learn the trade of butcher (ll. 645–8).

Chaungere, meaning 'money-changer', perhaps implies 'man of commerce': a tradesman who exchanges, buying and selling. Such work contradicts the self-image of the knightly class, to which *fraunchyse*, liberality and *largesse* are central. The commercial associations of apprenticeship soon clash with Florent's hereditary nature. His foster father, initiating the butchery appren-ticeship, sends him with oxen to the bridge. Instead of trading them, Florent uses them to buy a falcon. The foster father beats him. The mother, more per-ceptive that this child is not as other tradesmen's sons are, suggests he be not apprenticed but kept at home, serving his parents.

The plot traces a parallel process to conventional knightly education, this genetically aristocratic youth progressing through self-invented stages equivalent to Octavian's standard chivalric education. The apprenticeships to money changing (='commerce'?) and butchery are inversions of knightly indicators of *largesse* and hunting (having lost the oxen, his foster father tells him sarcastically to get his meat in future through his new kite). Butchery is perhaps also an inversion of knightly military activities. Later Florent will show enormous *largesse* and win great reputation as a warrior. A second episode shows the boy instinctively transmuting his commercial duties into a further step in the sequence of chivalric acquisitions. Sent on an errand carry-ing forty pounds through the streets to one of his tradesman foster brothers, he uses it to buy a steed, silk bridle and gilt bit. As with the falcon, he proves instinctively gifted at looking after noble beasts. His foster father wants to punish him but his mother recognizes he is born to a higher calling which causes his behaviour (ll. 753–6).

This narrative contrasts the education for the urban apprentice and young aristocrat, shows Florent obeying his *blode* (l. 755) and instinctively but sys-tematically passing through equivalents to the stages of becoming a knight that his bourgeois fostering denies him. After acquiring falcon and steed, he goes on to gain arms, showing an urge for the knight's role of defending others. When a giant threatens the city, he insists on having brought out of store old armour and weaponry: they are rusty, 'All sutty, blakk and vnclene' (l. 885). When he brandishes the sword, his lowborn parents collapse in ter-ror. He laughs at them. Mounted on his steed, with his armour and, his father now acknowledges, having spent *his* money well, educating himself in knightly skills (ll. 952–7), Florent, unaided by conventional chivalric nurture (but backed by involuntary diversion of his tradesman father's money) has performed a do-it-yourself evolution of boy into adult knight.

Octavian is a fable showing approvingly the economics and ideological validation of the 'noble' class. Florent's unofficially acquired accoutrements and skills prove adequate to the highest requirements of his hereditary pro-fession: he slays the giant, protects the townspeople and gains an heiress's love. It presents the naturalization and mystification of the economic basis of knighthood: we see irrepressible natural superiority and proclivities, depicted as positive, admirable forces (especially through the motif of Florent's defending the townspeople) and as a justification of the highborn male appropriating the profits of the tradesman. While so doing, the youth and the knightly group he joins snobbishly despise the tradesman's habitual exercise of commerce that – in the economic relationship (exchange) this text simultaneously reveals and represses – both funds the chivalric lifestyle and potentially challenges it for some recompense.

After his first military success he gains the name Florent of Paris, and is dubbed (ll. 1142–237). Even now his tradesman father embarrasses him, and is mocked for his commercial attitudes, but the ceremony goes ahead in appropriate form: Florent is dressed in 'atyre of golde' (l. 1144); comes before the emperor accompanied by his sponsors, one king on either side and the king of France walking before him, while minstrels play (ll. 1145–9). There is dancing, the new knight sits in the place of honour between the French king and the emperor (l. 1181) and, though without the formal training, shows himself at the feast courteous and open-handed, and the emperor perceives that he has gentle blood (ll. 1186–7). His father angrily wants payment, exchange, for the banquet he has provided. The knightly ones laugh, though the king of France then offers to cover the expenses. The emperor discovers Florent is his son and he is renamed Sir Florent of Rome. Rites of passage in *Octavian*, ceremonies and procedures marking transitions from birth to adulthood – christening, name-giving, education, dubbing and wedding – do not function, as in a novel, to convey the felt experiences of a fictional individual (Zoé Oldenbourg's *La Pierre angulaire*, 1972, set in the twelfth century, is a good example), but as marks tracing the biologically inevitable rise of the youth toward social success, and to differentiate the knightly class from the bourgeois. Like many romances, *Octavian* presents the skills of a class as inborn. Paradoxically it invokes rites of passage and aristocratic nurture only to present them as irrelevant to maturation as a knight. That urge of the nobly born to become knights, whatever form their education has taken, even against what loving guardians wanted for them, was an established fictional motif, going back to Chrétien's *Perceval*. In the mid-thirteenth-century *Fergus*, a boy with an aristocratic mother and villein father, vows, on first seeing knights, to become one; his mother thinks this shows ancestral blood coming out, though the boy's lack of appropriate education makes him look foolish at court. Only *Octavian* systematically contrasts the knightly instinct with a commercial education. Tales of the 'fair unknown' type, the poor boy coming from nowhere, superficially enlist sympathy for heroes who better themselves, but they are based on a mythology of immutable upper-class superiority. Their heroes are really upper-class; their upward mobility, through trials and against the odds, represents restoration of the status quo, not a challenge to it. *Le Roman de Silence* (c. 1270) depicts a disguised noble girl successfully undergoing knightly education. Inherited knightly identity is sometimes contrasted with animals and monsters, beings lower on the scale of creation (like trades-men); some romances use marvels like lost royal babies, bear-parents or were-wolves not only for sensationalism but also for exploring the concept at the heart of the chivalric myth of a class set apart from other classes by birth, superior honour, courage and refinement. This may include differentiating true nobility of heart from externalities. In *Bisclavret* the werewolf shows the truest nobility. Diamond sees *William of Palerne* contrasting the nobility of a gentle heart with nobility of birth, rank and power, and partly through the *gentil* characters' interactions with the animal kingdom.[25]

Octavian's emphasis on *largesse* in contrast to exchange – commercial money-making – as defining the gently-born may reflect older literary trad-itions of war-lords' ostentatious liberality (and the actuality of distributing booty) but also belongs to the late medieval socio-economic world, where landowners disassociate themselves from commerce, even if participating in it.[26] This motif in *Octavian* illuminates a moment puzzling to modern readers in *Gawain and the Green Knight*, when Gawain defines his sin as cowardice and 'couetyse'.[27] Fear of death led him to 'couetyse', a characteristic he specifically says is alien to the nature of knighthood: 'Þat is larges and lewté þat longez to knyȝtez'. Gawain may have committed cowardice and disloyalty, but why this self-accusation of 'couetyse'? The text has already stressed that covetous-ness, in the ordinary sense, was not involved (ll. 1846–50). If, however, we see this contrasting of 'couetyse' with 'larges', as defining the knight by separat-ing him from merchants and commerce, it makes sense in relation to contem-porary cultural assumptions. Through tests, Gawain, though not a youth undergoing standard rites of passage, attains to a higher concept of knight-hood (see below) and, in a romance abounding in the imagery and diction of exchange and contract, the poet's cultural paradigm is one that distinguishes between the bargains that true knights make, of self-forgetful loyalty ('lewté') and honour, and those that the unknightly make, for personal gain.

In contrast to Florent's contempt for, and laughing exploitation of his tradesman foster father, Havelok, the royal foundling throws himself into becoming a worker to help his adoptive family, saying he must learn to earn money since 'It is no shame forto swinken', to help pay for his food (ll. 785–966). Cuckoo-like, Havelok grows bigger than his plebeian family, a sign of superior lineage. Gamelyn too grows large, while growing up in reduced circumstances. He adopts his own equivalent to the knightly sword that is the formal sign at dubbing of achieving knighthood: a large pestle.[28] Perceval in the wilderness uses a homemade javelin. Young Gowther makes

---

[25] Diamond, 'Loving Beasts', p. 155.

[26] See Keen, *Chivalry*, pp. 146–8.

[27] *Sir Gawain and the Green Knight*, ed. J. R. R. Tolkien and E. V. Gordon, 2nd edn (London, 1967), l. 2381.

[28] *Gamelyn, Robin Hood and Other Outlaw Tales*, ed. S. Knight and T. H. Ohlgren (Kalamazoo, 1997), pp. 184–226, ll. 121–62.

his own terrifyingly massive falchion, matching his alarming physical growth and growth in evil, between fifteen and sixteen. Gowther becomes a fighter but not yet a correctly socialized fighter as his society constructs that role.[29] Such departures from formally bestowed swords can be positive or negative: signs of instinctive chivalry, where a boy lacks conventional nurture, or of that nurture's disastrous failure.

Sir Gowther (c. 1400) depicts adult violence without the moderating chivalric ideals of 'cortaysye', mercy and respect for the Church.[30] Gowther undergoes two different rituals, each designed to mark transition to a new, higher identity: dubbing, belonging to the secular code of chivalry, and penance, belonging to the theological model for spiritual progress. The dubbing (ll. 147–8) fails. He does not after it perform knightly acts correctly: he fights with his idiosyncratic sword and analogous lack of conformity to the model of the knight as defender of the Church: 'Now is he duke of greyt renown / And men of holy kyrke dynnggus down' (ll. 166–7). Similarly he loves hunting, distinctively aristocratic behaviour, but makes nuns his prey: 'He went to honte apon a day; / He see a nonry be tho way [. . .]', (ll. 178–9). Another mismatch in his bungled transition to knighthood: he wins 'greyt renown', but from outrages; raping and burning nuns spreads 'his name full wide' (ll. 185 and 188–9).

Krueger says that one of recent criticism's

> most sobering [critical] reassessments is the claim that many Arthurian romances 'aestheticize' or romanticize women's role as helpless victims of rape or male violence and thus make crimes against women a seemingly 'normal' aspect of the fabric of chivalric life.[31]

The potential for such reassessment seems already present in this fable of a youth whose aristocratic socialization does not proceed as it should. Gowther, the hyper-ferocious knightly youth, cured by the period of ritually imposed subhuman behaviour, ends as a hyper-socialized knight, fulfilling every literary criterion for perfectly achieved knighthood: fame, prowess, wife and realm, becoming an emperor ('Of all Cryston knyghttus tho flouwre',

---

[29] Swords in romances symbolize the romanticizing vision of the landowner as knight (Riddy, 'Middle English Romance', p. 238); also masculine sexuality, and legitimation, often involved when a youth's parentage or recognition as a knight are in question. Belting on the sword was part of the knighting ritual; Lancelot contrives that Guenevere, not Arthur, shall do this for him (*Lancelot*, p. 165). Degare's sword without a point accompanies him till he finds his father, who gives him the point, completing his legitimation and identity. Gowther points his own unknightly, deviant, sword at his mother till she tells him of his similarly unknightly and deviant father.

[30] *Raoul de Cambrai* depicts a highborn hero lacking these qualities, but in realistic literary mode. Raoul armed (= dubbed) Bernier, who feels consequently unable to oppose him even after Raoul disinherits his father and murders his mother. When young Gautier agrees to defend his uncle Raoul's memory, his armour is carried at Pentecost into mass in the church and then donned ceremoniously (CLXXXIV–CLXXXV).

[31] Krueger, 'Questions of Gender', p. 149.

l. 706), dispensing *largesse*, serving the Church: helping the poor, founding an abbey and always following good counsel. His ferocity now targets Saracens, the paradigmatic foes of Christendom, not nuns, the Church's own. Here penance performs three functions: in its normal theological role; as alternative *rite de passage* for this incomplete knight, on whose tainted genetics dubbing wrought no advance; and as an unspelling test, reversing the effects of his mother's rape by a fiend (baptism and a good mentor do this for Merlin in *Arthour and Merlin*). This romance's transformation of its hero is both a tale of wonder and a Christian blueprint for reformation through suffering. Its spectacle of a young man out of control, psychotic in modern terms, represents also repressed awareness of the aggressive basis of the concept of chivalry, which ceremonies of knighthood functioned, in theory, to civilize, curb and christianize.

Like the earlier *Queste*, *Gowther* subjects secular knighthood, and its developmental goals, to some potentially destructive questioning, but without replacing it with spiritual knighthood, though Gowther's suffering is defined by the Pope as Christian penance. Instead, Gowther's perversion of chivalric ideals, in the areas of violence and sex, ultimately gives stronger religious sanction to the values of secular knighthood: his unnatural, devilish lineage naturalizes those chivalric values. The implications of the devil's interference in the genetics of this Duke's son provide a reassuring message that normally nobly begotten youths will demonstrate during maturation a series of acts confirming their fitness for that identification. As in *Gawain*, using a fantastic form of penance to solve distortions in knighthood leaves unquestioned the issue of whether it is the construction of chivalry itself that is at fault: penance is a ritual built on the assumption that failures are a personal, not a socially constructed problem.

The *gentil* boy's superior size and warlike spirit, a recurrent romance topos, raises in *Gowther* the issue of violence: this youth with precociously massive physique and grotesque proclivity for fighting converts into extreme form, *in malo*, the stereotype of the born aristocrat's special strength and spirit. The phenomenon acknowledges a dark potential in a privileged warrior class, while safely containing this within the fiction that such a child's birth to a knight must be unnatural.[32] His reformation, through the ritual period of demotion to an animal-like lifestyle, losing human speech and civilized eating customs, symbolically appropriates and neutralizes the fear it addresses, of brute instincts in the highborn. Exploring the same anxieties, *Valentine and Orson*'s lost royal baby, reared by a bear, acquires no *gentilesse* even after transfer back to a court and

---

[32] See R. Kaeuper, 'The Societal Role of Chivalry in Romance: Northwestern Europe', in *Cambridge Companion*, ed. Krueger, pp. 97–114; P. C. Maddern, *Violence and Social Order: East Anglia 1422–1447* (Oxford, 1992), pp. 75–110, analyses internally contradictory attitudes to violence in chivalric doctrines that knights were rightly and naturally warlike, like lions, yet their violence would be justly employed, for good and in the defence of the people.

baptism, grabbing food 'as a famisshed wolfe' and sleeping on the earth.[33] This wild boy's lack of knightly education, contrasting with his conventionally reared brother, privileges education over nature, while also separating out aggressive and uncouth elements from the acceptable image of warrior adulthood. As in *Octavian*, two brothers reared differently (one at court, one among bears) create a fable to explore nurture and nature in the differing life-passages of medieval boys from higher and lower classes. Both romances invoke religious rites, penance and baptism, besides social rites of passage. These three tales – *Octavian* celebrating *gentil* nature, *Valentine and Orson* celebrating nurture, but pessimistic about the efficacy of the sacrament of baptism, and *Gowther* celebrating nurture, and even more the rite of penance in the eventual production of an acceptable mature knight – prove not finally very different from each other in their negotiation of conflicts within the concept of a hereditary noble class. The comic antics of Valentine, the wild boy, and the sensationalism of Gowther, the psychotic devil's son, resemble the mocked commercialism of the *Octavian* tradesman: all three provide negative counter-images to the model of knighthood, extreme caricatures to contrast with the ideal image of upper-class manhood, which their heroes, sooner or later, despite bad starts in life, achieve. We could read the animal-like boy, the devil-begotten psychopath and crude tradesman father as constructions invoking and then exorcizing the spectre of the possibility that the *gentils* might not be biologically superior to those they exploit: a fictional structure for separating knights from their own lower selves and from the lower classes, who consequently merit contempt or exploitation with impunity.[34]

Gawain and the Green Knight's wild man is elegant, courtly – in short, knightly – as well as massive, aggressive and endowed with symbols of nature, a double construction which challenges conflicts within the concept of the formation of a knight more tellingly than a wilder wild man would. This hybrid monster-knight, who brings trials for Gawain that resemble rites of passage, represents tensions within knighthood, not just an external hostile Other (somewhat as Morgan also is presented as the Enemy Within: 'thyn aunt, Arthurez half-suster', l. 2464). Some critics read him as superior, *qua* knight, to Gawain and the Round Table, a reaction showing how far the poet creates an ambiguous enemy: evil-intentioned, deceitful, yet challenging the assumption that Arthur's young knights are automatically the 'best' (l. 261). In my view, he embodies a revelation not that Camelot is decadent but of the potential for deconstructing chivalry's equivocal concepts such as

---

[33] *Valentine and Orson*, ed. A. Dickson, EETS OS 204 (London, 1937), p. 74. Chrétien's Perceval has natural chivalric gifts but grotesquely lacks understanding or responsibility, requiring a process of learning through precept and hard experience.

[34] *Silence*, with a girl hero raised as a boy, contains a debate between Nature and *Noreture*: Reason warns the child that unless she undergoes an upbringing to turn her into a male and a knight (breeches, boys' games, archery, a horse and a chariot), she cannot inherit her father's land. This romance poses, with particular subtlety, the question of whether being a knight, and masculinity and femininity, are matters of birth or training.

civilized aggression, or Christian luxury, pride and courtly love. *Gawain* shows personal effort and vigilance are required even by those who are already made knights (*Lancelot du Lac* also demonstrates effort working together with nurture and inborn knightliness). For Chênerie the conflict of nature *versus* nurture and effort, whether knights are born or made, was a troubling question from the earliest romances: the forest boy Perceval asks the first knights he meets, 'Fustes vos ansi nez?' ('Were you born like this?'). Chênerie asks, 'On ne nait pas chevalier, mais on le devient; or comment l'élite ainsi constituée ne serait-elle pas reservée à la noblesse, dans la réalité comme dans la fiction?'[35]

Besides animal-reared or supernaturally monstrous knights, transvestite heroines like Silence, acquitting themselves at knightly skills, pose analogous challenges to the social myths of noble youths' innate chivalric potential, of patriarchal power and 'the feudal politics of lineage'.[36]

Gawain does not literally depict its hero's *enfances* or rites and may seem a strange inclusion in this study of rites of passage. However, Arthur and the Round Table are introduced as knightly but also youthful, in their first age, even 'childgered' (l. 86), preparing us for a progression towards fuller maturity (which turns out to be a chastened understanding of knighthood) lying ahead, through the educative testing and humiliation of their representative, Gawain. Its sequence of trials and mystifications, akin to rites of passage, leads to enlightenment. Gawain experiences a variant of the second accolade, the nick in his neck, and emerges from lonely trials reborn as a penitent: a new kind of knight combining chivalry with the experience of penitence enjoined on all Christians. The narrative re-dubs its already-dubbed knight into a reformulated identity: the knight as consciousness-raised Christian adult, an Everyman (Every-Adam) accepting his own Original Sin – as well as re-incorporating him into a band of brother knights, themselves now reformulated into a new Order, with its penitential badge signifying 'Þe faut and þe fayntyse of þe flesche crabbed' (l. 2435). The Enemy Within, finally revealed as human proclivity to sin (symbolized in fitt three as female), is common humanity not just knighthood. Maturation and triumph over that enemy entails recognition of inadequacy, as in Deguileville's *Pèlerinage de vie humaine*, a possible inspiration for the Gawain-poet. Many elements encourage readers to think in terms of rites of passage: emphasis on the cycle of the seasons suggests corresponding human developmental cycles; fitt two's arming passage and fitt four's neck wound parody the dubbing and accolade, parallels strengthened during both passages by a listing of knightly duties. Gawain enters Hautdesert temporarily identity-less; the welcoming castle, appearing so mysteriously, like the uncanny Green

---

[35] Chênerie, *Chevalier errant*, pp. 42–3.

[36] S. Kinoshita, quoted in E. Archibald's discussion of cross-dressing heroines in 'The *Ide and Olive* Episode in Lord Berners's *Huon of Bordeaux*', in *Tradition and Transformation in Medieval Romance*, ed. R. Field (Cambridge, 1999), pp. 139–51 (p. 150); See Crane, *Gender and Romance*, pp. 76–92; Krueger, 'Questions of Gender', pp. 137–46.

Chapel (simultaneously chapel, devil's oratory and simple cave) are liminal spaces where tests, personal revelation and re-orientation occur. Romances like to take their heroes into mysterious, separated zones, whether the strange lake of *Lancelot du Lac*, grail castles, isles of ladies or magic territories like the land of Gorre, where they lose their certainties and emerge changed. Gawain's loneliness is stressed ('Ferre floten fro his frendys [. . .]', and 'mon al hym one': see ll. 696, 714, 735 and 749), riding through a Cheshire landscape that seems strangely depopulated, making it both familiar and one of these mythic terrains of separation. Extra strain is imposed on him, like an initiate, by withheld facts, his undisclosed destination and his assailants' disguised identities. The conclusion may not show a youth winning through to the conventional fictional acme of success – acclaim for prowess, a kingdom and wife – but Gawain and the youthful Round Table attain a higher stage of the concept of what it means to be a knight.

In several romances chivalric maturation is cross-fertilized with the ritual of penance.[37] *Gawain* has affinities with this group, which includes *Sir Gowther*. Romances also often have similarities with saints' lives. Medieval youths had more then one path to adulthood: religion was the career of many. Hybridization between the genres of romance, hagiography and penitential *exemplum* produces some narratives where two alternative life paths and identities, secular and religious, are central topics. The potential for conflict between them reflects both the prominence of penitential and transcendental ideals in medieval Christianity, and the contradictions in the idea of a Christian chivalry that included violence, pride, sexual desire, worldly display and luxury. Grail romances are the obvious sites for this conflict, presenting the two cultural paradigms in opposition for the allegiance of young knights: entry into the knightly military class and spiritual development.

Perceval's fascination with knights typifies one and his encounter with, and testing in, the Fisher King's castle typifies the other. The Cistercian view of life's journey in the *Queste del Graal* is relatively unequivocal about the absolute superiority of the spiritual path, whereas Chrétien's and Malory's negotiation of the two paths seems ambiguous.[38] Chrétien's Perceval, whose inherited knightly proclivities (nature) require mentoring, humiliation and training (nurture) to secure the desired identity, fails initially in his secular progress towards growing up as a knight and completely fails the spiritual test. Development involves first leaving the female world but later adapting to the need to relate to a woman and experience sexual desire, channelled into correctly socialized forms of *cortois* sensitivity, self-control and semi-mystical adoration: a sentimental education watched over by Gauvain as Perceval's

---

[37] A. Hopkins, *The Sinful Knights: A Study of Middle English Penitential Romance* (Oxford, 1990).

[38] On ambiguities in the *Queste*'s religious approach to romance see S. Gaunt, 'Romance and Other Genres', in *Cambridge Companion*, ed. Krueger, pp. 45–59 (pp. 55–7).

mentor.[39] In grail romances, contemplation of the grail, for chosen initiates, is an epitome of that liminal state ideally experienced through the Eucharist. It is unclear towards which model of masculine identity, secular or religious, Chrétien would have directed his incomplete romance, or whether incompleteness, as often with Chaucer, suggests tension between irreconcilable worldviews.

Secular and religious models of masculine adulthood both involve rituals to formalize correct relations with the female: marriage or vows of celibacy. The ideal woman, once found, is often separated by a gulf, a categorical otherness: in some romances she is a Muslim; the only loving female in Lanval's world is a fairy; the woman may be socially superior: a king's daughter or, for Lancelot and Tristan, the king's queen. In these narratives, like *Gawain*, where attraction to a female is lethally dangerous, society is essentially single-sex masculine, with women featuring as isolated figures: figures, for good or ill, of the power of masculine desire. Crane sees romance, with its remote females and courtly love, providing a 'distancing and protective function for male lovers [. . .] removing them from engagement with the female' and any potentially adversarial voice. The trials of *Gowther* and *Lanval* produce successful marriage, as well as admiration from the masculine group from which the hero was earlier excluded. In *Gawain*, however, lone trials unfold into an escape from the perils of interacting with women, the masculine group's approbation in this dénouement taking the form of re-defining a lady's girdle as a badge of membership of a new masculine knightly order.

Weddings were relatively common in *chansons de geste*, with their robustly practical interest in family advancement and winning estates. *Gerbert* describes a sequence: wedding, the subsequent birth of sons, the mother's churching and their baptisms (ll. 11482–594). For Alice in *Raoul de Cambrai*, her weddings have social and life-changing significance, but primarily for *men*: the king uses marriage to her, and her revenues, as counters in homosocial power relationships in the opening scenes' aggressive political drama. Fictional weddings illustrate rituals: giving money (in *Garin*, l. 7140, the bridegroom gives gold and silver); giving rings (two rings, perhaps for bride and groom, are mentioned in *Raoul de Cambrai*, l. 6166). Romances rarely describe weddings in detail except where they have emotional or symbolic significance for the wider drama. The wedding description forms the climax of *Libeaus*, marking the lady's release from enchantment as a 'worme' (dragon). *William of Palerne*'s triple wedding unites its three young men in comradeship after many trials. From windows townspeople dressed in their best watch aristocratic guests spur their horses along streets strewn and hung with cloth of gold and coloured draperies; there are many priests and amazingly loud music

---

[39] The English *Sir Perceval of Galles* lacks the Grail and spiritual dimension, contrasting earthly and heavenly knighthood (even Perceval's final expedition to Jerusalem is an opportunity to sack cities, not partake in a Crusade).

(ll. 5005–14). The brides enter the church magnificently dressed, each escorted by a great man. Priests in procession advance and bid the king kiss the cross. There is a solemn marriage 'bemaked at cherche' (wedding in church was not yet the absolute rule), said in the correct way, and month-long feasting, with splendid gifts for minstrels (ll. 5034–74). After a blunt man-to-man contract arranged with her father (the bride apparently not consulted), Arthur 'treuthed' Guenevere in *Arthour and Merlin* (1250–1300) (l. 8639), not betrothal but the crucial pledge 'I plight thee my troth': binding if followed by intercourse (see also *King Horn*, l. 672).[40] After the seven-day feast, Guenevere arms Arthur for fighting Saracens and he kisses her as she puts on each piece, a symbolic union of love and chivalry. The ceremony of the bridegroom laying money, the dower, on the service-book appears in *Havelok* (ll. 1173–4), 'penies þicke tolde / Mikel plente upon þe bok', a detail with bitter irony in context: by forced marriage to this unfree man, the bride is being deprived of her inheritance. Rymenhild's first wedding is on a Sunday; Horn arrives after the Matins bells have rung and Mass finished; Rymenhild refuses consent, stating she will not be married 'wiþ golde' (l. 1118), but is carried off to her bridegroom's castle. At the feast she circulates, pouring drink for the men, a ritual giving Horn the chance to reveal himself and plot their revenge. Her second unwanted wedding is at night. The custom of banquet minstrelsy enables Horn, disguised as a minstrel, to defeat their enemies. *Ponthus* describes a custom of feeding thirteen paupers in memory of Jesus and the apostles: at Sidone's unwanted wedding the bride goes round with drink for the paupers, providing a chance for her disguised, equally marginalized, lover to reveal himself. *Perceval of Galles* details lavish presents bestowed when Arthur gives his sister to a brave knight, and magnificent jousting, but these are the preliminaries to tragedy: the young husband's death.

Families and sweethearts are frequently lost and found. Occasionally (especially, it seems, in early romances) masculine relational and emotional development forms a central theme: the crises and tests Yvain and Erec endure are concerned with their maturation as husbands as well as knights. *Guigemar* presents heterosexual awakening as a necessary part of a young noble's growth, with failure to develop heterosexual desire as a *lack*, a disablement, in young Guigemar's psyche. It can only be healed and turned into wholeness by – paradoxically – a wound, followed by a magical, symbolic, experience of separation and initiation into love. Perhaps the rarity of such direct confrontation of masculine sexual and relational development in later romances' plots, despite their continuing motifs like advantageous marriages, loyal fiancées, perilous seducers and ecstatic desire, reflects their uneasy containment of sexual relationships. Krueger sees romances as fables

---

40 *Arthour and Merlin*, ed. O. D. Macrae-Gibson, 2 vols., EETS OS 268 and 279 (London, 1973, 1979). Berlenger, *Damedieus*, pp. 94–106; Riddy, 'Middle English Romance', pp. 240–1; Rymenhild's second marriage, starting with private 'troth', is 'a process rather than an event, just as it was in contemporary society'.

of powerful men's life-journeys and as upholding the traditional marginalization of women yet creating a fictive space where tensions within norms of
gender relations and identity, and resistances to them, can be explored.[41] The
Roman de la Rose, a hybrid of romance and allegory, is structured on the drama
of the protagonist's initiation into love and progress to sexual success.
Perhaps thereafter masculine emotional turmoil is still found, but in different
genres: dream poem and *dit amoureux*.

Giving, losing, changing and recovering names is linked in romance to
turning points and events apart from conventional baptism.[42] Baptism ceremonies, like other rites of passage, interest authors most when non-standard
or susceptible to symbolism, though occasionally we see simple concern that
the Christian ceremony shall have been performed. A Saracen's conversion
and baptism, however, is not uncommon in *chansons de geste* and romances:
part of the Christian hegemony that informs the ethos of knighthood. The
alacrity with which beautiful highborn Muslim women fall in love with
Christian heroes and desire baptism functions as a pattern of capitulation by
Islam: a triumphant, orientalist demonstration of Christian men's capacity to
defeat men of other societies, including through superior attractiveness to
their women. It parallels the victorious image of the higher-class male attracting the womenfolk of lower-class men which is aggressively celebrated by
medieval comedies like the *Miller's* and *Reeve's Tales*. *Gerbert* describes a
Muslim king's baptism after defeat, mentioning godparents and three fonts,
perhaps a trinitarian motif (ll. 12502–30). In *The Sowdon of Babylon*, though the
sultan's son accepts baptism and his sister capitulates eagerly to the Christian
hero and baptism, their father mocks the pope's tonsure, attacks the bishop
with a sword and spits in the font, choosing death rather than baptism. *The
King of Tars* (c. 1320) hinges on baptism: though the heroine accepts Islam and
marriage to a sultan, her child is born as shapeless flesh; she is accused of lack
of a true conversion to Islam, but the child after Christian baptism becomes a
beautiful baby, a miracle prompting the sultan's baptism (he changes from
black to white) and mass conversion of the Tartars. Similarly, in *Arthour and
Merlin* the newborn devil's baby, Merlin, can speak immediately after baptism
to defend his innocent mother. Anointing ceremonies are occasionally mentioned. Deguileville's *Pèlerinage de vie humaine* describes the hero's baptism
and anointing with chrism. *The Awntyrs off Arthure* (after 1375) mentions the
queen's christening and chrisming (ll. 138 and 224–5) and the apotropaic

---

[41] Krueger, 'Questions of Gender', p. 145.
[42] Name-giving or discovery as quasi-ritual reward for prowess is a frequent fictional
variant on christening, e.g. Perceval and Lancelot, whose name (multiply changed)
is restored after conquering Dolorous Gard. In *De ortu Waluuini*, the hero is first 'boy
with no name', then, after dubbing, 'knight with the surcoat' and, when restored to
his royal family, revealed as Gawain, nephew of Arthur. Like *Octavian*, this has a
foundling reared by a tradesman; *The Rise of Gawain, Nephew of Arthur (De ortu
Waluuini nepotis Arthuri)*, ed. and trans. M. L. Day (New York, 1984).

function of baptism, implicitly linked to her torture by demons in Purgatory.[43] Christening, which modern culture perceives as a gentle rite of passage combining name-giving with welcoming a new member into the Christian community, retained in medieval culture a stronger cosmic spiritual purpose, protecting the new Christian against demons. The *Prose Merlin* contains a rare allusion to coronation anointing, a detail demonstrating Arthur as exemplary medieval king ruled by his baronial council: agreeing their timetable for this 'sacring' at Pentecost.[44]

Detailed death rites are relatively rare in romances, commoner in *chansons de geste*.[45] In the *Moniage Guillaume* the dying hero asks forgiveness, bequeaths possessions to his sons and the Church and receives anointing.[46] *Garin* mentions a funeral Mass, vigil and endowment of a chantry (ll. 10819, 11354 and 11625–30). *Raoul de Cambrai* describes four gold crosses at the head of Raoul's bier, incense, priests saying the office and speeches of lamentation and vengeance over the bier; his 'aimie' recalls their betrothal 'dans une chapelle', swears eternal chastity and kisses his body; he is finely robed for burial and offerings are given to fund prayers (ll. 3309–543). Bernier, dying, forgives his murderer, confesses and gives himself communion with three blades of grass (a common motif); his body is washed with water and wine, sewn in a linen shroud and fine silk cloth covers the bier. There is tearing of hair, speeches of lamentation and vengeance and a vigil by the body (ll. 8230–350).

There have been changes of emphasis in anthropologists' and critics' use of 'rites of passage' over the last century, though the relevance to romance studies of the evolving and overlapping concepts remains strong. Critical perspectives on romance also changed, from early pre-occupations with myth, or an expectation of simple historical reflectionism, or discussion of romances as if essentially proto-novels, to approaches derived from cultural materialism and a new historicist focus on power; analyses of reception, readership and patronage; and psychoanalytic, gender and postcolonial perspectives. Many romances emerge as complex and conflicted in their presentation of masculine upper-class maturation and its goals: knighthood and success through prowess, war, marriage and rule. The study of rites of passage also raises issues of the presentation of violence, gender, socialization and class.

Van Gennep's foundational definition of rites of passage included separation: a private experience that fitted the individual to take up a role in his public community. Trial through separation takes many fictional forms:

[43] H. Phillips, 'The Ghost's Baptism in the *Awntyrs off Arthure*', *Medium Aevum* 58 (1989), 49–58.
[44] *Merlin*, ed. H. B. Wheatley, 2 vols., EETS OS 10 and 36 (London, 1899, 1910), I, 105–17.
[45] Chaucer, *Knight's Tale* (ll. 1969–2108), following Boccaccio, visualizes pagan rites and pyre, with 'lich-wake' and 'wake-pleyes' (l. 2102), conflating classical funeral games and English customs. See also V. E. B. Richmond, *Laments for the Dead in Medieval Narrative* (Pittsburgh, 1966).
[46] *Les deux rédactions en vers du Moniage Guillaume*, ed. W. Cloetta, 2 vols., Société des anciens textes français (Paris, 1906, 1911), I, ll. 41–50.

displaced babies, loss of family, rank, name, hideous incarnation as a were-wolf or devil's son, lonely quests, fights and temptations. In *Lanval*, *Guigemar* and *Erec* separation becomes the arena for sexual maturation. The 'peniten-tial knight' romances fit this template, penance being an individual ritual action for transition from an old self to a new: Lancelot does penance for adultery and this marks a transition from the old Lancelot of the prose *Lancelot* to the reformed one of the *Quest del saint Graal*, now enabled to see the Grail. *Sir Gowther, Robert of Cisyle* and *Gawain*, depict personal transform-ation through isolation, trial and humiliation all of which are specifically identified with penitence.

Gawain's tests and dénouement confirm Humphrey and Laidlaw's theory that ritual actions raise issues about interpretation resembling those raised by language and games.[47] The 'beheading' contract and bedroom tests, pre-sented as games (knightly sports, the game of love-talking), are challenges for Gawain in terms whose correct interpretation is hard to determine. He returns to his community a failure – in heroic terms – but contrition and recognition of human proclivity to sin is the Christian success story. By the end nothing is what it initially seemed, including knighthood, maturity and success. Waiting to receive the Green Knight's blow, he faces what appears to be death but is play-acting: another motif found in rites of passage. *Gawain*'s villains resem-ble the *Magic Flute*'s: apparently hostile tests are benign towards their victim, furthering his true maturation, an educational process more akin to rites of passage than to conventional romance models of heroes defeating unambigu-ous enemies. As in the *Magic Flute*, the symbolic acts and progress are defined according to distinctive cultural discourses (medieval penance or freemasonry) that create a drama of overt containment and conflict, most obviously in rela-tion to fear of the female.

Familial patterns in romances early attracted anthropologists' interest: recurrence of uncles as mentors to nephews was interpreted as a relic of matrilineal society.[48] Romance plots abound in mysteries and coincidences that reunite family members; an example with apparently ritualistic roots is Caradoc's 'beheading game' which restores his father to him. More easily than real life, romances heal family crises, fictionally and fantastically; these acts of healing are game-like symbolic acts and analogues to rites of passage. Critics who invoke rites of passage have concentrated most on family dramas, in relation to masculine development.[49] Brewer observes that English romances often end with reconciliation within the family, their plots tracing

---

[47] C. Humphrey and J. Laidlaw, *The Archetypal Actions of Ritual: A Theory of Ritual Illustrated by the Jain Rite of Worship* (Oxford, 1994).

[48] W. O. Farnsworth, *Uncle and Nephew in the Old French Chansons de Geste: A Study in the Survival of Matriarchy* (New York, 1913, repr. 1966); R. G. Koss, *Family, Kinship and Lineage in the Cycle of Guillaume D'Orange*, Studies in Medieval Literature 5 (Lewiston, 1990), pp. 3, 55–7, 129 and 185–6.

[49] See especially D. Brewer, 'Escape from the Mimetic Fallacy', in *Studies in Medieval English Romances*, ed. D. Brewer (Cambridge, 1988), pp. 1–10.

the 'multiple play of forces round the emerging adult', showing the youth escaping from childhood and parents, proving individual worth and then marrying; they are 'essentially stories of the successful *rite de passage*'.[50] Simpson reads *Sir Degare* as structured on rites of passage, which he defines as patterns of self-realization for individual men within the winning of a happy family. Degare is separated from his family and returned to it; *en route* he nearly kills his grandfather, nearly sleeps with his mother and nearly kills his father. In avoiding these, he rediscovers each family member, while becoming an adult himself through prowess and marriage, a plot Simpson calls 'clearly [. . .] a *rite de passage*'.[51] Such readings assume broadly Freudian readings of 'rite of passage' and a universal pattern for (masculine) maturation. Arguably, however, different cultures specify particular goals and crises to be addressed by rites of passage: medieval culture defined the purposes of historical and fictional rites of passage, as well as their format. The *Romance of the Rose*'s dramatization of initiation into love, appropriating chivalric rituals such as homage, clearly conflates that initiation with *entrée* into court society: a culturally specific idea of key stages in the path towards sexual union within a culturally specific idea of a particular class-community. Gaunt stresses the perception in *Éneas*, *Erec* and *Yvain* that young men learn to negotiate a 'competition' between the masculine and feminine worlds, whereas Crane sees a deeper medieval association between combat and love, extended here from homosocial to heterosexual encounters.[52]

Deguileville's *Pèlerinage de vie humaine*, widely known and translated, is the fullest medieval exposition of life as a journey and the richest compendium of rites of passage.[53] It plays off different identities and life-journeys against each other: the knight-errant's series of single combats, the pilgrim's journey through dangers and finally an entirely passive transportation by ship, representing the life of a monk. These are presented as three successive steps on a journey to a state of grace and death and also a journey towards understanding. Like *Gawain*, it subverts the chivalric paradigm of progress by individual effort: the goal is the soul's life-journey to the heavenly Jerusalem; success comes through experience of failure, the theological moment of triumph when the protagonist acknowledges that only throwing himself into the agency of Grace will secure a successful end. As a *remaniement* of the *Roman de la Rose*, it rewrites that symbolic narrative of an upper-class youth's initiation into sex. It unites the narrative genres of romance, allegorical psychomachia and dream

[50] D. Brewer, *Symbolic Stories: Traditional Narratives of Family Drama in English Literature* (Cambridge, 1980), pp. 11 and 90.
[51] J. Simpson, 'Violence, Narrative and Proper Name: *Sir Degaré*, "The Tale of Sir Gareth of Orkney" and the *Folie Tristan d'Oxford*', in *The Spirit of Medieval English Popular Romance*, ed. A. Putter and J. Gilbert (Harlow, 2000), pp. 122–41 (pp. 129–30).
[52] Gaunt, 'From Epic to Romance', cited in Crane, *Gender and Romance*, pp. 39–54.
[53] 1st version c. 1330, *Le Pèlerinage de vie humaine*, ed. J. J. Stürzinger (London, 1893); 2nd version c. 1350, ed. J. J. Stürzinger (London, 1895).

poem.[54] This is the chivalric romance where, after the grand arming ceremony, the hero takes his armour off. Later he does not stay long enough in the bath of penitence (symbol of cleansing from an old life, similar to the ceremonial baths at dubbing). Tribulation forges men's crowns by beating them and, in this progress through life which is, by conventional romance standards, an anti-progress, the turning point is a recognition that, having tried to fly upwards and failed, he resembles a fallen leaf blown into a corner. He emerges from tribulation to the refuge of Grace, not to personal triumph. Defeat, not heroism, is the context for new understanding – as in *Gawain*.

This narrative of the achievement of a non-self, compared with heroic narratives, is witty and action-filled: an *aventure* as sensational, violent and zestful as any romance. The hero encounters terrifying and bizarre foes. Deguileville designed it for laity: the hero ends up as a monk but the rites common to all Christians are prominent, with knights' dubbing, priestly ordination and monastic vows added to them. The narrative of the hero's own 'life journey' and its ritual stages begins after nine months in the 'house of dirt': he is baptized, plunged thrice in a cleansing bath, signed with the cross (the *Tau*: Deguileville frequently relates Jewish and Christian traditions) and anointed on head, breast and back (ll. 440–532). Rites of anointing are itemized, as ointments for champions and pilgrims: baptism, confirmation, extreme unction, coronation, ordination, the consecration of bishops and altars. Marriage is briefly mentioned (ll. 801–20). Then comes tonsure and initiation into the priesthood: Reason teaches new monks to adhere to her, use self-control and abjure carnality as illustrated by the *Roman de la Rose*. As an anti-*Rose*, the text allegorizes the tonsure as an enclosed garden (ll. 890–932), its open space symbolizing the monk's heart, open to God. Rituals for ordaining minor orders follow: porters, exorcists, acolytes, readers and sub-deacons (ll. 940–61). There is instruction on rites of penance and absolution (ll. 571–622, 1112–22 and 1381–412). The protagonist experiences Christian education and confirmation. The arming ceremony by Grace Dieu includes the allegorizations of arms, derived from biblical texts such as Ephesians, used in real-life dubbing *ordines*.[55] The author cunningly keeps the accolade for later (like Gawain's second accolade). The hero receives the gambeson of patience, habergeon of fortitude, gorget of sobriety, helmet of temperance, gloves of continence, sword of justice, scabbard of humility and shield of prudence. When he abandons all this, because it is too heavy, Grace initiates him into a second identity, giving him the satchel and staff of a pilgrim. These have magic jewels for defence, symbolizing the theological hope for mercy, a hope centred on the Virgin and Jesus. These, like other magic aids that save him later, represent the earliest stages of Christian teaching for medieval children: the Pater Noster, Ave, Creed and ABC; as in *Piers Plowman*'s journey the truths

[54] See S. Wright's perceptive 'Deguileville's *Pèlerinage de Vie Humaine* as "Contrepartie Edifiante" of the *Roman de la Rose*', *Philological Quarterly* 68 (1989), 399–422.
[55] Flori, 'Sémantique'.

humans will need most are the ones they always knew. The hero fails as a knight, and does not stay long enough in the bath of penance (recalling the ritual bath at dubbing, so common in French romances), a failure making possible his acceptance of grace. The hero's third identity, becoming a monk, is the occasion of his delayed accolade (ll. 12580–632), administered by Timor Dei with a mace, called Vengeance of the Lord and Fear of the Pains of Hell. The narrator says that secular knights would benefit from such a tough 'colee' (ll. 12630–1). Deguileville combines a blow of defeat and the dubbing to create a new honourable identity. The allegory of the cords recurs: in the monastic vows (we are told that religion is a binding together; Deguileville demonstrates his characteristic anti-individualism), where Obedience binds monks; Poverty makes music; the rule of silence becomes a tie on the tongue; the monk's feet are tied so that he cannot roam in self will; Chastity lies in bed with good monks. Life's journey ends with Sickness, Age, Death and divine Mercy. This ends the narrator's dream, an end that becomes a beginning: he wakes up, attends chapel and another day begins. This narrative of the 'vie humaine' as a journey differs from others we have considered in progressively devaluing and deconstructing notions of progress and the attainment of heroic identity. The most important truths a human can attain are ever-present, as is grace, ensuring victory over foes when this is denied to mere human effort. It concludes, like *Pearl* and *Piers Plowman*, leaving reader and hero with a personal journey still to make, in contrast to conventional chivalric narratives that offer closure, a completed narrative of masculine struggle, temptation, warfare and lone questing, producing triumphs and reconciliations. Death is the last initiation and metaphorically a return to babyhood: he drinks the milk of Misericorde, God's salvific mercy, that will preserve his infant soul during the journey into the Next Life. Medieval art presented souls as infants as they left the body. The life-journey has come full circle. Milk and blood in medieval physiology were one: this life-giving final rite is also the Eucharist, that symbolic enactment of the end which is a beginning, a defeat that is a victory.

Fictional narratives and rites of passage are both, Burke suggests, symbolic acts; Jameson defined symbolic acts as inevitably containing tensions and contradictions.[56] The tests, fights and ceremonies confirming knightly identity in romances embody contemporary visions of maturation (and of conflict, aggression and domination) for upper-class males. As such they resemble real-life culturally symbolic performances such as tournaments. Narratives of trial and battle, leading to the winning of success, peers' acclaim, the restoration and founding of families, relate a particular cultural narrative of masculinity, the most influential one of the medieval period, which survived vigorously into early modern culture. The conflicts and contradictions romances open up, particularly in chivalry's interactions with issues of gender, social dominance,

---

[56] K. Burke, *The Philosophy of Literary Form* (Berkeley, 1941), pp. 8–9; F. Jameson, *The Political Unconscious: Narrative as a Socially Symbolic Act* (Ithaca, 1980), p. 80.

violence and the opposing theological model of the human personality and its maturation, are unsurprising in narratives which so closely enact culturally symbolic acts. The potential for subversion of the masculine narrative of adventure, struggle and triumph is ever-present in romance. Its hero is, Jameson points out, typically naïve, inexperienced and puzzled.[57] He is close to being feminized; Crane suggests this is why the desired woman is often presented as Other, remote, exotic or dangerous.[58] Certainly the life-passages of the young heroes of romance turn out to be uncertain terrains, presenting as many conflicts within the realm of knightly identity and ideals as in battles with external foes.

---

[57] James, *Political Unconscious*, p. 113.
[58] Crane, *Gender and Romance*, pp. 184–96.

Becoming Woman in Chaucer:
'On ne naît pas femme, on le meurt'

Jane Gilbert

This essay considers the different relations between female characters, ideals of femininity, and death in two poems by Chaucer, the *Book of the Duchess* (hereafter *BD*) and the *Legend of Good Women* (hereafter *LGW*).[1] My argument on *BD* will be a version of that line of criticism which sees the poem as a funerary monument to the lady; the anthropological model here presented enhances understanding of this aspect of the poem. The absence in *LGW* of such a close fit between theory and text is itself productive, enabling us at once to refine the anthropological model and to argue that *LGW* works against certain normative constructions of femininity exemplified in *BD*. My focus will be on one specific rite of passage: that by which a deceased person is detached from the community of the living and integrated into the community of the dead. In both *BD* and *LGW* this process relates to a female character idealized as feminine exemplar. Hence my subtitle, which derives from the opening line of volume two of Beauvoir's *Le deuxième sexe*: 'on ne naît pas femme, on le devient', which I gloss as 'it is not birth that produces a woman, but social and cultural life'.[2] My adaptation is intended to read: 'it is not birth that produces a woman, but social and cultural death'. In *BD* the lady's

---

[1] All references to works by Chaucer are to *The Riverside Chaucer*, ed. L. D. Benson *et al.*, 3rd edn (Oxford, 1987). *BD* is generally dated between 1368 and 1376; see A. J. Minnis, with V. J. Scattergood and J. J. Smith, *Oxford Guides to Chaucer: The Shorter Poems* (Oxford, 1995), pp. 79–80. Of the two versions of *LGW*'s prologue, F is now generally accepted to be earlier, although there remains disagreement. The *Riverside Chaucer* dates the F prologue to 1386–8, G (which appears only in the earliest surviving manuscript) to 1394–6 (p. 1060); some of the legends may have been written earlier. For a full description of the manuscripts, see Geoffrey Chaucer, *The Legend of Good Women*, ed. J. Cowen and G. Kane (East Lansing, 1995), pp. 1–19. Minnis provides a review of major critical issues relating to *BD* and *LGW*; *Shorter Poems*, pp. 73–160 and 322–454, respectively. This paper has benefited from discussion at the Second York Interdisciplinary Conference on the Fourteenth Century and the Cambridge University Medieval English Graduate Seminar, and from the kind advice of Elizabeth Archibald, Ardis Butterfield, Paola Filippucci, Malcolm Gilbert, Sarah Kay, Helen Phillips and Nicolette Zeeman.

[2] S. de Beauvoir, *Le deuxième sexe*, 2 vols., folio essais 37 and 38 (Paris, 1949), II, 13. 'One is not born, but rather becomes, a woman', S. de Beauvoir, *The Second Sex*, ed. and trans. H. M. Parshley (Harmondsworth, 1972), p. 295.

idealization depends on her laudable willingness to leave the land of the living for that of the dead, whereas the virtuous women of *LGW* take their stand in an intermediate zone between earthly and heavenly life, resisting both passage into the afterlife and the rites designed to facilitate it. This resistance is an act of political, ethical and poetic significance, and the idealized representation of these ladies is consequently of a very different order from that found in *BD*.

DOUBLE OBSEQUIES

French anthropologist Robert Hertz, a pupil of Durkheim's, published in 1907 an essay on the collective representation of death.[3] Hertz focuses on societies in which the funerary process has two phases: death is followed initially by the temporary disposal of the body and by a period of mourning, which ends only some while later with a secondary burial involving the permanent disposal of the body and the memorialization of the deceased. With this, in Hertz's words, the death will be 'fully consummated'.[4] The intermediary period between death and the final obsequies permits a process of social disaggregation, gradually detaching the dead person from the collectivity to which he or she belonged in life. During this period the dead person is placeless, belonging fully to neither the land of the living nor the land of the dead.[5] 'Pitiful and dangerous', it exerts a continued claim on its mourners' solicitude (which must ensure its successful passage to the afterlife) while threatening them: 'It finds the solitude into which it has been thrust hard to bear and tries to drag the living with it.'[6] The mourners themselves mirror the deceased's 'illegitimate and clandestine' existence beyond the bounds of the community.[7] Considered to be impure, 'they can no longer live the way others do' but must remain isolated, distinguished by their dress, diet and activities.[8] Hertz uses paradoxical and sometimes poetic expressions to articulate the strange existence in which both deceased and mourners are trapped during this intermediary period, life in death for the former and living death for the latter. Secondary burial ends this temporary suspension of everyday life and social cohesion, and brings about a dual restoration. On the

[3] R. Hertz, 'A Contribution to the Study of the Collective Representation of Death', in *Death and the Right Hand*, trans. R. Needham and C. Needham (London, 1960), pp. 25–86; originally published as 'Contribution à une étude sur la représentation collective de la mort', *Année sociologique* 10 (1905–6), 48–137.
[4] Hertz, 'Contribution', p. 52.
[5] '[The soul] lives, as it were, marginally in the two worlds: if it ventures into the afterworld, it is treated there like an intruder; here on earth it is an importunate guest whose proximity is dreaded'; ibid., p. 36.
[6] Ibid., pp. 36–7.
[7] Ibid., p. 36.
[8] Ibid., p. 52. 'They live in darkness, dead themselves from a social point of view, because any active participation on their part in collective life would only spread abroad the curse they carry in them.'

one hand, by its 'liberation of the living' it functions 'to end the mourning of the relatives of the deceased and to bring these back into communion with society'.[9] On the other hand it marks the soul's rebirth as a full member of the invisible community of the dead.[10] Secondary burial regenerates the survivors and revitalizes earthly society; while the deceased finally casts aside its polluting mortal remains to emerge in a purified, idealized form, 'reborn transfigured and raised to a superior power and dignity' consonant with the status of the afterworld.[11] Only once the deceased is fully separate from the world of the living can a lasting memorial be constructed marking the absence of what it commemorates. In its new incarnation the soul may become a benign guardian spirit protecting and guiding the living. The purpose of the intermediary period between physical death and final burial is to perform this metamorphosis of 'a familiar person [. . .] like ourselves' into 'an ancestor', 'sometimes worshipped and always distant'.[12] Hertz describes the function of this metamorphosis as psychological and psychosocial. The belief that the soul 'only gradually severs the ties binding it to this world' expresses the emotional challenge facing the survivors who must let the dead person go. Similarly society, the collective formed of individuals, confronts the loss of 'the social being grafted upon the physical individual', a being which society has carefully formed over a long period.[13] The notion of death's finality threatens to annihilate the very terms on which life can be lived, and must be deflected into the idea of regeneration and rebirth. A crucial point which remains only tangential to Hertz's work is that this final reconciliation, a function of the living's deliverance from the disorientation of grief, makes the deceased available for political exploitation.[14] The definitively dead and gone are henceforth conjured as spirits to serve the interests of the dominant survivors, constrained only – although significantly – by the degree to which social conventions defy manipulation. Given that the dead enter the transcendent world on terms set by the living, secondary burial

---

9   Ibid., pp. 61–2.
10 '[T]here is a complete parallelism between the rite which introduces the deceased, washed and dressed in new clothes, into the company of his ancestors, and those which return his family to the community of the living: or rather it is one and the same act of liberation applied to two different categories of persons'; ibid., p. 64.
11 Ibid., pp. 56–7, 63–4 and 79–80.
12 Ibid., p. 82.
13 Ibid., p. 77. 'Death is an initiation. This statement is not a mere metaphor; if death, for the collective consciousness, is indeed the passage from the visible society to the invisible, it is also a step exactly analogous to that by which a youth is withdrawn from the company of women and introduced into that of adult men. This new integration, which gives the individual access to the sacred mysteries of the tribe, also implies a profound change in his personality, a renewal of his body and soul that gives him the religious and moral capacity he needs'; ibid., p. 80.
14 See the powerful but somewhat schematizing 'Introduction' by Maurice Bloch and Jonathan Parry to their edited volume *Death and the Regeneration of Life* (Cambridge, 1982), pp. 1–44. Bloch and Parry understand ritual as serving the dominant authority.

transforms a traumatic perception of physical loss into an orderly, healing apprehension of a greater pattern in which death is necessary to and a source of life.

THE BOOK OF THE DUCHESS

Told in the first person, *BD* recounts how after prolonged insomnia the narrator reads the story of Ceyx and Alcyone and eventually falls asleep.[15] Waking in his dream he follows a courtly party hunting a hart and meets a knight in deep mourning. His uncomprehending interrogation of this knight prompts the latter to recall in lengthy detail his beloved lady. Her fate is initially referred to through the mediation of courtly forms, but because the narrator fails to understand the fact of her recent, untimely death, the knight finally states it in a blunt form which the narrator immediately acknowledges, bringing both dream and poem to a rapid close.

The Man in Black's lady has been brutally torn out of her own and others' lives. It is clear from her lover's emotional state that this loss is unresolved; voluntarily outcast from society, 'Always deyinge and [. . .] not ded' (l. 588), his deathly life is closely reminiscent of Hertz's description of the mourner.[16] Unable even to contemplate engaging with life, the Man in Black feels excluded from and yearns for death (ll. 679–90). If, as Hertz has it, 'mourning is merely the direct consequence in the living of the actual state of the deceased', then the Man's condition implies that his lady's death remains unconsummated.[17] Her treatment to date has only functioned as a partial ritual, which cries out to be made whole. *BD* represents itself as responding to this need in a way which corresponds to the lady's secondary burial. The narrator elicits from the Man in Black an elegiac portrait and narrative which conjures his lady and their love in an ever more idealized form. This process involves a forgetting which becomes increasingly evident, for instance when the knight does not record the actual words by which the lady initially rejected him, only their import for himself (ll. 1236–44).[18] His experiences and emotions come into focus while hers remain indistinct; she is generalized as

---

[15] My reading of *BD* is generally indebted to A. Butterfield, 'Lyric and Elegy in *The Book of the Duchess*', *Medium Aevum* 60 (1991), 33–60; M. Ellmann, 'Blanche', in *Criticism and Critical Theory*, ed. J. Hawthorn, Stratford-upon-Avon Studies 2nd series (London, 1984), pp. 99–110; L. O. Fradenburg, '"Voice Memorial": Loss and Reparation in Chaucer's Poetry', *Exemplaria* 2 (1990), 169–202; L. O. Fradenburg, '"My Worldes Blisse": Chaucer's Tragedy of Fortune', *South Atlantic Quarterly* 98 (1999), 563–92; P. Hardman, 'The *Book of the Duchess* as a Memorial Monument', *Chaucer Review* 28 (1993–4), 205–15; G. Margherita, 'Originary Fantasies and Chaucer's *Book of the Duchess*', in *Feminist Approaches to the Body in Medieval Literature*, ed. L. Lomperis and S. Stanbury (Philadelphia, 1993), pp. 116–41.

[16] 'Contribution', pp. 37–53.

[17] Ibid., p. 51.

[18] On commemoration and forgetting see Adrian Forty's introduction to *The Art of Forgetting*, ed. A. Forty and S. Küchler (Oxford, 1999), pp. 1–19.

he is particularized. Knight and Lady act out the purgative process which is the *raison d'être* of Hertz's intermediary period, ending with their tranquil departure in opposite directions. Memorialized as the perfect woman, 'goode faire White' (l. 948) enters the transcendent beyond and passes out of her former lover's life, her death consummated by his performative admission that 'she is ded' (l. 1309). The knight's return to the land of the living coincides with and is to some extent effected by his account of his successful suit: 'As helpe me God, I was as blyve/Reysed as from deth to lyve' (ll. 1277–8).

The poem draws out the public implications of these private rites. Because his mourning is demoralizing and slowly killing the Man, it is damaging the society in which he ought to hold a prominent place and which cannot function properly without him. His return to the living community at the end of the poem is represented poetically by the abrupt shift into a different mode of signification in the closing lines:

> With that me thoughte that this kyng
> Gan homwarde for to ryde
> Unto a place, was there besyde,
> Which was from us but a lyte –
> A long castel with walles white,
> Be Seynt Johan, on a ryche hil,
> As me mette; but thus hyt fil.   (*BD*, ll. 1314–20)

The Man is identified as John of Gaunt by the references to the saint, the *ryche hil* – Richmond, of which Gaunt was earl for part of his life – and the *long castel* – Lancaster, which Gaunt acquired through his wife Blanche, the real-life prototype of the lady in the poem, who died in 1368. As he moves towards historical specificity and agency, Blanche the Duchess moves in the opposite direction. Initially translated in the poem's intermediary fiction, she is now further metamorphosed into the *walles white* of Lancaster.[19] Successful and definitive translation into the land of the dead means that the lady ceases to threaten the living and becomes socially useful once more. Secondary burial installs her as protectress of her house, in both senses: the building and the social group that constructs its identity around it, first and foremost her former husband. Her final separation from the everyday world guarantees her symbolic authority but simultaneously deprives her of human identity, form and autonomy. The poem's funeral effigy in language operates within the narrative not as a lasting memorial but as a temporary construction which eases the lady's disappearance.[20] Blanche and White are gradually erased

---

[19] The *whit wal* (l. 780) unites the lovers; Ellmann, 'Blanche', p. 103.

[20] An analogous example of commemoration by obliteration is the destruction of the palace of Sheen ordered by Richard II after Anne's death; replicated (if the G prologue is later than the F) by the elision from the text of Sheen and Anne, as noted by D. Wallace, *Chaucerian Polity: Absolutist Lineages and Associational Forms in England and Italy* (Stanford, 1997), p. 373. On the other hand, the text of *BD* stands as a lasting memorial presenting the effigy it contains, which both is and is not Blanche's.

from figuration, commemorated by being incorporated into the physical sub-stance of her own former castle, which thus becomes her non-figurative monument. Leaving the here and now altogether, she moves simultaneously into the fully abstract and the fully material domains. However, the lady is not evicted from history; rather there is an attempt to fix her historical mean-ing. In the final stage of her transfiguration, Blanche benevolently safeguards the declared prominence of the house of Lancaster and promotes the further rising of its star. The lady's secondary burial thus works to reinforce her lord's authority.[21] Gaunt and the Man in Black leave the poem with ancestral pres-tige thanks not only to the lady but also to the legendary companions the Man invokes when describing his love.[22] Gaunt benefits from this even more than the Man, since the dream's closing move between worlds allows the presti-gious otherness of the ancestral realm(s) to be conflated with Gaunt's (repre-sented) real life, which thereby acquires the air of legend. Here as everywhere, the eternal and the transcendent as well as the private and domestic serve specific political ends.[23]

Key to the lady's idealization is the opposition between her and Fortune.[24] As the Man in Black evokes it, Fortune is not simply a force within which all human beings exist under God's law, but stands for an unbearable vision of life without the comfort of transcendence. Ruled by Fortune, earthly life is characterized by meaningless and traumatic accident and mutability. Pendant to this is a vision of death as a process of bodily decay and incapacitating grief which eats away at deceased and survivor, threatening to annihilate both; death, that is, conceived without the secondary burial which transforms it into a meaningful part of the greater life cycle. According to her mourner, however, White's virtues of *trouthe*, constancy and moderation freed her from Fortune's whims and made her the living proof of a transcendent sphere. Although the Man does not appear to grasp them fully, the logical implications are clear:

[21] Rituals 'are not productions from cultural templates or "expressions" of structure, but instead are acts of power in the fashioning of structures: acts that make gods, kings, presidents, and property-rights by declaring that the authority of the priest, judge, or police officer resides in a higher source, a *mana, dharma* or constitution'; J. D. Kelly and M. Kaplan, 'History, Structure, and Ritual', *Annual Review of Anthropology* 19 (1990), 119–50 (p. 140). The view of ritual as performative differs from Hertz's Durkheimian view that ritual represents and reinforces existing social structures.

[22] Initially related to contemporary male and female characters like (although inferior to) themselves, the lady and her lover are afterwards surrounded only by ancestors, the legendary figures of western culture (ll. 1054–87 and 1117–25). At the same time the knight records his own adoption of the idealizing mode of lyric, itself given a classical pedigree in ll. 1159–70.

[23] Compare E. H. Kantorowicz's account of royal funerary effigies in the late Middle Ages; *The King's Two Bodies: A Study in Mediaeval Political Theology* (Princeton, 1957), pp. 419–37.

[24] Hardman, 'Memorial Monument', p. 209; H. Phillips, 'Fortune and the Lady: Machaut, Chaucer and the Intertextual "Dit"', *Nottingham French Studies* 38 (1999), 120–36 (pp. 132–3).

because even in her earthly life she made manifest the existence of God, White is the Man's means of redemption, his path to faith when he is in danger of despair because of her bodily death.

The vision of White as Beatrice-like mediator between earthly life and Christian transcendence results, of course, from the secondary burial which her lover's reminiscence gives her.[25] In the Man's portrait of her, White is purified of Blanche's lived (and her own fictional) singularity; those aspects of their biographies and characters which would suggest that they lived under Fortune's sway or within time's flow are discarded and forgotten, coded thereby as inessentials and imperfections. This process can be compared to the physical transformation which Hertz insists must be undergone before secondary burial can take place. The soft parts of the corpse must disappear leaving only those which are considered immune to time: bones, ashes or a mummy. Reduction to 'immutable elements' represents purification from life's corruption, but also corresponds to the construction of a new, incorruptible body fit for the soul to inhabit in the afterlife.[26] Similarly, White/ Blanche's newly pure self emerges phoenix-like (compare ll. 982–3) from the ruins of the old mortal being. This new self is suited to ideological exploitation by her survivors, who themselves construct it to that end.

Ancestral patrons might be male or female, but in *BD*, transfiguration into the Lancastrians' tutelary spirit is a highly gendered process. The opposition between the lady and Fortune delimits the kind of woman she can be. Fortune, 'the trayteresse fals and ful of gyle' (l. 620), epitomizes the negative idealization of femininity as fickle, dangerous and sexually uncontrolled.[27] Against this stands the Eternal Feminine. Beauty, chastity, good sense, modesty and a kind heart are necessary but not sufficient qualities of this idealized Woman. Her fundamental attribute is her location beyond the world of change and contingency. The Eternal Feminine, unchanging and incorruptible, inhabits that death beyond death achieved by secondary burial: a timeless, spiritual land which lies entirely beyond material existence but which bestows symbolic authority relating to the life continuing on earth.[28] Secondary burial thus construes life as safe and meaningful, under the protection of a higher power which orders its events for the best in accordance with a greater plan. Earthly life and eternal life bridge the temporary state of death to render it almost insignificant. And in *BD* the spirit embodying this transcendent vision is uncompromisingly feminized.

[25] Hardman, 'Memorial Monument', p. 209.
[26] 'Contribution', pp. 41–8 (p. 43). '[D]eath is not a mere destruction but a transition: as it progresses so does the rebirth; while the old body falls to ruins, a new body takes shape, with which the soul – provided the necessary rites have been performed – will enter another existence, often superior to the previous one' (ibid., p. 48).
[27] '[S]exuality is [. . .] opposed to fertility. It is associated with flesh, decomposition and women, while true ancestral fertility is a mystical process symbolised by the tomb and the (male) bones'; Bloch and Parry, 'Introduction', p. 21.
[28] Hertz, 'Contribution', pp. 78–80.

For living women, accessing the symbolic authority granted to the Eternal Feminine is problematic. Already in Hertz's account it is evident that entry into the company of ancestors requires the dead person to accept the necessity of his or her own death, bowing to the general interest and gracefully exiting the mortal scene. By accepting individual fate the deceased allows society to renew itself and earthly life to continue in others. The small opportunity for dissent is decreased when ancestor status is identified with the Eternal Feminine. It seems from *BD* that individual women participate in this ideal type only by adopting its lofty indifference to incident and time as well as its other virtues. This further discourages women from behaving with singularity. It is true that White is elevated to universality by the rhetorical construction of her uniqueness; according to the Man she was superlative in every way, a hapax in femininity. But these qualities are not abnormalities, on the contrary they are highly normative. Insofar as they are validated by their virtues, women appear to be all the same, avatars of the Eternal Feminine. Any peculiarities which might distance them from the ideal must be forgotten, as Blanche's are; to insist on them would be perverse and invalidating, and might even suggest a disastrous identification with Fortune.[29] Hence the symbolic authority granted to the Eternal Feminine is limited to activities and uses which demonstrably accord with that ideal. Furthermore, the woman who wishes to exercise this authority must recognize that she is merely a conduit for power. White is represented as authoritative only in proportion to her usefulness for those who promote her memory. As she becomes Woman, the lady ceases to be an independent agent; she must either be or behave as if her autonomous self were dead. *BD* thus gives exemplary form to a specific connection for women between power, death and an ideal of femininity.[30]

Blanche's absorption into the castle of Lancaster, material symbol of a clan's political power and longevity, makes her patron and protector of that clan and therefore available to sponsor whatever course its prime representative chooses to follow in order to advance its interests. She becomes a potentially important piece in a strategy which aims both to bring about a desired political state and to extend it into the future. Marriage may very well play a part in this strategy. According to Hertz, during the intermediary period a widow or widower is considered to be still married to 'a person in whom death is present and continuous'.[31] Only after secondary burial is the relict

---

[29] '[A]s against the dispersed, contingent, and multiple existences of actual women, mythical thought opposes the Eternal Feminine, unique and changeless. If the definition provided for this concept is contradicted by the behaviour of flesh-and-blood women, it is the latter who are wrong: we are told not that Femininity is a false entity, but that the women concerned are not feminine'; de Beauvoir, *Second Sex*, p. 283.

[30] E. T. Hansen, *Chaucer and the Fictions of Gender* (Berkeley, 1992), pp. 73–4.

[31] 'During this entire period when death is not yet completed, the deceased is treated as if he were still alive [. . .]. He retains all his rights over his wife and guards them jealously. The widow is literally the wife of a person in whom death is present and continuous; thus she is considered during that period as impure and accursed and

free to return to a place in society. The interpretation I have been outlining might therefore have some bearing on the question of *BD*'s date in relation to Gaunt's remarriage in 1371. It is obvious that the secondary burial which *BD* performs on its lady is symbolic and suggestive, not legal and formal. There was no official prohibition to prevent Gaunt remarrying before this poem was written, nor did its composition alter his position in law. However, Hertz's work does suggest that memorializing Blanche is not incompatible with urging Gaunt to remarry, or even with retrospectively endorsing such a project.[32] Assimilation into the Eternal Feminine, the outcome of White's secondary burial, increases the possibilities contained in Blanche's fruitful absence. For the Man in Black to marry another good woman will be tantamount to having White back again, for all good women are in a sense avatars of the type she is brought to represent. Marrying another version of his dead lady is a way to express performatively not only his continuing love for her but also hers for him. Secondary burial allows the deceased to be enlisted as an advocate of her own former husband's remarriage, as she joins the community of guiding spirits which preside over social renewal. Not that the poem presumes to instruct the lordly widower. The contingent and dependent nature of White's authority is demonstrated by its pliability in the service of various potential strategies on Gaunt's part.

Hertz stresses the dead person's progression through the troubling period during which it is uncontrolled by and even hostile to society, to a final resting-place in which it is socially integrated once more. He emphasizes how survivors move correspondingly through unliveable grief towards a comfort which accommodates the altered aspects of their lives. He analyses the ways in which death is worked into a stage on the path to regeneration, allowing potentially traumatic changes in social and individual lives to be recuperated as part of a cycle by which life endlessly renews itself. Such a model permits variations in the social order so long as they can be anchored in some way in a framework of continuity and tradition. Although change itself is acceptable, the potentially disruptive forces which may bring it about cannot be tolerated while they appear as such. This traditionalist process is illustrated by the passing of both White and Blanche in *BD*. However, a different account might emphasize the intermediary period as a possible site from which opposition to the socio-political order and its renewal could be elaborated.[33] With this

is condemned in a great many societies to the abject existence of an outcast; it is only at the time of the final ceremony that she can be freed and allowed by the kin of the deceased either to remarry or to return to her family'; Hertz, 'Contribution', pp. 48–9. Hertz does not distinguish between widows and widowers.

[32] Referring to the anniversary services which Gaunt ordered for Blanche, Ellmann suggests that the act of burial 'demanded repetition every year' ('Blanche', p. 103). Compare the double tomb which Gaunt had built for himself and Blanche in 1374–5 (Hardman, 'Memorial Monument', p. 206).

[33] There are correspondences between the theory of double obsequies and that of 'between two deaths'; J. Lacan, *The Seminar of Jacques Lacan, VII: The Ethics of*

alternative vision in mind, we can turn to *LGW*. In a poem which focuses on women true in loving all their lives, we might expect to encounter a series of Whites, and indeed Alceste is often described in terms which recall White's transcendence. However, the notion of dual obsequies, utilized in this analysis of *BD*, can be useful in suggesting a profound opposition between the poems. It allows us to appreciate the deep-seated differences which separate Alceste and her cohorts from White, and still more strikingly from Blanche.

THE LEGEND OF GOOD WOMEN

LGW consists of nine short narratives with a prologue which survives in two versions, F and G. In the prologue the poet declares that his devotion to books is interrupted only by his preference for going out to the fields in spring to worship the daisy flower. He falls asleep and dreams that he sees a regal god of Love leading by the hand a lady whose dress recalls the daisy. They are accompanied by a host of other women, all true in love. The daisy-lady is named as Alceste early on in the G version and towards the end of the F version. The god of Love reproaches the poet-narrator for having produced in English the *Romaunt of the Rose* and *Troilus and Criseyde*, poems which the god claims attack him and his devotees.[34] In particular, the poet is accused of choosing to retell only women's *wikednesse* even though wicked women are rare exceptions to the general rule of female *goodnesse* (G, ll. 268–9 and 277).[35] Alceste intervenes to disarm the god's threats by discoursing on tyranny and on the responsibility of a ruler to uphold justice and exercise mercy, at the same time advancing a series of arguments absolving the author of responsibility for the content of the works under dispute. She lists other works by Chaucer, some of which are positively friendly to love (including *BD*), others being Christian in theme. The lady then suggests that the poet be required to repair the damage he has caused, and sets what she calls his *penaunce*:

> Thow shalt, whil that thow livest, yer by yere,
> The moste partye of thy tyme spende

Psychoanalysis, 1959–60, trans. D. Porter (New York, 1992), especially the discussion of Antigone, pp. 243–87. According to Lacan, the subject in whom physical death is disconnected from symbolic death may occupy an uncanny space outside society. This space provides a basis from which to challenge the social system because it draws attention to that system's necessary incompleteness and hence incoherence. Lacan therefore focuses on ethical and political resistance, whereas Hertz, working in the Durkheimian tradition, emphasizes society's tendency to assimilate and adapt.

[34] On the poem as palinode, see F. Percival, *Chaucer's Legendary Good Women* (Cambridge, 1998), especially pp. 151–70.

[35] Against the usual view that the sources cited in G by the god of Love are antifeminist, see H. Phillips, 'Register, Politics, and the *Legend of Good Women*', *Chaucer Review* 37 (2002–3), 101–28 (p. 114).

> In makynge of a gloryous legende
> Of goode women, maydenes and wyves,
> That were trewe in lovynge al here lyves;
> And telle of false men that hem betrayen,
> That al here lyf ne don nat but assayen
> How manye wemen they may don a shame;
> For in youre world that is now holden game.   (G, ll. 471–9)

The poet begins his legend but the text is incomplete. The life of Alceste which the god instructs the poet to make the concluding piece has been lost, if it ever existed. The lives that do survive are those of Cleopatra, Thisbe, Dido, Hypsipyle and Medea, Lucrece, Ariadne, Philomela, Phyllis, and Hypermnestra, this last lacking an ending.

LGW has not been popular in recent years.[36] Modern commentators have typically found it repetitive and limited in range, while its insistence on a particular idea of female virtue and the way it reshapes its source material to fit that idea have caused unease. It is strange to modern eyes, for example, to see Medea rub shoulders with Lucrece as virtuous victims of male betrayal. In BD (ll. 726–7) Medea is said to have killed her children in response to her abandonment by Jason, but in LGW she confines herself to writing him a letter.[37] Some critics argue that LGW's true subject is poetic activity, while others focus on the poem's relevance to issues of kingship, government and statecraft, linking this to the contemporary political situation. Critics who engage with the poem's treatment of women generally argue either that the poem endorses medieval ideas and practices relating to female virtue (and understood to be unacceptable today) or that it ironizes such ideas; some impute to Chaucer an antifeminist position, others an anti-antifeminist one. Despite these various approaches, the poem remains today largely unpalatable. Moreover, arguments constructed around it often seem to leave the text behind or even to obscure it; it is almost traditional to appeal to the poem's 'obvious' qualities even while contending that this surface conceals a deeper meaning requiring additional, often allegorical interpretation or information which must be supplied from outside the text. LGW today is at once unappealing and spectral, difficult to enjoy and difficult to capture. In the present essay I do not offer an apology for these qualities but interpret them as essential to the poem.

---

[36] Spurgeon's evidence suggests that LGW was never one of Chaucer's more popular works; C. F. E. Spurgeon, *Five Hundred Years of Chaucer Criticism and Allusion, 1357–1900*, 3 vols. (Cambridge, 1925), I, especially the table on lxxix.

[37] On Medea in LGW, see Minnis, *Shorter Poems*, pp. 371–8, Percival, *Legendary Good Women*, pp. 203–20 and N. F. McDonald, 'Doubts about Medea, Briseyda, and Helen: Interpreting Classical Allusion in the Fourteenth-Century French Ballade *Medee fu en amer veritable*', in *Studies in English Language and Literature: 'Doubt Wisely'. Papers in Honour of E. G. Stanley*, ed. M. J. Toswell and E. M. Tyler (London, 1996), pp. 252–66. Much more broadly, see R. Morse, *The Medieval Medea* (Cambridge, 1996); Chaucer is discussed on pp. 224–30.

I shall argue that *LGW* is difficult to enjoy not because it is overly conventional or because it enshrines long-dead cultural practices but because it
pays insufficient regard to conventions which govern our lives as readers
and as social beings today. It is difficult to capture because its own partiali-
ties of vision produce blind spots in its readers, so that what tends to slide
away from our attention is not what the poem omits but, surprisingly, that
which it highlights. Drawing on psychoanalytic insights as well as on the
anthropological material presented above, my analysis will focus on three
central features of the poetic programme laid out in the prologue which
have proven resistant to critical analysis. These relate respectively to Alceste
as revenant, to repetition and to the proper topic of poetry. Comparison
with *BD* in each case highlights the significance of certain characteristics
of *LGW*.

LGW is placed under the aegis of someone who has returned from the
grave. When the poet fails to recognize the classical figure of Alceste in the
daisy-lady before him, the god of Love reminds him of her story:

> [. . .] and that thow knowest wel, parde,
> Yif it be so that thow avise the.
> Hast thow nat in a bok, lyth in thy cheste,
> The grete goodnesse of the queene Alceste,
> That turned was into a dayesye;
> She that for hire husbonde ches to dye,
> And ek to gon to helle rather than he,
> And Ercules rescued hire, parde,
> And broughte hyre out of helle ageyn to blys?   (G, ll. 496–504)

The emphasis on Alceste's return is the more evident if we compare the brief
summary of her story in *Troilus and Criseyde*. Troilus objects to Cassandra
when she announces Criseyde's infidelity with Diomede:

> As wel thow myghtest lien on Alceste,
> That was of creatures, but men lye,
> That evere weren, kyndest and the beste!
> For whan hire housbonde was in jupertye
> To dye hymself but if she wolde dye,
> She ches for hym to dye and gon to helle,
> And starf anon, as us the bokes telle.
> (*Troilus and Criseyde* V, ll. 1527–33)

Troilus ends Alceste's story with her dying in her husband's place, the act
which makes her the paragon both of *fyn lovynge* and *of wifhod the lyvynge*
(*LGW*, G, ll. 534–5). In *LGW*, however, this death has a sequel, as Alceste is res-
cued and returned to *blys* by Hercules. In the mythographic works from
which Chaucer is thought to have drawn her story, Alceste is restored to
wedded bliss, an idealized human marriage. However, the echo of the
Harrowing of Hell in Chaucer's text confers overtones of a life beyond the

human, as also does the reference to metamorphosis into a daisy and the subsequent mention of stellification (G, ll. 513–14).[38]

Figuring Alceste's situation in Hertz's terms, we may say that the Narrator and the god of Love discuss Alceste as if she were not only dead but had undergone secondary burial. Buried in a book which is itself entombed in a coffin-like chest, she is said to lie dormant within the poet's memory, at once familiar and comfortably forgotten. She is presented in the aspect of an artefact, submitted to the natural cycle as the heliotropic daisy, occupying that world of legend and idealized nature inhabited by White:

> In remembraunce of hire and in honour
> Cibella made the dayesye and the flour
> Ycoroned al with whit, as men may se;
> And Mars yaf to hire corone red, parde,
> In stede of rubies, set among the white.   (G, ll. 518–22)

By speaking as if Alceste had already undergone secondary burial, the male characters attempt to perform that rite. The image they conjure aligns Alceste with the idealized female who is the final product of *BD*; both are figures of authority who dispense solace to living men. As in *BD*, the product serves the interests of her male sponsors, becoming in *LGW* the patron of domesticity and of the gender roles associated with it. But Alceste's actual manifestation in the prologue suggests a curious affinity with Hertz's intermediary period. The returned Alceste does not seem to be in an identifiable afterlife, whether Christian or pagan; if she is not in the land of the living, nor is she exactly in the land of the dead. Her intermediary condition is however not identical to that of *BD*'s undead lady, which cries out for secondary burial. After her physical death that lady's image is a construct manifested only in her lover, at first in his physical and psychic deterioration and latterly in his memorial to her; Alceste has a positive presence of her own, surging beyond death and appropriation. Whereas Lady White exemplifies Hertz's model in her initially destructive effect on the living and in her progressive enhancement, as an artefact, into a wholly benevolent patron spirit, Alceste is consistently creative, saving the poet from the god's wrath and furnishing him with material and occasion for future productions. She nevertheless remains an ambiguous figure, restricting and domineering, never in this text safely dispatched into the symbolic land of the benignly dead.[39] While White's authority over the living is derived from her

---

[38] Alceste's story was apparently known in the Middle Ages through brief accounts in mythographic works, see the *Riverside Chaucer*, p. 1065; W. Wetherbee, *Chaucer and the Poets: An Essay on* Troilus and Criseyde (Ithaca, 1984), pp. 141–3; and V. A. Kolve, 'From Cleopatra to Alceste: An Iconographic Study of *The Legend of Good Women*', in *Signs and Symbols in Chaucer's Poetry*, ed. J. P. Hermann and J. J. Burke (University, 1981), pp. 130–78 (pp. 171–4).

[39] 'The return of the living dead [. . .] materializes a certain symbolic debt persisting beyond physical expiration'; S. Žižek, *Looking Awry: An Introduction to Jacques Lacan Through Popular Culture* (Cambridge, MA, 1991), p. 23.

status as a legitimized member of the eternal, spiritual community, Alceste's is associated with her survival of both physical death and attempted secondary burial.[40] With Alceste, the intermediary period becomes an other place, a zone outside the concrete sequence of life, death and new life proposed by Hertz.[41] This spectral quality is far from being associated with weakness.

The problematic authority of this resilient revenant manifests itself throughout the prologue. Alceste shows little of White's malleability. Unlike White's, her authority actually finds expression within the poem, in a direct command to the narrator and in assertion of her own wishes against those of her male companion and sponsor, the god of Love. Her decrees are not negotiable. After she has won forgiveness for the narrator by arguing that he cannot be considered responsible for those works to which the god of Love objects, the narrator himself intervenes to claim rather more authorial status. Alceste silences him sternly:

> And she answerde, 'Lat be thyn arguynge,
> For Love ne wol nat countrepleted be
> In ryght ne wrong; and lerne that at me!'   (F, ll. 475–7)

These lines are sometimes held to show how reasonable Alceste is by comparison with the tyrannical god of Love. Yet it is she who wins in argument against the god and who refuses to countenance any point of view other than her own. This uncompromising absolutism also characterizes her attitude towards her husband. Her inflexible fidelity could be interpreted as tantamount to a demand for death, but death finds itself marginalized where Alceste is concerned. She dismisses its power over her not only when she dies for her husband, but much more spectacularly when she returns to his side. If there was ever a love that would brook no counterplea, surely this is it. It may seem ironic that it should be Alceste's utter refusal to accept separation from her husband which results in her final independence of that husband (nowhere present in the prologue) and in her ability to bend to her own wishes the god of Love, a character often of dubious benefit to women.[42] However, Alceste's

---

[40] Her experience affords her knowledge designated in the prologue's opening lines as inaccessible to mortals; C. Sanok, 'Reading Hagiographically: The *Legend of Good Women* and its Feminine Audience', *Exemplaria* 13 (2001), 323–54 (p. 332, n. 25). The human condition, which necessitates mediation between earthly and transcendent, excludes Alceste.

[41] F, which concentrates on the daisy-muse, gives greater prominence to the transformed, benevolent, useful Alceste, whereas the uncompromising and gloss-resistant Alceste is stronger in G, as is the contrast between this figure and the product of secondary burial. If Alceste is to be identified with Richard's queen, Anne of Bohemia, who died in 1394 and to whom the F prologue is to be presented (F, ll. 496–7), then F might be seen either as performing her secondary burial in a manner analogous to Blanche's, or as idealizing her during her lifetime in line with the Eternal Feminine archetype.

[42] For J. Simpson, 'Ethics and Interpretation: Reading Wills in Chaucer's *Legend of Good Women*', *Studies in the Age of Chaucer* 20 (1998), 73–100, the god is a figure for exploitative male desire.

appearance in the prologue without her husband but with her story suggests that the fact of her love has primacy over its object: that her unparalleled *trouthe* should be understood above all as truth to her own desire, partially coincident with but not reducible to fidelity to her husband. In herself she exceeds the domestic framework within which the god of Love wishes to contain her.

It is Alceste's demand which generates the repetitive scenario which is so prominent a feature of the legends. Their repetitiveness has been a major cause of the low critical esteem in which *LGW* is held, but it is evident from Alceste's prescription that the project is conceived of as a repetitive one. Variations between the individual legends are irrelevant to what is identified at their inception as their primary characteristic: the single scenario to be played out again and again. This scenario defines the male role as serial betrayal, and the male characters do indeed repeat themselves – notably Jason, betrayer of both Hypsipyle and Medea – as well as repeating each other, most conspicuously in the case of Theseus and Demophon, father and son, but also more widely, as each male protagonist takes the same path as his predecessors and successors in the *Legend*. Similarly, the heroines each follow Alceste's example, replicating her and each other. Within the text itself there is repetition of word and imagery. Some of these features can be evaluated as developing patterns which organize meaning and literary effect, as one usu-ally expects of literary texts, but repetition here far outruns any such justifi-cation. It becomes wearisome repetitiousness, anything but aesthetic. Not only the existence of two redactions of the prologue but also their standard printing strengthens the sense that repetition is central to *LGW*'s impact.[43] The text gives the impression of proceeding not from an artistry of which the poet is fully in control, but from irrational compulsion generated by the need to resolve an insoluble but unavoidable problem.[44] Rather than trying to free the legends of Alceste's prescriptive constraint by emphasizing their individ-uality, I want here to keep in sight the poem's monotonous, monologic and obsessive quality. Moreover, I interpret this quality as central to the text's resistance to dominant norms.

This 'perpetual recurrence of the same thing' (to borrow a phrase from Freud)[45] originates with Alceste. She demands of the narrator that he spend

---

[43] Other of Chaucer's poems extant in substantially different versions are not generally printed as separate texts. See, for example, Geoffrey Chaucer, *Troilus and Criseyde: A New Edition of 'The Book of Troilus'*, ed. B. A. Windeatt (London, 1984), pp. 36–54.

[44] Compulsion and loss of self-control are differently figured in the abdication of authorial authority to the poem's commissioners. It must be stressed that I am not here concerned with whether or not Chaucer was fully in control of the processes and themes I am analysing or in his conscious position on the political questions discussed.

[45] *Beyond the Pleasure Principle* (1920), in *The Standard Edition of the Complete Psychological Works of Sigmund Freud*, trans. under the general editorship of J. Strachey, 24 vols. (London, 1953–74), XVIII, 22.

the rest of his days repeating a single, extremely limited, rigid and essential-izing version of gender roles and relations. Her version is not, however, that recommended by the god of Love; he again echoes *BD*, and again Alceste dis-sents. *BD* and *LGW* present pre-emptive variations on Edgar Allan Poe's famous assertion that 'the death [. . .] of a beautiful woman is, unquestion-ably, the most poetical topic in the world'.[46] In *BD* the Man in Black is inspired to lyric by the death of a woman who, as (re)created by him, is not only beau-tiful but virtuous, while his dream motivates the narrator to write. In *LGW*, the god of Love urges the poet to write the stories of women of the following sort:

> [. . .] to hyre love were they so trewe
> That, rathere than they wolde take a newe,
> They chose to be ded in sondry wyse,
> And deiden, as the story wol devyse;
> And some were brend, and some were cut the hals,
> And some dreynt for they wolden not be fals;
> For alle keped they here maydenhede,
> Or elles wedlok, or here widewehede.   (G, ll. 288–95)

In the god of Love's formulation, a *trewe* woman will recognize that severance from her man (however involuntary or undeserved) is equivalent to death; her actual suicide seems thus to be only a belated acting out, an obedient translation into the physical of patriarchally determined symbolic reality. In the poem's pagan setting suicide is the ultimate good death for a woman and grants her instant passage into the Eternal Feminine. By this act she declares her superiority to Fortune; to do otherwise would threaten her social identity in ways which have been spelled out above.

Alceste, however, proclaims the proper topic of poetry to be the single scen-ario in which women are faithful *al here lyves* (G, l. 475) while men spend *al here lyf* (G, l. 477) betraying women. Her prescription differs from the god's because it cuts out the variations between the women's stories (the *sondry wyse* of their deaths, which might provide distraction) and because it con-structs gender difference around dissimilar modes of living, not around the distinction between life and death. The single form of life Alceste proposes for poetic women does however keep them in some relation to death, since in order to have been true all their lives they must have been true unto death. In the legends themselves, some of the heroines die immediately, others after a lifetime which is presented as a sort of long-drawn out death, as in Hypsipyle's case:

---

[46] E. A. Poe, 'The Philosophy of Composition' (1846), in *Essays and Reviews*, selected and with notes by G. R. Thompson (New York, 1984), pp. 13–25 (p. 19). C. Dinshaw, *Chaucer's Sexual Poetics* (Madison, 1989), pp. 65–87 (p. 77), relates the phrase to *LGW*. Poe continues, 'and equally is it beyond doubt that the lips best suited for such topic [*sic*] are those of a bereaved lover'.

> And trewe to Jason was she al hire lyf,
> And evere kepte hire chast, as for his wif;
> Ne nevere hadde she joye at hire herte,
> But deyede for his love, of sorwes smerte.   (*LGW*, ll. 1576–9)

Although she is no longer Jason's wife in the full sense of the word, Hypsipyle's fidelity prevents her from living in any other social role. From the moment of their abandonment the heroines' futures are foreclosed; they are set apart from everyday life even before their physical death. Their refusal to participate further in life nevertheless does not make them the acquiescent suicides commended by the god of Love. For it is not in fact her severance from her man which seals each heroine's fate but her wilful refusal to be detached from her former partner. Nor does her decision imply submission to male desires; we can rather say that each heroine refuses to allow her partner to detach himself from her. Whether they enact their defiance by dying or by remaining alive, the heroines of the legends do not pass quietly out of their erstwhile lovers' lives.[47] There are no liberating secondary burials in *LGW*. On the contrary, the women go to extraordinary lengths to ensure that these men will never be free of them, nor licensed to remodel the women's personae to suit their own political ends. Thus the emphasis in Alceste's prescription of the most poetical topic lies on women's rejection of normal existence and the masculine authority decreeing it. Physical death is not in itself momentous and does not bring this rejection to an end but instead preserves it. Choosing to exist suspended beyond the masculinist cycle of normal life and consummated death, *LGW*'s heroines withhold the regenerating power which their deaths ought properly to contribute to the social order. In place of the exemplary bearers of patriarchal meaning proposed by the god of Love, Alceste links the making of poetry to the presentation of a group of women who defy the *boundes* that they *oughte kepe* (G, l. 536): the confines of social life and of the social death which is an integral part of that life. It is Alceste's totalizing, monologic project which ensures for these women a spectral presence which outrages recognized forms but is nonetheless immoveable.

The legends themselves are sometimes considered to undermine Alceste's prescription and sometimes to disappoint the expectations it arouses. However, in certain respects Alceste's command is precisely realized in the legends.

---

[47] The decision of those heroines who choose to follow their lovers into death is coloured by Alceste's return from the grave and therefore exceeds the 'impassioned expression of emotional union' described by J. Mann, *Geoffrey Chaucer* (Hemel Hempstead, 1991), p. 44. Nor is it merely the turning upon themselves of a violence impotent to harm its true object (ibid.). In *LGW*, women's suicide functions as an assertion of autonomy more akin, in Mann's account, to Augustine's judgement on Lucretia (p. 45). Compare Bloch and Parry's discussion of suicide as 'an act which, by its apparent similarity, almost parodies the death which is the ultimate manifestation of altruistic self-abnegation' ('Introduction', p. 17). See also the denunciation of suicide in *BD*, ll. 723–39.

Each heroine repeats the intransigent position that Alceste articulates in the prologue. *Pace* those critics who see them dying for love, monogamy or their men, these women die for nothing but to uphold their own desire.[48] Unlike the ladies of *BD*, the heroines of the legends could never be transformed into patrons of remarriage. In declining to be replaced they repudiate the idea of women's essential interchangeability and combat the endless recycling of ideal types associated with the Eternal Feminine. Paradoxical though it may appear, the poem's repetitive quality is key to its heroines' uniqueness.[49] The ladies' re-enactment of Alceste's adamant resolution preserves their personal couplings perpetually in human memory (a ploy whose success is borne out by *LGW*'s own reproduction of their stories).[50] The repetitiousness that originates with Alceste must therefore be distinguished from the repetition which characterizes the supposedly eternal cycle of life and death: whereas the latter erases and discourages singularity and promotes conformity in favour of a socially useful norm, the former is allied with an inassimilable particularity which is all the balder for being independent of accidental biographical details, pared down to the bare facts of desire and assertion of self.[51] Central to the embarrassment which makes us avert our gaze from the poem's surface, an embarrassment often coded as boredom, is *LGW*'s insistence on its ladies' undying protest.[52]

Alceste's heroines refuse to be passed along into the transcendent realm from which Blanche and White preside puppet-like over their own replacement, and by this means resist conscription as patrons of social renewal. Female resistance to a patriarchal order could easily be coded as misogyny, but in *LGW* it is couched in positive moral terms. Alceste is no less a paragon than

---

[48] Some of the heroines 'are primarily or partly victims of themselves'; J. M. Cowen, 'Chaucer's *Legend of Good Women*: Structure and Tone', *Studies in Philology* 82 (1985), 416–36 (p. 433). 'Lucrece dies for her high principles of wifely fidelity rather than for her actual husband'; Minnis, *Shorter Poems*, p. 436. My argument concurs with other critics of *LGW* primarily where they note the text's departures from the explicit ideological message.

[49] This effect might be lost or much diminished in manuscripts such as Ff, P and R, which contain only one or a few legends. However, such manuscripts may produce their own patterned effects, such as the sequence of female complaints into which manuscript Ff, the Findern Anthology, inserts the legend of Thisbe; see N. F. McDonald, 'Chaucer's *Legend of Good Women*, Ladies at Court and the Female Reader', *Chaucer Review* 35 (2000–1), 22–42 (pp. 36–9).

[50] Phyllis 'warns Demophon that she will make of her dead body a sign of her "trouthe" to him'; Dinshaw, *Chaucer's Sexual Poetics*, p. 83.

[51] Investigating why people repeat unpleasurable experiences, Freud in *Beyond the Pleasure Principle* distinguishes between repetition which ultimately produces pleasure and that which has no pleasurable yield, illustrated respectively by the *fort-da* game and by traumatic dreams (pp. 12–17) The former is experienced as calming and soothing, the latter as destructive and disruptive. In my view, the unsettling repetitiousness of *LGW* falls into the second category.

[52] Dinshaw refers to readerly boredom with *LGW* as a form of defence against it but aligns it with the poem's 'soothing and reassuring' use of repetition (see above, n. 51); *Chaucer's Sexual Poetics*, p. 86.

White, and the quality she and her heroines exemplify is once again *trouthe*. I can hardly overstate the difference between *LGW* and *BD* where this value is concerned. Whereas Lady White's *trouthe* is the prime mechanism inducting her into the politically manipulated symbolic realm beyond time and change which is the land of the dead, Alceste's *trouthe*, realized in the poem as her unshakeable demand, rescues her from that realm without integrating her into everyday life. *Trouthe* makes White doubly socially useful, easing her through ideal normativity into the universal and thus back into substitution on earth, but it fixes Alceste and her ladies in the intermediary zone outside society's living and deathly manifestations. Their *trouthe* represents the women's rejection of the customary identification of femininity with lack (G, l. 298). *LGW* provides its heroines with a positive ethical position which gives them the power to engage seriously in debate with other views. It creates out of traditionally feminine virtue a place distinct from the Eternal Feminine ideal and the current social system, and critical of both. Spectrality and lack of orthodox aesthetic appeal produce poetic as well as ethical and political possibilities. Since the narrator is to have no other subject until he dies, *yer by yere* (G, l. 471) his life is as foreclosed and dominated by repetition as that of the ladies he is to write about. His poetry is henceforward to occupy a domain analogous to theirs. Alceste's gift to the narrator's poetic production is expressed in the ballade in her honour inserted into the prologue. This ballade lists paragons of 'trouthe in love' (G, l. 221) (all feminine except for two masculine names at the beginning in the first stanza), with the repeated refrain 'Alceste is here, that al that may desteyne'. The *MED* gives three principal glosses for *disteinen*:

1. (a) To color or stain (sth.); (b) fig. to disguise (one's purpose).
2. (a) To deprive (sth.) of color, brightness, or beauty; (b) fig. to dim or obscure (sth.), put in the shade; (c) fig. to fade away, vanish.
3. (a) to sully (someone's reputation); desecrate (the name of God); ~ **tonge**, speak vilely; (b) to dishonor or defame (sb.); defile.

The refrain is commonly understood to suggest that Alceste's pre-eminence is such that she extinguishes all other claims, a reading which relies on sense 2 (b).[53] However, attention to the other glosses alters our appreciation. Alceste's effect is to cast a particular colour or stain over – even, given the negative connotations of sense 3, to discolour – any woman she stands next to. The heroines of the *Legend* all acquire Alceste's livery, turning a corpse-like pale or taking on a bloody flush as they manifest the uncompromising *trouthe* that projects them into the zone beyond life and death and opposes them to the life cycle.[54] Seen

---

[53] The *Middle English Dictionary* gives the refrain as an example of sense 2 (b). The lines following the ballade in F (F, ll. 272–5) support this reading, but are absent from G.

[54] '[P]hysical loss of control' (Dinshaw, *Chaucer's Sexual Poetics*, p. 75) here represents a step beyond the order of everyday life. Its involuntary nature reflects the essential (not necessarily conscious) drive to resist that order.

in the light she casts they appear quite different from their realizations in other texts. Testifying to the revenant's effect, each lady resists being appropriated to the reproduction of the established order. This explains the peculiar treatment of source material in *LGW*: to tell a story under Alceste's aegis is to distort its natural (which is to say its usual) ideological purposes.[55] Compare Slavoj Žižek's discussion of the Lacanian notion of anamorphosis:

> If we look at a thing straight on, i.e., matter-of-factly, disinterestedly, objectively, we see nothing but a formless spot; the object assumes clear and distinctive features only if we look at it 'at an angle', i.e., with an 'interested' view, supported, permeated, and 'distorted' by *desire*.[56]

The formless spot of (boring and conformist) *LGW* comes into focus when the desire of Alceste and her heroines is made the basis for the critical gaze. No wonder that the ballade's pantheon of conventional exemplars of true love are urged to hide and be silent. If these names represent figures who, like Blanche and White, have undergone secondary burial, Alceste comes to disinter them. The warning signalled by the ballade's insistent refrain is a real one, for through Alceste this lyrical, symbolic domain (the domain to which Blanche and White are dispatched) will be dismantled in the name of a different, awkward and singular femininity. *LGW*'s prologue suggests that distortion is not so much a valid as an inevitable interpretative principle, for desire intervenes in even the most supposedly disinterested of accounts. Its achievement is to grant to Alceste's refractory desire an effective authority usually reserved for the representatives of the established order. The secondary burial and translation into the Eternal Feminine professedly achieved in *BD* contrast with the inflexible revenant, obsessive repetition in form and content and assertiveness of female *trouthe* which give *LGW* its spectral and unpalatable quality. These attributes of the later poem are, in a sense, blindingly obvious: simultaneously impossible to ignore and impossible to confront directly, they invite us to *disteyne* the literary material before us if we are to see clearly the reality it sets before us.[57] *LGW* opposes the possibility that we may assimilate it comfortably into an existing system, thereby challenging our potential appropriation of it as much as it does that of the god of Love in

[55] '[P]oetically disfigured' by their single scenario, the legends distort notions of narrative and *trouthe*; E. W. Leach, 'Morwe of May: A Season of Feminine Ambiguity', in *Acts of Interpretation: The Text in Its Contexts, 700–1600. Essays on Medieval and Renaissance Literature in Honor of E. Talbot Donaldson*, ed. M. J. Carruthers and E. D. Kirk (Norman, OK, 1982), pp. 299–310 (p. 305).
[56] Žižek, *Looking Awry*, p. 12; italics in original.
[57] Žižek defends and reworks Paul de Man's thesis of interpretation as 'a violent act of disfiguring the interpreted text' based on close reading but opposed to 'historical archaeology': 'it is through the very "pullback" from direct experience of "reality" to the textual mechanisms that we are brought closer to the traumatic kernel of some Real "repressed" in a constitutive way by so-called "reality" itself'; S. Žižek, *The Plague of Fantasies* (London, 1997), pp. 95–6.

the prologue.[58] Taking their stand in the intermediary zone through which their system's rites are designed to hurry them, the legends' heroines contest the social vision consecrated by those rites. As woman after woman ceremonially upholds her singularity she not only protests against the sacrifice of women to a male-dominated order but also creates new ethical and political possibilities. Insistent poetic repetition elevates behaviour into ritual and the cumulative effect of Alceste's and her heroines' actions is to replace the ritual they challenge with one of their own: a 'ritual of resistance'.[59] Although Hertz does not consider the possibility, an altered rite can be an engine of social change. Alceste's exemplarity is of a new and radical kind: refusing the satisfaction of sublimation it remains resolutely demanding, geared not to social reproduction but to critique, not to the normative but to the alternative.[60]

---

[58] 'Fiercely monogamous' (Minnis, *Shorter Poems*, p. 406), these women can, of course, be reclaimed for the domestic ideology proposed by the god of Love. However, monogamy in this poem appears not as a manifestation of masculine authority but as a mode of feminine resistance to that authority.

[59] 'If a system of domination controls the representation of what is possible and what is natural, then a ritual of resistance breaks the hegemony over the subjective consciousness of the ritual participants. It makes them conscious of the oppression and allows them to envision new communities and possibilities'; Kelly and Kaplan, 'History, Structure, and Ritual', p. 135.

[60] Medieval texts regularly show pagan society disrupted and defeated by Christian saints and by uncompromisingly virtuous pagans; S. Kay, *Courtly Contradictions: The Emergence of the Literary Object in the Twelfth Century* (Stanford, 2001), pp. 216–31. *LGW* borrows the framework of martyrdom to produce actively resistant and politically radical deaths, but removes the Christian content, thereby doubly exploiting the pagan setting.

John Gower's Fear of Flying:
Transitional Masculinities in the
Confessio Amantis

Isabel Davis

Aviation and social challenge

Icarus, in the classical fable and Book IV of John Gower's *Confessio Amantis*, flies too high on artificial wings, against the advice of his father Daedalus. As the wax holding his flying machine together melts in the heat of the sun, Icarus goes into tailspin, plunges into the sea and drowns. Phaeton, on the other hand, again in contravention of paternal wisdom, pilots a flying chariot too low; he also submits to a watery death. The tales of these early aviators were regularly told together in the Middle Ages and operated as a double warning against the dangers of contravening the laws of nature and patriarchal authority.[1] In a discussion of altitude these stories configure natural law on a vertical axis; the warning is specifically about violating the hierarchical structures of social condition.[2] Gower's poem does not deviate from this medieval tradition as shown in the link between the tales of the two mythological airmen:

> In hih astat it is a vice
> To go to lowe, and in service
> It grieveth forto go to hye.   (IV, ll. 1035–7)[3]

Icarus and Phaeton warn those who would abandon the fixity of social categories that alternatives can be insubstantial and mutable zones of risk.

[1] E. M. Kavaler, *Pieter Bruegel: Parables of Order and Enterprise* (Cambridge, 1999), p. 64. The research for this article was done as part of my doctoral work, generously funded by the Arts and Humanities Research Board. I am indebted to my supervisors, Felicity Riddy and Jeremy Goldberg, who helped me to formulate my ideas, the participants in the Second York Interdisciplinary Conference on the Fourteenth Century, Craig Taylor for his advice on matters chivalric and, in particular, footnote twenty-one, and Lara McClure, Richard Rowland and Nicola McDonald who commented on drafts of this work.
[2] A famous example is Pieter Brueghel's mid-sixteenth-century depiction of *The Fall of Icarus*. See also K. A. Zipf Jr, 'The Tale of Icarus (CA, IV, 1035–71)', in *John Gower's Literary Transformations in the* Confessio Amantis: *Original Articles and Translations*, ed. P. Beidler (Washington, 1982), pp. 37–9 (p. 38).
[3] John Gower, *The English Works of John Gower*, ed. G. C. Macaulay, 2 vols., EETS 81 (London, 1900). All quotations will be from this edition.

My title, of course, refers to Erica Jong's 1974 novel *Fear of Flying*.[4] Written at the height of the second wave feminist movement, Jong's novel tells the story of Isadora Wing, a young Jewish woman trying to find her feet, or rather wings, amongst the contradictory and changing models of feminine behaviour at that time. The novel charts the heroine's rite of passage as she steers a course between freedom and acceptance in order to reconcile her fantasies with her life. *Fear of Flying* is given mythological and thematic unity by the idea of flying. This is understood in the literal sense of plane travel – the novel opens with Isadora on a flight to Vienna – but also in the metaphorical sense of emotional and sexual liberation. The narrator is afraid of transgressing the social codes and personal inhibitions that she imagines are the barriers to perfect and guiltless passion. Flying, in the novel, represents independence, bravery and confident womanhood. Just as Jong has described her work as a 'novel of apprenticeship and growing up [which] has been mistaken for a work of pornography', Gower too structures his narrative of tutelage as erotic fantasy and similarly, as I shall show, has a preoccupation with ideas of travel and flight.[5]

It has been argued, however, that Jong finally resorts to a conservative ending to her text. The novel has not traditionally been included in the corpus of feminist writing, partly because she invokes Icarus – the symbol of social impudence – to describe Isadora's attempts at sexual liberation as *hubris*.[6] John Gower too has been described as a conservative, who was uncomfortable with the shifting social arrangements of post-Black Death England.[7] Yet, by opening up fictional spaces in which their characters can transgress and challenge social orthodoxies, however briefly, these authors show themselves to be intrigued by the possibilities presented by a society which – with hindsight – we might see as undergoing liminal transition, defined in its broadest sense by V. and E. Turner as a phase

> of decisive cultural change, in which previous orderings of thought and behaviour are subject to revision and criticism, when hitherto unprecedented modes of ordering relations between ideas and people become possible and desirable.[8]

---

4   Erica Jong, *Fear of Flying* (London, 1974, repr. 1998).
5   The quotation comes from E. Jong, 'Fear of Flying Turns Twenty', in ibid., pp. viii–x (p. x).
6   For the reference to Icarus see Jong, *Fear of Flying*, p. 329. For a discussion of the conservatism of this novel see R. Felski, *Beyond Feminist Aesthetics: Feminist Literature and Social Change* (London, 1989), p. 14.
7   For a general assessment of Gower's tone, see, for example, J. Coleman, *English Literature in History 1350–1400* (London, 1981), pp. 126–56, esp. pp. 126–7; P. Strohm, 'Form and Social Statement in the *Confessio Amantis* and the *Canterbury Tales*', *Studies in the Age of Chaucer* 1 (1979), 17–40 (p. 27).
8   The discussion of rites of passage here and in section I refers to: V. Turner and E. Turner, *Image and Pilgrimage in Christian Culture: Anthropological Perspectives* (Oxford, 1978) especially pp. 2, 4, 8–9, and 231–3. See also M. Rubin, 'Introduction' to this volume.

These transitional – or liminal – spaces characterize social change and challenge in Gower's poem. In particular I shall argue that the demilitarization of
the aristocracy in the late fourteenth century was a transition of some significance which inspired John Gower to create a character, in Amans, who questions the relevance of traditional ideals of noble manhood. By using the work
of Victor and Edith Turner on rites of passage, but contesting some of their
conclusions about medieval religious practice, I shall investigate the precarious flights that take off in the *Confessio Amantis*, and Book IV in particular, in
order to show John Gower's complex attitude to the changes that were taking
place in his society.

The liminoid and the liminal: late-medieval Christian experience

Victor and Edith Turner broaden the discussion of rites of passage beyond
consideration of the structured tribal rites which accompanied transitions
between generations or occupations, as described by Arnold Van Gennep, to
consider the interior spiritual rituals of medieval religious practice, amongst
other things. In particular they focus upon pilgrimage as a 'liminoid' transition – that is an open, voluntary, anarchic and populist event – and a spiritual
passage marked by a physical journey. Liminoid transition, unlike liminality,
is less about the pre- and post-liminary states, less about passage in a
diachronic sense and more about the synchronic experience of being a pas-
senger. Thus pilgrimage does not usually entail the kind of altered social status that, for example, the 'puberty rites' that are assessed by Africanist
scholars do. In this way, the Turners, following on from the preoccupations of
Victor Turner's seminal work, *The Ritual Process: Structure and Anti-Structure*,
were more interested in the textures and meanings of transition itself rather
than the way in which it related to the sequential progression of an individual
within the hierarchies of their community.[9]

That is not to say, however, that the Turners are uninterested in the way in
which threshold phases and social structure relate. On the contrary, they are
most interested in pilgrimages which are not yet routinized and institutional-
ized by the organized Church, which grow up in spontaneous response to
rumours of miracles; they are palpably fascinated by the subversive potential of
pilgrimages which exist at some spatial and ideological distance from both the
ordinary structures of daily life and the regulated forms of worship which characterize the spiritual dimensions of that life. This subversive quality is contrasted with those transitional experiences – the examples given are the
sacraments of the Eucharist and Penance – which serve to confirm the hege-
monic arrangements of an integrated religious polity. However, the Turners
argue too that pilgrimages have a tendency to be claimed by organized religion
and incorporated into the obligatory round of ritual practice. This they pejora-
tively describe as a 'regression' from liminoid to liminal or pseudo-liminal

---

[9]   V. Turner, *The Ritual Process: Structure and Anti-Structure* (London, 1969), p. 94.

status – an assessment that reveals an antipathy to the conservatism of both medieval and tribal communities.

The Turners make a distinction between liminoid events – such as pilgrimage – which foreground the individual's interior development, and liminal processes – such as Penance and the Eucharist – in which an 'initiand seeks a deeper commitment to the structural life of his local community'. The Turners admit that this distinction is not clear cut and they use, as an example, crusade and *jihad* to show the way in which fanatical forms of pilgrimage serve to reinforce established religion, rather than offering a liberating holiday from profane social structure during which self-examination can take place. The assumption that is made here is that liminal processes, conservative and socially affirming events, offer no space for meaningful self-scrutiny and meditation on the nature of private desire. However, medievalists know that there are ways of reading cultural responses to Eucharistic devotion and Confession, for example, as subversive, creative and voluntary as well as culturally corroborative.[10] Indeed, it may be that the same discourse may mean very different things when deployed by different commentators: women's relationships to the humanized Christ and the Mass, for example, were very differently described by female mystics like Julian of Norwich and those male clerics writing the *vitae* of penitentially ascetic female saints.[11] Similarly the scholarship on the appropriation of the confessional mode in life-writing practices indicates that the confessional, as well as being a place where parish priests could regulate and monitor the appetites of parishioners, had the potential to be a creative and reflexive space radically energized by the confessing subject.[12]

I do not share the Turners' cynicism about the medieval Church and its capacity to control and subjugate its members. Necessarily, corporations are made up of individuals who are complicit beneficiaries as much as people whose vivacity – spiritual or otherwise – is supervised and resisted by external pressures. While the Turners see liminoid experience as always – and liminality as never – generative of art, I would see the tensions between liminal and liminoid experiences, that is the interplay of social power and interiority,

---

[10] See the debate about the Eucharist as a rite of passage set out in M. Rubin, *Corpus Christi: the Eucharist in Late Medieval Culture* (Cambridge, 1991), pp. 2–3.

[11] See, for example, C. W. Bynum, *Fragmentation and Redemption: Essays on Gender and the Human Body in Medieval Religion* (New York, 1991), pp. 171 and 149; C. W. Bynum, *Holy Feast and Holy Fast: the Religious Significance of Food to Medieval Women* (Berkeley, CA, 1987), pp. 208 and 260; K. Biddick, 'Gender, Bodies, Borders: Technologies of the Visible', *Speculum* 68 (1993), 389–418 (p. 415); Rubin, *Corpus Christi*, pp. 10–11.

[12] L. Gilmore, 'Policing Truth: Confession, Gender, and Autobiographical Authority', in *Autobiography and Postmodernism*, ed. K. Ashley, L. Gilmore and G. Peters (Amherst, MA, 1995), pp. 54–78; M. Foucault, *The History of Sexuality: an Introduction*, trans. R. Hurley, 3 vols. (London, 1990), I, 61; J. Tambling, *Confession: Sexuality, Sin, the Subject* (Manchester, 1990), pp. 2–3.

as a creative dynamic.[13] This is especially true in the literature of the late four-teenth and early fifteenth centuries, which is often concerned with the rela-tionship between a desiring individual and the ethical codes, both traditional and novel, with which his behaviour is compared.[14] John Gower's *Confessio Amantis* is just such a liminal text which flirts with the liminoid: a poem which is heavily invested in the idea of a corporate and holistic society, with some radical moments, in which new, individually-determined models of behav-iour are tentatively proposed.

High flying: the Confessio Amantis, *rites of passage and the second estate*

The poem's narrative is about initiation, and yet the expected passage – of the narrator, Amans, into the court of Venus – does not take place. The text, then, is about frustrated passage: the narrator, it is revealed, cannot be integrated into the retinue of lovers because he is too old. Excluded from the heterosex-ual pairing process, the narrator is forced to accept a substitute rite of passage in Confession and absolution, which is an anti-climactic compromise. Thus the poem is less interested in the pre- and post-liminary states but instead focuses on the complexion and significance of threshold experience. As such the *Confessio* looks very much like a liminoid text: its ending is not a satisfying resolution in which the narrator's status is altered or upgraded in a logical way. At the same time, however, the poem is structured as educative dialogue and confession that takes the seven deadly sins as its organizing principle. The poem seeks to find a 'middel weie' (Prologue, l. 17) that has often been read as a search for 'bourgeois moderation'.[15] In this liminal way Amans is encouraged to measure himself against and implicate himself in the ethics of his social *milieu*. However, the confessional format of the poem is disrupted by its 'erotic code' which complicates it, pushing it away from the stabilized genres of advice and confessional dialogue.[16] There is a tension in the

---

13 Turner and Turner, *Image and Pilgrimage*, p. 232.
14 William Langland's *Vision of Piers Plowman*, for example, has a narrator who is at odds with, and measured against, the text's moral agenda. See, for example, J. Burrow, *Langland's Fictions* (Oxford, 1993), pp. 28–9.
15 See, for example, A. Middleton, 'The Idea of Public Poetry in the Reign of Richard II', *Speculum* 53 (1978), 94–114 (pp. 95 and 102).
16 For a discussion of the intersections of the Christian schema and the 'erotic code' of the poem, see C. S. Lewis, 'Gower' in *Gower's* Confessio Amantis: *A Critical Anthology*, ed. P. Nicholson (Cambridge, 1991), pp 15–39 (pp. 15–16), first published in *The Allegory of Love* (London, 1936), pp. 198–222; N. Zeeman, 'The Verse of Courtly Love in the Framing Narrative of the *Confessio Amantis*', *Medium Aevum* 60 (1991), 222–40; Strohm, 'Form and Social Statement', p. 27; J. Davis Shaw, 'Lust and Love in Gower and Chaucer', *Chaucer Review* 19 (1984), 110–22 (esp. p. 113); J. Simpson, 'Ironic Incongruence in the Prologue and Book I of Gower's *Confessio Amantis*', *Neophilologus* 72 (1988), 617–32 (p. 617); A. J. Minnis, 'John Gower, Sapiens in Ethics and Politics', in *Gower's* Confessio Amantis: *A Critical Anthology*, ed. Nicholson, pp. 158–80 (p. 158), first printed in *Medium Aevum* 49 (1980), 207–29.

Confessio between sin-proper and sin-in-love, which is also a tension between the narrator's romantic or erotic desires and his social conscience.

The poem is self-consciously positioned on the cusp between stable alternatives – 'lust' and 'lore' and 'ernest and game' – as is stated in an early manifesto in the Prologue and a summarizing coda in the eighth Book (Prologue, ll. 17–20 and 462; VIII, l. 3109). However, this article will focus upon Books IV and V, which appropriately enough, if we are thinking about mid-way points, are in the centre of this eight-book work. It was common practice in medieval poetry to put those issues that are most central themat-ically into the physical centre of the poem. Nicola McDonald has argued that this is true of Book V and I suggest that Book IV shares this position; both are related discussions of the economics of love.[17] Book IV is the most equivocal book in the poem, being the point at which the narrator and his confessor, Genius, disagree, enlarging the gap between them and the polarities of 'lust' and 'lore' which they might be said to represent. The 'middel weie' may be about 'bourgeois moderation', but such ideals were in the process of being devised and debated; that indeterminacy is reflected in the disparity between Amans and Genius.

Book IV is dominated by a discussion of men-at-arms that is similarly centrally positioned and of a length that emphasizes its thematic relevance (IV, ll. 1608–2363). It is in this part of the text that the views of Amans and Genius diverge most profoundly – Genius proposes knighthood as a suitable masculine mode and Amans rejects it – opening an unstable textual space between the two interlocutors. In contradicting and refuting the arguments of his Confessor, Amans delays his own passage; as an unwilling ritual subject he makes this threshold discussion more significant. In Book IV there is also, uniquely in the poem, a deliberate separation of men and women. The Confessor begins by discussing Rosiphelee and Jephthah's daughter and their sloth in love (IV, ll. 1245–595) but is interrupted by Amans who wants to hear about men and receive more applicable advice (IV, ll. 1596–607). In this distinction can be seen a concern with the rites and passages associated specifically with men's moral and social lives.

The significance of the discussion of knighthood lies in the conflict between nostalgia and innovation, between sentimentality about a classic masculine model and scepticism about its universal relevance. Becoming a knight is often acknowledged as a rite of passage in traditional generational and occupational terms.[18] Chivalric manuals describe the knighting ceremony, or dubbing: an elaborate purification ritual undertaken, by those who are eligible in terms of class, age and status, in order to qualify for a heightened and glamorous

---

[17] N. F. McDonald, 'Lusti tresor': Avarice and the Economics of the Erotic in Gower's *Confessio Amantis*', in *Treasure in the Medieval West*, ed. E. M. Tyler (York, 2000), pp. 135–56 (p. 144).

[18] Turner, *The Ritual Process*, p. 105; P. Coss, *The Knight in Medieval England, 1000–1400* (Stroud, 1993), pp. 64–5.

estate.[19] How far such rites were actually practised is subject to some discussion.[20] There may also have been other ritual markers of this progression; the one that I shall discuss here is foreign travel and, in particular, crusading. Gower focuses not on ceremonial dubbing but upon travel and crusade. Geoffroi de Charny, in his *Livre de chevalrie*, places a similar stress on travel, beginning his account of ideal chivalric practice with a discussion of the relative merits of local and distant military expeditions, leaving discussion of ritual initiation to a later section of the text.[21] There is an implicit assumption in de Charny's *Livre* that younger knights will prove their military worth locally before travelling to a distant campaign; travelling marked out social adulthood.[22]

The *Confessio Amantis* moves the ideal knight as far away from the home as possible, locating him in 'strange londes' and 'sondri place' (IV, ll. 1611 and 1614), using language which replicates the fascination with variety and exoticism found in de Charny's *Livre*, which is admiring of those who journey through 'pluseurs paÿs estranges et lointains'.[23] Because of the superiority of travelling knights, Gower chooses the image of the crusading knight rather than the, perhaps more familiar, figure of the soldier on the front line in France. Genius offers a suitable itinerary for the ambitious fame-seeking knight:

> So that be londe and ek be Schipe
> He mot travaile for worschipe
> And make manye hastyf rodes,
> Somtime in Prus, somtime in Rodes,
> And somtime into Tartarie.   (IV, ll. 1627–31)

Although the 1390 date of the original dedication in the *Confessio Amantis*, by which time at least a first draft of the poem must have been written, coincided with a truce in the war with France, it was this European war, rather than more distant campaigns, which dominated the military agenda of the fourteenth

---

[19] For a discussion of this ceremony and medieval accounts of it, see M. Keen, *Chivalry* (New Haven, 1984), pp. 64–82.

[20] Coss, *The Knight*, p. 64.

[21] Geoffroi de Charny, *The Book of Chivalry of Geoffroi de Charny: Text, Context, and Translation*, ed. R. W. Kaeuper and trans. E. Kennedy (Pennsylvania, 1996), pp. 166–70. It does not seem that this text circulated in England; I do not suggest that Gower would have known of this text in particular. I use this as a comparative text because of its importance as a statement of chivalric ideology and as a 'portrait' of French chivalric culture, which was so 'decisive in finalising the shape of chivalrous modes and ideology' as noted by Keen, *Chivalry* (New Haven, 1984), pp. 12–15 and 31. It is also one of the rare chivalric manuals written by a military figure rather than a cleric like Ramon Lull. Keen, *Chivalry*, p. 12.

[22] de Charny, *The Book of Chivalry*, p. 92: 'Et par ceste maniere se partent de leur paÿs avant qu'il soit nul compte d'eulx par nul fait d'armes, et plus volentiers demorassent en leur paÿs se il peussent bonnement.'

[23] Ibid., p. 90.

century.[24] However, Gower chooses to concentrate on campaigning grounds in Prussia and Rhodes because they are further away, because the journeys to them were more risky and more expensive and because crusaders were more stellar than their counterparts fighting in the more local war.

The crusaders' motivations were very different from those of the men at war with the French. While the nearer conflict promised financial reward, the further proffered social renown as well as spiritual profit.[25] Crusaders in the late fourteenth century were noblemen who, by purchasing their own equipment and paying for their own passage to the front line, proved their economic power and social worth.[26] But there was no small financial risk in neglecting one's property at home, which, if the supposition that Gower worked in the Chancery court in some capacity is right, our poet would no doubt have known.[27] Maurice Keen has described a revival of interest in crusading by the English aristocracy, but admits that an English soldier was more likely to have had experience of active service across the channel than in the crusading regions.[28] With fewer men joining the armies heading to the crusades, the movement became more exclusive and increasingly the preserve of men of the highest status: men like Henry earl of Derby, soon to become Henry IV, who engaged against the pagans in Prussia in 1390. In 1393 Gower rededicated the *Confessio Amantis* to this man whom he described as 'Ful of knyhthode and alle grace' (Prologue, l. 89).[29] At a time when the word 'manhode' had both its modern meaning of 'manly virtue' and conveyed the sense of 'nobility – a pun which Gower often uses in the *Confessio* – the

24 For a discussion of the date of the text, the various revisions and dedications, see Macaulay's introduction to Gower, *The English Works*, I, xxi–xxviii (p. xxi); J. Fisher, *John Gower: Moral Philosopher and Friend of Chaucer* (New York, 1964), pp. 116–22; P. Nicholson, 'Gower's Revisions in the *Confessio Amantis*', *Chaucer Review* 19 (1984), 123–45 (*passim*); P. Nicholson, 'The Dedications of Gower's *Confessio Amantis*', *Mediaevalia* 10 (1984), 159–80. For a discussion of the truce years in the Hundred Years War, see A. Curry, *The Hundred Years War* (Basingstoke, 1993), p. 74.

25 This is a subject of some debate. See T. Jones, *Chaucer's Knight: the Portrait of a Medieval Mercenary* (Baton Rouge, 1980); M. Keen, 'Chaucer's Knight, the English Aristocracy and the Crusade', in *English Court Culture in the Later Middle Ages*, ed. V. J. Scattergood and J. W. Sherborne (London, 1983), pp. 45–61 (pp. 46–7 and 58).

26 For a discussion of the increasing elitism of English knighthood, see, W. M. Ormrod, 'The Domestic Response to the Hundred Years War', in *Arms, Armies and Fortifications in the Hundred Years War*, ed. A. Curry and M. Hughes (Woodbridge, 1994), pp. 83–101 (p. 86).

27 A. Ayton, 'English Armies in the Fourteenth Century', in *Arms, Armies and Fortifications*, ed. Curry and Hughes, pp. 21–38 (p. 23); Fisher, *John Gower*, p. 54.

28 M. Keen, *English Society in the Later Middle Ages, 1348–1500* (London, 1990), pp. 142–5.

29 For a discussion of this shift of political allegiance, see E. Siberry, 'Criticism of Crusading in Fourteenth-Century England', in *Crusade and Settlement*, ed. E. W. Edbury (Cardiff, 1985), pp. 127–34 (p. 131); Fisher, *John Gower*, pp. 68–9; L. Staley, 'Gower, Richard II, Henry of Derby and the Business of Making Culture', *Speculum* 75 (2000), 68–96 (p. 69).

crusader was an unambiguous masculine role model; crusades, as rites of passage, offered access to this secure and elite masculine identity.[30]

Victor and Edith Turner identify crusades as fanatical or aggravated forms of pilgrimage and, as such, liminal events with a predominantly religious meaning.[31] Pilgrimages and crusades are singled out for comment because of the way in which they represent a physical separation from mundane social structures. Of course, the accepted rationale for crusading *was* religious, but the motivations of individual knights undertaking these passages must have been various – economic, political, social *and* religious. The Turners seem not to consider that crusaders had a different social profile to other kinds of pilgrims and that their ritual journeys, as much as their ceremonial initiations, were confirmatory not just of the organized Church but also of aristocracy and traditional forms of political authority. The knighting process, as a rite of passage, was, of course, conservative in maintaining a military aristocracy that accorded with traditional understandings of the proper constitution of the polity. Indeed, part of the problem for historians in assessing how far chivalric discourses were relevant or appealing in the later Middle Ages and beyond is surely that they were not characterized by innovation nor designed, with their emphasis on the patina of a past 'golden' age, to look particularly pertinent to more modern tastes.[32] Despite, or indeed perhaps *because* of its conservatism, knighthood, as a manly resort, had an enduring appeal: not surprisingly given what it appeared to offer knightly initiands in terms of social benefits.

Gower's poem, being a text about the education of a lover, suggests that the public popularity which follows from success on crusade, translates into sexual and domestic rewards. The knight's absence from his lady – his sexual abstinence – makes his military journeys look even more like rites of passage which, as ethnographers have noted, are so often characterized by a prohibition on the intiand's engaging in sexual intercourse.[33] The sexual dimension of this physical segregation indicates that Gower views crusades as rites of passage not only in social, generational or religious terms but also in sexual terms. Despite the retrospective nature of knightly ideals, the combination of political authority, military prowess, refined sensibilities and sophisticated forms of etiquette made knighthood ripe for association with sexual success, giving it iconic status in artistic and literary productions about love and sexuality both in the Middle Ages and in later, post-medieval pastiche. Part of the codified form of aristocratic love, so prevalent a theme in medieval literature,

---

[30] *Middle English Dictionary*: 'manhede': 2 (a) 'Manly virtue, character, or dignity; manliness; (b) the character befitting a knight or monarch; chivalric nature or dignity; courageous behavior, bravery, valor'; See, for example, *Confessio Amantis* (VII, l. 4230).

[31] Turner and Turner, *Image and Pilgrimage*, esp. pp. 8–9.

[32] R. C. McCoy, *The Rites of Knighthood: the Literature and Politics of Elizabethan Chivalry* (Berkeley, CA, 1989), p. 18.

[33] Turner, *Ritual Process*, p. 104.

was an accent upon a decorous distance between the sexes.[34] This elegant style of courtship owed much to the value placed upon virginity in the religious conventions with which it was inextricably intertwined.[35] However, this aloofness amplified, rather than limited, the sexual frisson within depictions of noble romance, fetishizing their quasi-religious actors and objects.

In Book IV, Genius describes aristocratic courtship as a very indirect process built upon an assumption of physical separation imposed by the knight's military duties. Knights should, Genius says, behave in such a way on the battlefield:

> So that these heraldz on him crie,
> 'Vailant, vailant, lo, wher he goth!'
> And thanne he yifth hem gold and cloth,
> So that his fame mihte springe,
> And to his ladi Ere bringe
> Som tidinge of his worthinesse;
> So that sche mihte of his prouesce
> Of that sche herde men recorde,
> The betre unto his love acorde
> And danger pute out of hire mod,
> Whanne alle men recorden good,
> And that sche wot wel, for hir sake
> That he no travail wol forsake.   (IV, ll. 1632–44)

A knight who would be a husband must be fêted in public opinion and his honour suitably broadcast via the feudal networks of social obligation, before his lady's consent to a union is given. A positive male reputation is said to transcend physical distance; indeed, as chivalric writers like Geoffroi de Charny observed, knightly honour was enhanced by foreign travel and honour was crucial in securing the admiration of women.[36] It was critical to a military project that travel was characterized as part of the glamour of risk-taking and, by the same token, that a physical remoteness of a man from his lady was given romantic appeal. It was very unusual for men to take their wives with them on campaign in the later Middle Ages.[37] What is more, the medieval authorities, certainly in the early fifteenth century, perhaps mindful of the prevalent notion that sexual intercourse was physically draining and reduced pugnacity in men, or observant of the disruptiveness of inter-male rivalry and venereal

---

[34] See, for example, the discussion of love etiquette in S. Kay, 'Courts, Clerks and Courtly Love', in *The Cambridge Companion to Medieval Romance*, ed. R. L. Krueger (Cambridge, 2000), pp. 81–96 (pp. 82 and 84–5).

[35] On the religious discourses in depictions of aristocratic love see, E. Salter, '*Troilus and Criseyde*: a Reconsideration', in *Patterns of Love and Courtesy: Essays in Memory of C. S. Lewis*, ed. J. Lawlor (London, 1966), pp. 86–106 (pp. 89 and 97).

[36] de Charny, *The Book of Chivalry*, pp. 90–2 and 120–2.

[37] A. Curry, 'Sex and the Soldier in Lancastrian Normandy, 1415–1450', *Reading Medieval Studies* 14 (1988), 17–45 (p. 35).

disease, made repeated attempts to regulate, or prohibit, prostitution in military camps.[38] The problem of controlling the sexual behaviour of soldiers presumably contributed to the generation of positive discourses of knightly abstinence and distanced married love.[39] There is, in the passage above, a presupposition that affection might be concomitant with public fame. This account of marriage-making relies on the glamour of celebrity, rather than emotional proximity, for its appeal. Genius places female consent to marriage within the context of a larger community. While it is wrong to suggest that medieval marriages were universally loveless and non-consensual, marriages of the nobility were more likely than those of the more modestly placed to have been politically, economically or dynastically motivated.[40] The romanticization of remoteness may well have responded to the need to make these marriages attractive options to young aristocratic people.

Flying in the face of convention: reassessing the benefits of knighthood

Amans, however, dismisses the appeal of knighthood and crusading on both romantic and religious grounds. First he argues against the romantic logic of leaving home in order to win a lady and establish a conjugal household, and secondly he contests the notion that pacifist Christian doctrine can be disseminated by violent means. Amans rejects the imperative to travel and undertake a rite of passage despite its multi-dimensional cultural significance, its ability to signal acquisition of noble adult masculinity. Amans's answers seem comically lethargic in a book that is thematically focussed upon sloth and informed by contemporary ideologies of labour; he betrays a fear of travelling (flying) that is far from heroic.[41] However, his pacifism has been

---

[38] Ibid., pp. 23–4. See also Langland, *The Vision of Piers Plowman: An Edition of the B-Text*, ed. A. V. C. Schmidt, 2nd edn (London, 1987), Passus IX, l. 183a.

[39] For a discussion of chaste love in the *Confessio Amantis*, see J. A. W. Bennett, 'Gower's "Honeste love"', in *Gower's* Confessio Amantis: *A Critical Anthology*, ed. Nicholson, pp. 49–61 (pp. 53–4), originally published in *Patterns of Love and* Courtesy, ed. Lawlor, pp. 107–21.

[40] For studies which suggest medieval marriage as loveless see, for example, L. Stone, *The Family, Sex and Marriage in England 1500–1800* (London, 1977), esp. pp. 70–1 and 81; E. Shorter, *The Making of the Modern Family* (New York, 1975), pp. 54–65. For a discussion of the influences on aristocratic marriage, see M. M. Sheehan, 'The Wife of Bath and her Four Sisters: Reflections on a Woman's Life in the Age of Chaucer', in *Marriage, Family, and Law in Medieval Europe*, ed. J. K. Farge and J. T. Rosenthal (Cardiff, 1996), pp. 177–98 (p. 189); J. Murray, 'Individualism and Consensual Marriage: Some Evidence from Medieval England', in *Women, Marriage and Family in Medieval Criticism: Essays in Memory of Michael M. Sheehan*, ed. C. M. Rousseau and J. T. Rosenthal, Studies in Medieval Culture 37 (Kalamazoo, 1998), 121–51 (pp. 126–7); P. J. P. Goldberg, *Women, Work and Life Cycle in a Medieval Economy: Women in York and Yorkshire, c. 1300–1520* (Oxford, 1992), e.g. p. 231.

[41] G. M. Sadlek, 'John Gower's *Confessio Amantis*, Ideology, and the "Labor" of "Love's Labor"', in *Re-Visioning Gower*, ed. R. F. Yeager (Asheville, 1998), pp. 147–58 (esp. pp. 147–8).

taken seriously by a generation of modern critics who have focussed on his lucid objections to religious warfare.[42] Amans's protestation that killing the infidel is no way to further the philosophy of Christ is a much quoted example of the kind of reassessments, in ballades and other poetry, that were being made about warfare and what it could achieve.[43]

While the narrator's discussion of his attempts at courtship have been read lightly, his romantic logic is inextricably intertwined with his rejection of crusading as a Christian practice. Amans does not see how the immediate religious and military successes of crusading can deliver a romantic prize:

> For this I telle you in schrifte,
> That me were levere hir love winne
> Than Kaire and al that is ther inne:
> And forto slen the hethen alle,
> I not what good ther mihte falle,
> So mochel blod thogh ther be schad.
> This finde I writen, hou Crist bad
> That noman other scholde sle.
> What scholde I winne over the Se,
> If I mi ladi loste at hom?   (IV, ll. 1656–65)

Amans separates out military and romantic fortunes, in a way that his Confessor does not, and expresses a desire to concentrate his energies on love without undertaking a heroic physical journey. In rejecting the appeal of honour and distance, Amans offers a critique of marriages that are not based upon a sophisticated affective bond, diffidently advocating what is often identified as a bourgeois ideal of conjugal love.[44] That diffidence reflects an anxiety that social under-reaching might be as dangerous as over-reaching, that Phaeton's error is as serious as Icarus's. The narrator, in emphasizing the word 'schrifte', draws guilty attention to his feelings of inadequacy. However, he puts a forceful case when he measures the treasures of Cairo, won through un-Christian and violent means, against his potential romantic conquests. In this way the perfect example set by the knight-errant is countered with a more logical, but less romantic recourse to static courtship and religious pacifism.

Amans delivers a long confessional speech in Book IV (ll. 1122–224) of which the following is a small excerpt. It is characteristic of the whole

[42] For a more detailed discussion, see R. F. Yeager, '*Pax Poetica*: On the Pacificism of Chaucer and Gower', *Studies in the Age of Chaucer* 9 (1987), 97–121 (pp. 97–8 and 104); J. Barnie, *War in Medieval English Society: Social Values in the Hundred Years War, 1337–99* (London, 1974), pp. 75 and 122–3; Siberry, 'Criticism of Crusading', p. 127.

[43] I disagree with Yeager's unsubstantiated assertion that Amans approves of crusading, see Yeager, '*Pax Poetica*', p. 105.

[44] See, for example, M. Howell, 'The Properties of Marriage in Late Medieval Europe: Commercial Wealth and the Creation of Modern Marriage', in *Love, Marriage and Family Ties in the Middle Ages*, ed. I. Davis, M. Müller and S. Rees Jones (Turnhout, 2003); Goldberg, *Women, Work and Life Cycle*, pp. 231 and 273.

section from which it comes in its deployment of the language of labour and
idleness:

> Thus hath sche fulliche overcome
> Min ydelnesse til I sterve,
> So that I mot hire nedes serve,
> For as men sein, nede hath no lawe.
> Thus mot I nedly to hire drawe,
> I serve, I bowe, I loke, I loute,
> Min yhe folweth hire aboute,
> What so sche wole so wol I,
> Whan sche wol sitte, I knele by,
> And whan sche stant, than wol I stonde:
> Bot whan sche takth hir werk on honde
> Of wevinge or enbrouderie,
> Than can I noght bot muse and prie
> Upon hir fingres longe and smale,
> And now I thenke, and now I tale,
> And now I singe, and now I sike,
> And thus mi contienance I pike.   (IV, ll. 1164–80)

The narrator's love service is hyperbolic and absurd. His attentive industry is
an inversion whose irony is deepened by the lady's needle*work*. The traditional maxim 'need hath no lawe', which was more conventionally used to
justify those crimes committed for survival, is used flippantly here to convey
a sense of melodramatic earnestness.[45] The comic tone of this excerpt and its
surrounding lines undermines the logic that Amans uses elsewhere to question the ideological basis of crusading. This tension is indicative of the fact
that, while his suggestions and criticisms are based upon sound, logical
assessments, they can hardly hope to produce as perfect, practised and
authoritative an ideal of masculine achievement as is represented by knighthood. They are poised between 'ernest and game'. The comedy of failed masculinity reflects a lack of conviction about the validity of alternative masculine
models, despite historical evidence which indicates that alternatives, for those
men who would traditionally form the second estate, were being developed
and were not simply dismissed as foolish and insubstantial. It is too simple to
say, as some critics have, that the portrait of the narrator is a feminized one; he
is the anxious construct of a transitional period – a cultural rite of passage –
in which men's social and economic choices were under review.[46]

The most nostalgic laments in the *Confessio* are directed at the imagined
collapse of feudal values and, in particular, the decline of chivalry:

> If I schal drawe in to my mynde
> The tyme passed, thanne I fynde

---

[45] See, for example, W. Langland, *The Vision of Piers Plowman*, B-text, Passus XX, l. 10.
[46] The idea of Amans as effeminate has been put forward by C. McCarthy, 'Love and
Marriage in the *Confessio Amantis*', *Neuphilologus* 84 (2000), 485–99 (p. 493).

> The world stod thanne in al his welthe:
> Tho was the lif of man in helthe,
> Tho was plente, tho was richesse,
> Tho was the fortune of prouesse,
> Tho was knyhthode in pris be name.   (Prologue, ll. 93–9)

The wistful, impassioned tone of this extract, conveyed through the accumulated rhythmic phrase 'Tho was', reflects a broader conservative disappointment with the changes taking place within both military ranks and the higher echelons of English society.[47] The number of knights in the English army declined with some rapidity, a process that was mirrored by a steadier trend in society more generally. The financial and administrative burdens of knighthood have been described as deterring men of good families from undergoing the formalities of dubbing.[48] This failure to seek admission into the orders of knighthood is accounted for by the economic pragmatism of a social group that, in the later fourteenth century, was under increasing financial pressure, especially as the price of land fell in response to the demographic shifts of the previous decades.[49] The demilitarization of the gentle-born was also indicative of a financial realism about the potentially sizable losses that might be incurred by those going to war, for which loot from Cairo or anywhere else could not compensate.[50]

Tellingly, the documentary evidence from which John Gower's biography has been speculatively constructed suggests him as a man reassessing the benefits of bearing arms. John Fisher's analysis of the evidence implies that the poet, despite having a background which would have qualified him for knighthood, failed to undertake this rite of passage, preferring to remain an *esquire*, the title given him on his tomb at Southwark cathedral.[51] Gower probably came from a Kentish gentry family. His near relative, Sir Robert Gower, with whom he may have lived as a child, was a retainer to the earl of Atholl and married to Margaret Mowbray, the daughter of Sir Philip de Mowbray, the ancestor of the later dukes of Norfolk. Many of Gower's associates and business contacts, with whom he appears in the documentary evidence of his life, were of aristocratic stock. It has been suggested, by Fisher, that Gower's eschewing of knighthood was a conscious refusal of a crucial medieval rite of passage, a choice that seems to accord with a trend amongst other men socialized in similar ways at this time.

[47] Barnie, *War in Medieval English Society*, p. 26 discusses this in relation to Gower's earlier poem *Vox Clamantis*.
[48] Ayton, 'English Armies', pp. 29–30; Keen, *Chivalry*, p. 144.
[49] Keen, *Chivalry*, p. 144.
[50] K. Fowler, 'Introduction: War and Change in Late Medieval France and England', in *The Hundred Years War*, ed. K. Fowler (London, 1971), pp. 10–11.
[51] For a description of the tomb, see W. Thompson, *Southwark Cathedral, its History and Antiquities of the Cathedral Church of St Saviour (St Marie Overie)*, 3rd edn (London, 1910), pp. 204–8. The biographical material discussed here is all derived from Fisher, *John Gower*, especially pp. 39, 43, 46, 54, 58 and 66.

It is speculatively assumed from internal evidence in Gower's earlier poem, the *Miror de l'omme*, that Gower was a lawyer of sorts, possibly in the Chancery court. The evidence that survives from his adept land deals and the disquisitions on the legal profession within his work seem to confirm this assumption. In this respect the poet was one of those secular men who took up clerical posts, forming a new professional bureaucracy recruited to respond to the increasing complexity of domestic administration. Much criticism of England's military policies, and the Hundred Years War in particular, came from these quarters and often focused upon the domestic damage done through taxation raised for the war effort.[52] Given this contemporary context, it is suggestive that Gower sets up foreign and domestic concerns as the crux of the debate over proper masculine conduct: 'What scholde I winne over the Se, / If I mi ladi loste at hom?' (IV, ll. 1664–5).

During the late fourteenth century the central administration of England was undergoing a period of laicization.[53] While in the past men who had jobs in this area would have been members of the regular clergy, laymen and secular clergy were increasingly being integrated into these professional circles.[54] This quasi-clerical group found it difficult to classify themselves within the standard medieval taxonomies. In particular, the ubiquitous estates model, which described an holistic social order built upon male status/occupation groups, could not accommodate a section of the community whose occupation suggested that they might be best placed in the first *ordo* but whose sexual or marital status allied them with the second or third. Gower himself seems to have been even more out of kilter, being a single secular man living in a monastic establishment in Southwark, London's most notorious red-light district.[55] As either a widower or, more probably, a never-married man at the time of writing, Gower's did not replicate the standard pattern of residency of many of his contemporaries, amongst whom marriage was the normative option.[56] While the ethical indeterminacy of this untested kind of lifestyle may have been uncomfortably ambiguous, at liminoid moments it must have augured new possibilities and opportunities, which the literary

---

[52] Yeager, '*Pax Poetica*', p. 97 has noted that much war criticism came from bureaucratic circles. Ormrod, 'The Domestic Response', p. 86 outlines the historiographical debate on the broader economic situation and concurs with M. M. Postan that the Hundred Years War contributed to the 'economic stagnation' of the fifteenth century. See, also, Barnie, *War in Medieval English Society*, p. 24.

[53] E. Knapp, 'Bureaucratic Identity and the Construction of the Self in Hoccleve's *Formulary* and *La Male Regle*', *Speculum* 74 (1999), 357–76 (p. 360).

[54] P. H. Cullum, 'Clergy, Masculinity and Transgression in Late Medieval England', in *Masculinity in Medieval Europe*, ed. D. Hadley (London, 1999), pp. 178–96 (esp. p. 180).

[55] Fisher, *John Gower*, pp. 58 and 65; M. Carlin, *Medieval Southwark* (London, 1996), p. 210.

[56] It seems that Gower married for the first time, to Agnes Groundolf, in 1398, some five or more years after writing the *Confessio*. Fisher, *John Gower*, p. 64.

renaissance of the late fourteenth century, led as it was by bureaucrat-poets, explored and exploited.

Test flights: experimental and alternative rites

What Amans proposes, instead of the rarefied patterns of aristocratic courtship organized around daring foreign adventures, is pretty insubstantial. The action in these sections is located in the strange airy spaces between sleeping and waking which draw attention, once more, to the importance of threshold experience in this poem. The fourth Book's theme of sloth necessarily requires a consideration of somnolence, but tarries in the in-between states of dreaming and insomniac anxiety. Further, at crucial moments in the poem, in Books IV, V and VIII, Amans is subject to various trance-like states and paralyses, experiences that are extreme, psychophysical manifestations of initiation. Here, for example, the narrator describes falling into an erotic dream from which he is unwakeable:

> I am tormented in mi slep,
> Bot that I dreme is noght of schep;
> For I ne thenke noght on wulle,
> Bot I am drecched to the fulle
> Of love, that I have to kepe,
> That nou I lawhe and nou I wepe,
> And nou I lese and nou I winne,
> And nou I ende and nou beginne.
> And otherwhile I dreme and mete
> That I al one with hire mete
> And that Danger is left behinde;
> And thanne in slep such joie I finde,
> That I ne bede nevere awake.   (IV, ll. 2893–905)

In this passage the dreamer moves from a state of turmoil to one of supreme bliss. In the transitional phase between these two states he is poised between extreme positions and is uncertain of how to respond. His environment becomes classically liminal and disorientating, losing its definition as laughing and weeping, losing and winning, and ending and beginning become indistinguishable as polarities.[57]

In an experimental medium the narrator can explore his darkest fantasies without jeopardizing the integrity of his world. Indeed, it is the fear that he might damage his social environment that brings on his physical paralysis in Book IV:

> Min herte is yit and evere was,
> As thogh the world scholde al tobreke,
> So ferful, that I dar noght speke

[57] Turner, *Ritual Process*, p. 95.

> Of what pourpos that I have nome,
> Whan I toward mi ladi come,
> Bot let it passe and overgo.   (IV, ll. 355–63)

Reminiscent of, and a probable source for, T. S. Eliot's J. Alfred Prufrock, Amans is scared by the strength of his own desires and the reception that they might receive, asking 'Do I dare / Disturb the universe?'.[58] In his Book IV confession, Amans admits to being pusillanimous and forgetful because of the strength of his desires; both conditions lead him, he complains, into inaction and silence or, as seen above, deep sleep.

Amans's slothfulness in love is informed, of course, by depictions of aristocratic male lovers elsewhere, who are entitled to the idle leisure time which makes them vulnerable to the ravages of love-sickness.[59] However, Amans's precursors – perhaps the Man in Black in Chaucer's *Book of the Duchess* or Troilus in *Troilus and Criseyde* – do overcome their trepidation and gain some favour with their ladies, however temporary, either through their own agency or that of a go-between like Pandarus respectively.[60] Further, both Troilus and the Man in Black are knights of unquestionable integrity: the latter is described as a 'wonder wel-farynge knyght' (*Book of the Duchess*, l. 452), the former as a war hero of renown; their status, if not their toughness in battle, contrasts with and balances their sensitivity as lovers. Amans, on the other hand, having rejected the identity of man-of-arms, has neither the military credentials, the inner resources, nor a man willing to serve his interests to counter his romantic fecklessness.[61] In a poem which exemplifies good male lovers as having a knightly occupation beyond their domestic and romantic lives, Amans seems to have none beyond his; he remains static in his lady's house entertaining her pets and servants like a household fool while she, who does have alternative work, 'besien hire on other thinges'

---

[58] T. S. Eliot, *The Lovesong of J. Alfred Prufrock* (1917). John Gower's influence on Eliot's work has been noted before. See, for example, F. X. Roberts, 'A Source for T. S. Eliot's Use of "Elsewhere" in "East Coker"', *American Notes and Queries* 6 (1993), 24–5; G. Schmitz, 'Rhetoric and Fiction: Gower's Comments on Eloquence and Courtly Poetry', in *Gower's* Confessio Amantis: *A Critical Anthology*, ed. Nicholson, pp. 117–42 (pp. 117 and 142).

[59] Famously in *Roman de la Rose*, Oiseuse gives or denies access to the garden of love. See, Guilaume de Lorris and Jean de Meun, *La Roman de la Rose*, ed. F. Lecoy, 3 vols. (Paris, 1983), I, 19, l. 580; C. F. Heffernan, 'Chaucer's *Troilus and Criseyde*: The Disease of Love and Courtly Love', *Neophilologus* 74 (1990), 294–309 (p. 301); M. Wack, *Lovesickness in the Middle Ages: the* Viaticum *and its Commentaries* (Philadelphia, 1990), p. 61.

[60] See, for example, the exchange of rings between these couples: Geoffrey Chaucer, *The Book of The Duchess*, ll. 1269–73 and *Troilus and Criseyde*, III, ll. 1366–72, both in *The Riverside Chaucer*, ed. L. Benson *et al.*, 3rd edn (Oxford, 1987).

[61] For another comparison of Troilus and Amans, see R. Levin, 'The Passive Poet: Amans as Narrator in Book 4 of the *Confessio Amantis*', in *Essays in Medieval Studies Vol. 3 1986: Proceedings of the Illinois Medieval Association*, III, ed. R. E. Hamilton and D. L. Wagner (Chicago, 1986), 114–30 (p. 125); Lewis, 'Gower', p. 34.

(IV, l. 1183).[62] Unlike Troilus, he is not spared the day-to-day humiliations of courtship. Indeed, he looks a lot more like Pandarus himself, the prototype of the industrious bourgeois man, who, despite his best efforts, never gets the girl.[63] Again, Amans fails to make the passage, lacking the capacity to move through the transitional phase of suffering in courtship to sexual consummation.

Amans's physical insufficiencies are countered, but also produced, by his imaginative daring. In this fictional space Amans overcomes his fear of travelling (flying?). The text twice surmounts the distance between the house of the narrator and that of his lover as Amans's heart goes on an imaginary erotic journey into her home, chamber and bed. In these expressive transitional moments Amans imagines having terrible preternatural powers; the imagery of magic and miracle establishes these notional passages as rivals to more orthodox rites.[64] Amans denies being guilty of somnolence, the sixth branch of sloth, claiming that he is far too wakeful and entirely unable to sleep on account of his desire for his lady. He constructs a fiction in which his heart, unlike his body, is not confined by domestic architecture or the niceties of polite courtship:

> Thus ate laste I go to bedde,
> And yit min herte lith to wedde
> With hire, wher as I cam fro;
> Thogh I departe, he wol noght so,
> Ther is no lock mai schette him oute,
> Him nedeth noght to gon aboute,
> That perce mai the harde wall;
> Thus is he with hire overall,
> That be hire lief, or be hire loth,
> Into hire bedd myn herte goth,
> And softly takth hire in his arm
> And fieleth hou that sche is warm,
> And wissheth that his body were
> To fiele that he fieleth there.   (IV, ll. 2875–88)

The heart, portrayed here as an unstoppable penetrative force, is a sinister symbol of aggressive masculine desire. Personified as male, the disembodied heart sheds its usual emotional meanings as it disregards the impediment of consent – 'be hire lief, or be hire loth'. This reveals not just a lack of respect for

---

[62] Ulysses, for example, is finally forced to accept that he must do his military duty and respond to the Achaean draft (IV, ll. 1816–900). Geoffroi de Charny also mentions that while it is appropriate for women to be static in the household, men should be off adventuring and fighting. *Book of Chivalry*, pp. 120–2.

[63] See, Chaucer, *Troilus and Criseyde*, IV, ll. 397–9. On Pandarus's work and social status see, for example, B. A. Windeatt's notes to Geoffrey Chaucer, *Troilus and Criseyde: A New Edition of 'The Book of Troilus'*, ed. B. A. Windeatt (London, 1984), p. 291.

[64] Turner, *Ritual Process*, p. 108.

this hypothetically violated woman, but also for the legal doctrine of consent upon which medieval marriage was based.[65] The final lines cited here, with their tonal shift into pensive longing, do nothing to moderate this earlier impudence.[66] This is quite unlike the erotic service done by the aristocratic characters with whom I have already contrasted Amans.[67] The synecdochic heart behaves a lot like Pandarus who also has access to all areas, however intimate, overcoming the architectural boundaries which Criseyde relies on to protect her sexual reputation.[68]

Amans's second erotic fantasy works in a very similar way, again spiriting away the obstacles of physical architecture. This time Amans looks out across the city from his window and wishes he could master the black arts and send his heart on a flight over the rooftops:

> Whan I am loged in such wise
> That I be nyhte mai arise,
> At som wyndowe and loken oute
> And se the housinge al aboute,
> So that I mai the chambre knowe
> In which mi ladi, as I trowe,
> Lyth in hir bed and slepeth softe,
> Thanne is myn herte a thief fulofte:
> For there I stonde to beholde
> The longe nyhtes that ben colde,
> And thenke on hire that lyth there.
> And thanne I wisshe that I were
> Als wys as was Nectanabus
> Or elles as was Protheüs,
> That couthen bothe of nigromaunce
> In what liknesse, in what semblaunce,
> Riht as hem liste, hemself transforme:
> For if I were of such a forme,
> I seie thanne I wolde fle
> Into the chambre forto se
> If eny grace wolde falle,
> So that I mihte under the palle
> Som thing of love pyke and stele.   (V, ll. 6659–81)

---

[65] J. A. Brundage, *Medieval Canon Law* (London, 1995), pp. 73–4.
[66] The incongruence of these lines is also discussed by Levin, 'The Passive Poet', p. 124.
[67] Think, for example, of the way in which Troilus and Criseyde's relationship is characterized by mutual consent. J. Mann, 'Troilus' Swoon', *Chaucer Review* 14 (1980), 319–35 (esp. p. 321).
[68] On the ways in which Pandarus manipulates and dominates space in Chaucer's poem, see S. Stanbury, 'The Voyeur and the Private Life in *Troilus and Criseyde*', *Studies in the Age of Chaucer* 13 (1991), 141–58 (pp. 152 and 154–5); S. N. Brody, 'Making a Play for Criseyde: the Staging of Pandarus's House in Chaucer's *Troilus and Criseyde*', *Speculum* 73 (1998), 115–40 (*passim*).

Here the heart gains access to the lady's bedchamber by stealth rather than force, but this passage is just as threatening a portrayal of male sexual desire.[69] This passage is followed by two classical *exempla* – that of Leucothoe and the tale of Hercules and Faunus – both of which are narratives about attempted or actual rape, the presence of which confirm the sexual aggression in Amans's confession.[70] The composite portrait of the narrator as voyeur and master-thief, conjuring with the diabolic power of male sexuality is arresting and haunting. The morbid connotations of the word 'palle' – which could imply a shroud or a fabric in ceremonial religious use – and the violent phallic associations of 'pyke' make this a chilling episode, more 'earnest' than 'game'.[71] In particular the narrator's desire to become a shape-shifter is suggestive; hoping for an ambiguity which would disrupt the identity which exacts his social and sexual conformity, Amans wishes for, and imagines himself, not crashing like Icarus and Phaeton, but successfully passing through a new and alternative rite of passage which will bring him to sexual success.

Both of Gower's sexual narratives imagine that the impediment of domestic and urban architecture might fall away in a medieval version of Jong's 'zipless fuck', an idea that envisioned the dissolution of barriers to human passion:

> Zipless because when you came together zippers fell away like rose petals, underwear blew off in one breath like dandelion fluff. Tongues intertwined and turned liquid. Your whole soul flowed out through your tongue and into the mouth of your lover.   (*Fear of Flying*, pp. 11–12)

The physical obstacles of buildings in the *Confessio Amantis*, with their locked doors and impenetrable walls, are the manifestations of other, less tangible hindrances. Clothes in Jong's novel are worn both through choice and convention; so, too, the buildings in Gower's poem, represent the physical manifestations of social orthodoxy and, by using space in the accepted way, Amans allows them to describe his own inhibitions.

Amans's fantasy sweeps away those conventions and inhibitions, imagining a rite of access that will rival entry into, and compensate for his being barred from the Court of Venus. Social rites of passage, Van Gennep noted,

---

[69] This sinister stealth is discussed by K. Olssen, 'Love, Intimacy and Gower', *Chaucer Review* 30 (1995), 71–100 (p. 75) but he does not consider this as a rape fantasy.

[70] For a discussion of the problematic nature of Gower's sometimes immoral ideas on passion and sexual *mores* see C. D. Benson, 'Incest and Moral Poetry in Gower's *Confessio Amantis*', *Chaucer Review* 19 (1984), 100–9 (p. 108).

[71] *Middle English Dictionary*, 'pal': 3(a) 'A fine covering for an altar, a bed, or a seat; a bed-cover, an altar-cloth, a corporal; a coverlet, a shroud for a corpse or an icon'; 'piken': 8(b) '~ and stelen, steal (sth.)' and 1 'To work with a pick or other digging implement'.

are often imagined and ritualized as physical transitions into rooms or villages, as passing through doorways or streets.[72] As Monika Vizedom writes: 'If society is a house and each transition is the crossing of a threshold, then rites of passage are necessarily rites of access.'[73] In Gower's flights of fancy – dreams of erotic access – the rules on heterosexual intimacy, governing the conventions of residency, are transcended in a way which pays no heed to the institutions of 'marriage and the family, which legitimate structural status'.[74] Yet this is a text that, it is often noted, is heavily steeped in the contemporary discourses of marriage and ideas of Christian corporation.[75] The *Confessio Amantis* provides alternative and illegitimate, if hypothetical, access while simultaneously lamenting the breakdown of traditional ways of managing social relationships.

The enterprising presumption that Amans momentarily asserts in this fantasy world sympathizes with the late fourteenth century trend for breaking out of the spaces and stations that limited social and economic agency.[76] In his description of himself as a malcontent at his window at night, the narrator emphasizes his isolation, and yet it was not necessarily singular at the time of the poem's composition to call into question traditional assumptions about entitlement, and to consider taking things for oneself that had not been formally assigned. Contemporary conservative discourses about sloth and labour – which surely must have informed Book IV of the *Confessio* – expressed shock at the rising expectations, read as Icarian *hubris*, of an appetitive work force and the negligence of those employers and landlords who failed to curb them; they concentrated on the iconoclastic potential of appetition and the need to reassess and reaffirm people's social responsibilities

---

[72] N. Belmont, *Arnold van Gennep: The Creator of French Ethnography*, trans. D. Coltman (Chicago, 1979), p. 65.

[73] M. Vizedom, *Rites and Relationships: Rites of Passage and Contemporary Anthropology* (Beverley Hills, 1976), p. 45.

[74] Turner, *Ritual Process*, p. 111. Others have noted that, despite Gower's reputed 'moral' conservatism, there is a 'willingness', in the *Confessio Amantis*, to deal with, indeed a palpable fascination for, ideas which have been described as 'transgressive'. See, for example, D. Watt, 'Sins of Omission: Transgressive Genders, Subversive Sexualities, and Confessional Silences in John Gower's *Confessio Amantis*', *Exemplaria* 13 (2001), 529–51 (pp. 530–1); R. Woolf, 'Moral Chaucer and Kindly Gower', in *J. R. R. Tolkein, Scholar and Storyteller*, ed. M. Salu and R. T. Farrell (Ithaca, 1979), pp. 221–45 (p. 224).

[75] The *Confessio Amantis*, as many critics have noted, is primarily interested in marriage as opposed to any other form of romantic union. See, for example, J. A. W. Bennett, 'Gower's "Honeste love"', esp. pp. 58–9; Woolf, 'Moral Chaucer and Kindly Gower', p. 222; McCarthy, 'Love and Marriage', *passim*; A. Esch, 'John Gower's Narrative Art', trans. L. Barney Burke, in *Gower's* Confessio Amantis: *A Critical Anthology*, ed. Nicholson, pp. 81–108 (p. 84). For Gower's discussion of the three estates model and the dream of Nebuchadnezzar, see *Confessio Amantis*, Prologue, ll. 93–664.

[76] See, for example, Strohm, 'Form and Social Statement', p. 21.

in terms both of status and occupation.[77] Although discussions of *accedia* – in sermon literature and so on – were not new at this time, they took on new meanings in a period obsessed with the ethics of labour and acquisition. In this context the dramatization of Amans's grasping desires are at once horrendous and thrilling. The dream-fantasy form allows discussion of potential violence and its corollary, social disruption, and tragically segregates the desiring narrator from the comforts of community. The solidarity, or *communitas*, experienced by initiands in many rites of passage is notably missing from these visionary liminoid moments.[78] The anxiety manifested here about exclusion and marginalization says much about how the social conscience is confected, and how creative energy is generated, on the interface between conflicting desires to conform and/or pursue private impulses. It is no coincidence that such energy is produced at times of social change and sexual revolution – cultural rites of passage – when liminal nostalgia is countered, but also made more poignant, by liminoid innovation and enterprise.

[77] Sadlek, 'John Gower's *Confessio Amantis'*, p. 145 writes about the preoccupation in Gower's poem with the 'late-medieval ideologies of labor'. See, for example, William Langland's *Vision of Piers Plowman*, esp. Passus VI of the B-text, the statute legislation repeatedly reissued throughout the late fourteenth century, in *Statutes of the Realm*, 10 vols. (London, 1816), I and II, esp. I, pp. 307–13 or contemporary sermons e.g. Thomas Wimbledon, *Wimbledon's Sermon: Redde Rationem Villicationis Tue: A Middle English Sermon of the Fourteenth Century*, ed. I. Kemp Knight (Pittsburgh, 1967).

[78] For a discussion of communitas, see Turner, *Ritual Process*, p. 96; Rubin's Introduction to this volume.

'Le moment de conclure':
Initiation as Retrospection in
Froissart's *Dits amoureux*

Sarah Kay

This essay is concerned with initiation not as outward rites but as inner change. What does it mean to be initiated? Using *dits amoureux* by the fourteenth-century French poet Froissart I will argue that, from the point of view of the initiate, the fact of initiation is lost between the events that lead up to it and the retrospective awareness of it that follows. Initiation is thus experienced only as something that has already taken place. The short answer to my own question, then, is that being initiated means recognizing that one *has been* initiated. This account might be described as a 'phenomenology' of initiation were it not that the approach I shall be taking relies on psychoanalysis, and thus on unconscious processes. This essay thereby runs counter to the anthropological approaches adopted by some other contributors to this volume. Indeed, I shall be arguing that the logic which leads to recognizing oneself as having been initiated involves a certain collaborative misapprehension, a contention which may further deepen the rift with anthropology. Although focusing on love poetry, the argument outlined here has implications for political experience and for philosophical questions (such as the nature of memory), to which I return in my concluding section. Indeed, in their widest repercussions, the ideas advanced in this essay may affect the way we conceive our relationship to the past, and thus be relevant to historical preoccupations more generally.

Froissart's *dits* are full of material that prompts reflections on initiation. He follows medieval practice in envisaging human life not as an uninterrupted continuum but as a series of discreet stages or 'ages of man'.[1] In *Le Joli buisson de Jonece* he distinguishes seven phases each ruled by a different planet, and each represented by one of the branches of the great cosmic bush which provides the central image of the dream vision around which this *dit* is

---

[1] See Philippe de Novare, *Les Quatre ages de l'homme, traité moral*, ed. M. de Fréville, Société des anciens textes français (Paris, 1888); on the ages of man in Deschamps, see C. Attwood, *Dynamic Dichotomy: The Poetic 'I' in Fourteenth- and Fifteenth-Century French Lyric Poetry*, Faux Titre (Amsterdam, 1998), pp. 143–4; and in Froissart and his successors, see J.-C. Muhlethaler, *Poétiques du quinzième siècles*, (Paris, 1993), p. 149.

composed.[2] The infant is governed by the Moon, the boy by Mercury, and the young man by Venus. Growing seniority brings in turn the reigns of the Sun, Mars, and Jupiter, while death is presided over by Saturn.[3] The idea that life is divided into 'ages' has the effect of privileging a series of thresholds, and Froissart's accounts of his passage from one age to another, and especially from boyhood (Mercury) to youth (Venus), can be read as offering a purchase on the experience of initiation.

In his *Espinette amoureuse* (usually dated to 1369)[4] Froissart's first-person narrator describes his passage from the games of childhood to the bewilderments of love. Mercury appears, reminding the young Froissart that he has had governance of him since he was four years old. The god is accompanied by Juno, Venus and Pallas, who have been at loggerheads ever since Paris passed judgement on their respective merits and bestowed the coveted golden apple on Venus. The youthful Froissart is asked for his view and repeats Paris's choice, disdaining Juno's wealth and Pallas's might in favour

---

2 Jean Froissart, *Le Joli buisson de Jonece*, ed. A. Fourrier, Textes littéraires français (Geneva, 1975).

3 *Buisson*, ll. 1599–1707. The Moon runs from birth to age 4; Mercury from age 5 to 14; and then Venus from 15 to 24; the Sun 5 to 34; Mars 35 to 46; Jupiter 47 to 58 or more; and Saturn from then until death. Here in translation is Froissart's account of the key 'ages' referred to in this essay: 'Mercury (ll. 1628–35) takes delight in raising him for ten years and trains his tongue to speak. He takes command of him in this way, enables him to move and walk, makes him intelligent and responsive. During this age, the child loves to concentrate on those things to which he is most drawn. Thus Mercury teaches him. Then comes Venus (ll. 1637–45), who in turn takes him and takes care of him for ten years, with what care you should know: she washes away his ignorance and cleanses him, teaches him to know the world and experience the meaning of pleasure, whether of the table or the bedroom, and makes him gay, merry and smart, and acquaints him with all forms of fun. Then (ll. 1646–50) comes the bright and noble Sun who is not negligent of him at all, but makes him strain after honour of all kinds and set his heart on ample possessions, dissipates many a vice and nourishes him for as long as ten years. Afterwards (ll. 1653–67) comes Mars, who reigns for twelve years. This planet has a prolonged reign over man, because through it, man obtains knowledge of wealth and power. At this stage, man seeks out honour. It seems to him that the time has come for that. He will never be weary of recognition and advancement. This planet is harsh and fierce. There is none to compare with it in arrogance and fierceness. It loves all wars, conflicts, struggles and arguments. It takes delight in such things and inclines man to accumulate wealth, whether by art or by conquest. Then (ll. 1668–87) comes the course of Jupiter who assists man greatly because, as you well know companion, the planet delivers him from excesses and follies and the various kinds of melancholy in which he previously was stuck, and by which he has been assailed as much as a result of his own wrath as that of others. Jupiter delivers him to a more stable state that is to be valued and respected, and makes him enjoy peace for the body and rest for the soul, dispose his burial and tombstone, love the Church and fear God, and recognize and tremble that this world is but a step. This planet does not leave man be but governs him for twelve years or more.'

4 Jean Froissart, *L'Espinette amoureuse*, ed. A. Fourrier (Paris, 1963).

of love. Then, to Froissart's sorrow, Mercury departs and the other goddesses with him, leaving Froissart to become the tongue-tied and embarrassed recipient of Venus's gifts. *Le Joli buisson de Jonece* (generally dated four years later, in 1373) is a more complex work in which, as I have said, the theme of the ages of man is made explicit. Froissart again looks back at his initiation to the age of Venus, re-running in a dream, albeit in altered form, the experiences previously narrated in the *Espinette*.

By thus taking up one poem within a later, more ambitious one, Froissart is imitating Machaut who revisited and revised his *Jugement dou roi de Behaigne* in his *Jugement dou roi de Navarre*. The similarities between the two pairs of texts bring their differences into focus. In Machaut's case, the overlaps and differences between the two *Jugement* poems serve to question whether poetry can adequately represent and assess other people's experience of suffering, given the radically different relationship to it of men and women. The replication of material between Froissart's two *dits*, however, changes the focus from the other to the self. The question now is, to what extent can he represent and assess his own experiences, given that they have been undergone at different ages and filtered through more or less adequate degrees of perception? These *dits* are thus typical of Froissart, whose preoccupation throughout his *oeuvre* with memory and the experience of ageing is well known.[5]

Froissart retraces his own past with an odd mixture of intimate involvement and humorous detachment. At the beginning of the *Espinette*, for example, he wryly compares his current self with the self of his youth; both are driven by desire for pleasure but now his past pleasures elude him:

> En mon jouvent tous tels estoie
> Que trop volentiers m'esbatoie,
> Et tels que fui, encor le sui.
> Mais che qui fu hier n'est pas hui.   (*L'Espinette amoureuse*, ll. 22–6)

(In my youth I was such that I was over fond of fun and games; I am still the same as I was then, but yesterday is not today.)

In the second of these couplets the paradoxical convergence of continuity and discontinuity are emphasized by aphoristic phrasing and the internal rhyme *fui* : *sui*. In the final lines of the *dit* the poet remains entangled in the past experiences which he has been describing, 'languishing', as he puts it, in the complexities of love:

> Et quant il plaira a ma dame
> Que j'aie ossi grant q'une dragme
> De confort, adont resjoïs

---

[5] See for example M. Zink, *Froissart et le temps* (Paris, 1998); L. de Looze, *Pseudo-Autobiography in Fourteenth-Century France* (Gainesville, FA, 1997), chapter 4; P. E. Bennett, '*Ut pictura memoria*: Froissart's Quest for Lost Time', unpublished conference paper given at the University of Edinburgh, May 2001 (cited with thanks to Dr Bennett).

Serai de ce dont ne joïs
Ains languis, en vie ewireuse
Dedens l'Espinette amoureuse. (*L'Espinette amoureuse*, ll. 4193–8)[6]

(And when it pleases my lady that I should have so much as a dram of comfort then I shall enjoy a happy life in a way which, currently, I don't enjoy but instead languish in the little thorn bush of love.)

The distance of retrospection is greatly increased in the *Joli buisson de Jonece* which Froissart claims (l. 794) to have composed at the age of 35, that is, when he has just crossed the further boundary that divides the age of the Sun from that of Mars. This *dit*, then, reviews the narrator's initiation to erotic love some time after he has left it far behind him. Indeed, given the work's conclusion, the age from which the *dit* is composed may seem to be an even later one than his chronological age of 35. For, at the end of the *Buisson*, Froissart composes a pious palinode that recalls less the age of Mars, an age preoccupied with consolidating wealth and power, military dominance, and the respect of others, than that of Jupiter when a man puts secular cares behind him and takes thought for his immortal soul. Unlike in the *Espinette* he now reviews his initiation to the age of Venus with the changes of perspective consequent on having passed over at least two more of life's great divides. From one poem to the other, then, initiation to Venus's rule is looked back on with increased distance.

If initiation is something which is apprehended through retrospection, then the relation of experience to time needs to be considered. In the first instance I want to do this by showing how Lacan's essay on logical time throws light on Froissart's understanding of initiation; it is from this essay that the French phrase in my title, 'le moment de conclure' ('the moment for conclusion'), is drawn.[7] But I shall also frame that discussion within the broader problematic played out in Lacan's theory between causality and interpretation, drawing especially on Žižek's analysis of the Lacanian real in *The Metastases of Enjoyment*.[8] I shall use these to argue that the rationalizations of initiation to love which we find Froissart's *dits* – the passage from the age of Mercury to that of Venus, the story of his fumbling courtship, his flights of allegory, mythological analogies, clusters of exemplary tales, and outbursts of lyric *formes fixes* – are indeed all generated in retrospect, after the fact, from a position of greater age. At the same time, however, their accumulation traces the way the narrating subject has been produced in the wake of causes which remain concealed from him, but which persist in the way these rationalizations are framed.

---

[6] For the punctuation and interpretation of these lines I have followed Zink, *Froissart*, p. 150.
[7] J. Lacan, 'Le Temps logique et l'assertion de certitude anticipée. Un nouveau sophisme', in *Ecrits* (Paris, 1966), pp. 197–213 (written in 1945).
[8] S. Žižek, *The Metastases of Enjoyment: Six Essays on Woman and Causality* (London, 1994), chapter 2.

I hope this approach will contribute to the understanding of initiation as something which, while it is 'real', is nonetheless accountable for only in explanations that in some sense fail to include it; and also that it will constitute a fresh view point in Froissart studies. Froissart has influentially been read as preoccupied solely with the generation of texts, and as aspiring to situate the universe within a web of discourse.[9] This paper aspires to put the 'real' back into Froissart, even if only in the perverse and elusive sense which Lacan gives to the term.

* * *

I will start by reading Froissart in conjunction with Lacan's essay 'Le Temps logique'. In this essay, written early in his career, Lacan contrasts logical and chronological time. Chronological time is constituted by the sequential relations between phenomena, but logical time is to be defined by the way we make sense of those phenomena. It is still temporal (indeed, it is in a sense more temporal than chronological time which, because it is sequential, could be viewed as an essentially spatial arrangement), but its temporality depends on the positioning and activity of the subject.[10] Lacan starts from the *exemplum* of three prisoners sharing a cell. Their warden has decided to free one of them. He has prepared five disks, three white and two black, and proceeds to attach one disk to the back of each of the prisoners. None of them can see his own disk, but each must work out what colour he is wearing. The first to do so will be freed provided he reaches the answer by reasoning, not guesswork. In the event, all three prisoners step forward at the same time, having all reached the correct conclusion that the disk they are wearing is white. Logic and temporality come together because the argument each prisoner has staged in his head has been based on observing the successive impulses and hesitations of the two others, each of whom, of course, is doing exactly the same where his two fellows are concerned. Their reasoning, therefore, is sophistical since it has reached the right answer for reasons which are not themselves logically cogent: it is the concurrence of their behaviour that leads each of the prisoners to impute the same thoughts to the others as the others were imputing to him and so leads them all to act in concert. In this way, even though they may have argued mistakenly, all have arrived at the right answer.

---

9   Notably C. Nouvet, 'Pour une économie de la dé-limitation. La *Prison amoureuse* de Jean Froissart', *Neophilologus* 70 (1986), 341–56; S. Huot, *From Song to Book: The Poetics of Writing in Old French Lyric and Lyrical Narrative Poetry* (Ithaca, NY, 1987), chapter 10; P. E. Bennett, 'The Mirage of Fiction: Narration, Narrator and Narrative in Froissart's Lyrico-narrative *dits*', *Modern Language Review* 86 (1991), 285–97.

10   Compare the Introduction to this volume, which stresses both that initiation can fluctuate in the length of real time which it occupies and that it is often heightened by intense affective states.

In analysing his fictional prisoners' thought processes, Lacan distinguishes three different temporal modes, three aspects of this 'logical time'. There is the glance which takes in a situation (*l'instant du regard*), the time absorbed in comprehending it (*le temps pour comprendre*), and the moment in which a conclusion is arrived at (*le moment de conclure*). These three phases need not be arranged sequentially – they could easily be concurrent or overlapping, and their order could be reversed if, having concluded, the subject were to open up once again to contemplating the thought processes of others. Rather, the relationship between the phases is hermeneutic, and involves the way each subject positions himself relative to others and interprets what is going on in their thoughts as well as his own. As Žižek points out in his discussion of this essay, the way Lacan sees subjective positions emerging in the course this dynamic shows his distance from structural anthropology. 'Claude Lévi-Strauss conceived the symbolic order as an asubjective structure, an objective field in which every individual occupies, fills in, his or her pre-ordained place; what Lacan invokes is the genesis of this objective socio-symbolic identity'.[11] But although this genesis is based on (mis)interpretation, and it is (mis)interpretation which 'constructs' the answer, the example also turns around the real existence of the coloured disks, and the real prospect of liberation from the prison. Each of the prisoners reacts to the way he thinks that the other two are reacting to what he himself cannot possibly see: the reality of the disk on his own back.

In training Lacan's analysis upon Froissart's *dits*, I want to propose that the idea of the 'ages of man' does not only involve chronological, but also logical time. The transition from one age to another is, of course, in some sense a chronological phenomenon, and involves real causal processes. In Froissart's account, it is both clocked by actual age and governed by planetary influences. But we fail to grasp its nature unless we also see it also in terms of logical time, for the 'reality' which it represents is, in a sense, pinned out of sight behind our back. Initiation in Froissart is a phenomenon in which *le temps de comprendre* is always tied, on the one hand, to the experience of subjects other than himself, and, on the other, to *le moment de conclure*, a moment when the subject assumes to himself the significance of what he believes he has understood. Comprehension is itself comprehended in retrospect, from the perspective of its radical transformation from process to conclusion.[12]

As a small-scale instance of this multiple logic at work in Froissart, I will take the example of the prologue to the *Buisson* in which Froissart alludes to a serious failing which he committed in his youth, a crime against his Nature which is to be a writer composing for the pleasure of others.

---

[11] S. Žižek, *The Indivisible Remainder: An Essay on Schelling and Related Matters* (London, 1996), pp. 133–5 (p. 135).

[12] The complex interplay between chronological and psychological time in Froissart's poems would bear comparison with another work by Guillaume de Machaut, *Le Voir Dit*; see the suggestive remarks by J. Cerquiglini, '*Un engin si soutil': Guillaume de Machaut et l'écriture au xive siècle* (Paris, 1985), pp. 72–4 and 111–12.

Diex par sa grasce me deffende
Que ja Nature jamés n'offende!   60
Ja fu uns temps que l'offendi,
Mais le guerredon m'en rendi,
Car elle qui eslevet m'ot
Sans ce qu'onques en sonnast mot,   64
Elle me fist – chi se miron –,
Descendre ou piet dou somiron.
Or y eut tant de bien pour mi
Ensi qu'on dist a son ami   68
Et qu'on ramentoit les grans plueves!
En jonece me vint chils fleuves,
Car s'en viellece m'euïst pris,
J'euïsse esté trop dur apris.   72
Jonece endure moult d'assaus,
Mes en viellume nuls n'est saus.
Pour ce fu dit en reprouvier:
'En jone homme a grant recouvrier'.   76
Si fui je espris de grant anui
Si tost que je me recognui.
Mes tous seuls, pour oster l'esclandle
Dont je voel ores qu'on m'escandle   80
Me mesfis, dont moult me repens,
Car j'ai repris a mes depens
Ce que de quoi je me hontoie;
Dont grandement m'abestioie,   84
Car mieuls vaut science qu'argens.

(*Le Joli buisson de Jonece*, ll. 59–85)

(May God by his grace defend me from ever again offending Nature. For offend her once I did, but she paid me back for it. For she who had raised me up dashed me down without a word from the summit to the foot – let everyone take example from this! There was as much good for me in this as when a man speaks to his friend and reminds him of the heavy rains! This torrent came upon me in my youth, for if it had struck me in old age I would have learned too harsh a lesson. Youth can withstand many an assault, but no one is safe in old age. For this reason the proverb said: youth has great powers of recovery. And indeed I was overwhelmed with torment as soon as I realized what I had done. But in order to avoid the scandal which I now seek out I erred in secret, and I repent of this greatly now, and so I have publicly reproved on my own account my degeneration into bestiality, for knowledge is worth more than money.)

Like much of Froissart's writing, this passage is teasingly elusive and editors have disagreed about how to understand it.[13] The point, as I see it, is that there is a necessary time lag between wrongful acts and the possibility of assuming responsibility for them. On the one hand, wrongfulness is always retrospective;

---

[13] See Fourrier's notes to his edition; the translation offered here is my own.

and so, in a sense, there is no such thing as the crimes of youth since these can only be assumed by those who are no longer young. On the other, it is equally the case that youthful wrongdoing is the only kind of wrongdoing there is: older men would not be so foolish (ll. 70–4). Thus, though the interval between 'jonece' and 'viellece' may be in part objective and biological, it is also subjective and logical. The transition from one to the other introduces a warp in which the *chronological* time of the 'youthful act' is lost and only its *logical* time remains.

Society too plays its part in this logic of age, furnishing the subject with *le temps de comprendre*. The separation between the youthful act and its recognition is sustained by popular wisdom, which perpetuates the irresponsibility of youth. As a man might say to his friend, the effects of misbehaviour are like a heavy downpour – something that passes off without doing much damage (ll. 68–70); or as the proverb says, a young man recovers himself quickly (ll. 75–6). Sustained by social connivance at his 'failings', a young man need not feel greatly concerned since they aren't really failings until such time (i.e. when he is 'old') as society perceives them as such. These commonplaces, however, are double-edged for they also imply that this time will one day come. That is, the very reassurances that suspend the young man's wrongdoing also underline its reality, even though that reality cannot yet be recognized. Ultimately it will be, and so a 'right' answer is arrived at through reasoning which, though fallacious, is also psychologically revealing.

This passage from *le temps de comprendre* to *le moment de conclure* occurs in this passage in lines 77–8, and unleashes the orgy of self-reproach in the concluding lines. The focus on the first-person subject in these lines finds its pendant in Lacan's essay, which proposes that the various modes of logical time enact a dialectic between the subject and its others. The *moment de conclure* is a moment in which the subject, having subordinated itself to others in the *temps de comprendre*, is reborn. However, in its confidence in its decision, the subject also anticipates its imminent demise in favour of the 'objectivity' of certitude, when its view merges with those of others.[14] This move is also reflected in this passage in the way the 'reformed' Froissart offers himself as an exemplum of proverbial wisdom of his own (l. 85) and a model for others (l. 65).

I shall return to this passage later, but now I should like to jump to the ending of the *Joli buisson de Jonece*, where similar moves are replayed on a larger scale, and where the process of initiation is more obviously at stake. The dream that makes up the major part of this text could be said to be prompted by *l'instant du regard*, the moment when Froissart looks at the portrait of his

---

14 As Lacan puts it, 'Le *"je"*, sujet de l'assertion conclusive, s'isole par un *battement de temps* logique d'avec l'autre, c'est-à-dire d'avec la relation de réciprocité. Ce mouvement de genèse logique du *"je"* par une décantation de son temps logique propre est assez parallèle à sa naissance psychologique.[. . .] Ce qui fait la singularité de l'acte de conclure dans l'assertion subjective démontrée par le sophisme, c'est qu'elle anticipe sur sa certitude [. . .]' (*Ecrits*, pp. 208–9).

lady and begins his rediscovery of love (*Buisson*, ll. 615–24). *Le temps pour com-prendre*, occupied by the dream, leads him to an understanding of love via detours through cosmology and mythography, and places him in relation with various groups of personified abstractions. The contrast between the intersubjective time which this occupies and time as measured by the clock is brought out in Froissart's foolish gesture, when he wakes up, of feeling his moustache and finding it has barely grown; he can hardly believe the disproportion between the range and intensity of his dream experiences and the six hours which his dream actually took (ll. 5136–49).

As in the prologue passage considered above, Froissart's attention to the words of others during *le temps de comprendre* does not lead straightforwardly to the conclusions which he draws from them. The overall drift of these other figures has been reassuring. Jonece has told him stories to persuade him that to see his beloved as she was in her youth is far from exceptional; Desir has rehearsed *exempla* to prove that everyone suffers from the intensity of passion. Froissart's lady has not been unkind to him at all, and at the end of the dream the various personifications celebrate their eternal and unchanging natures. All this seems to reinforce the value of youthful love, and so it may come as a surprise that, when he gathers himself on waking for the *moment de conclure*, Froissart should dismiss his imaginings as idle. He is now convinced that the body burns to cinders in the fire of erotic love, whereas the soul alone is eternal and its Creator the sole worthy object of love (ll. 5156–73). To cleanse himself from sin, Froissart turns to the Virgin. The *lai* which ends the *dit* replaces the secular with the sacred, dismisses seduction in favour of virginity, and reverses the structure of intercession from the dream, where Jonece and Desir had pleaded Froissart's cause with his Lady, by begging the Virgin to intercede for Froissart with her Son.

This ending is not, however, perhaps as surprising as it seems. Froissart's preoccupation with preparations for death was signalled from the outset. Moreover, to focus my comments more specifically on Lacan's idea of *le temps de comprendre*, the reasoning he has attributed to his interlocutors in the dream has been largely specious. Partly it relies on misappropriating philosophical categories of argument, and in this deliberate travestying of scholastic methods Froissart shows himself a true heir of Jean de Meun.[15] Partly it operates – as many other scholars have remarked – on citing spurious or bungled *exempla*.[16] These inset stories seek to fortify the dreamer so that he can endure the heat of passion, but of course this very intention leads the tellers to dwell at some length on love's perils and delusions. Desir, for instance, provides Froissart with some hundred illustrations of lovers who died or went mad or both; the

[15] A crucial passage here is the bungled attempt by the personification Jonece to recall the instruction given to him by his philosophy teacher: *Buisson*, ll. 1563–95.
[16] See for example D. Kelly, 'Les Inventions ovidiennes de Froissart: réflexions intertextuelles comme imagination', *Littérature* 41 (1981), 82–92; Huot, *From Song to Book*, pp. 319–22; S. Kay, 'Mémoire et imagination dans *Le Joli buisson de Jonece* de Jean Froissart', *Francofonia* 45 (2003), 179–97.

fact that some of Desir's tales are invented and others distorted does not detract from their devastating unanimity. As in Lacan's narrative of the prisoners, the dreamer's *moment de conclure* follows sophistically from *le temps de comprendre*. If it is true, it is not because of the validity of the reasoning which led to it, but because of a certain collusion between Froissart's thought processes and those of others.

The progression to this moment shows more elaborately than the prologue how central Lacan's self-other dialectic is to initiation in this *dit*. The abstraction-dominated world of the allegorical dream poem is an excellent figure of how we endow the symbolic order with agency, turning it into what Lacan calls the big Other;[17] its population by indefinitely many doubles and parallels of the dreamer provides just the conditions of reciprocity which Lacan ascribes to *le temps de comprendre*. Equally, Froissart's *moment de conclure* propels him momentarily into agency before he effaces himself as a humble supplicant to the will of the Virgin. In this passage from near the end of the *dit*, for instance, the verb *voloir* (to wish, want or intend) is first associated solely with Froissart, then relinquished by the first person and passed to her as the embodiment of certainty. (For ease of identification, forms of this verb are picked out in bold.)

> Pour ce me **vodrai** retrenchier
> Que d'acroire a un tel crenchier
> Que pechiés est, qui tout poet perdre:
> Je ne m'i doi ne **voel** aherdre.
> Et s'en moi se sont espani
> Aucun villain visce, pas n'i
> **Voel** arester, mais mettre y ces
> Et principaument pour ycés
> Fourfaitures a coron traire
> Humlement je me **voel** retraire
> Viers la Mere dou Roi celestre
> Et li prie qu'elle **voelle** estre
> Pour moi advocate et moiienne
> A son Fil, qui tout amoiienne
> Et qui est vrais feus habondans,
> Caritables et redondans,
> Pour coers enflamer et esprendre.
>
> (*Le Joli buisson de Jonece*, ll. 5174–90)

---

[17] The big Other – Lacan's *Autre* with a capital *A* – is where the authority of the symbolic order is assumed to lie. Belief in such authority equates to supposing that there is something additional to the symbolic order which props it up, conferring density and substance on it. This is a delusion: the Other is not an agent, just a tissue of differences. This is why Lacan teaches that the big Other is nothing but an impostor, even going so far as to claim that the big Other does not exist. For help with Lacanian vocabulary consult D. Evans, *An Introductory Dictionary of Lacanian Psychoanalysis* (London and New York, 1996).

(For this reason I intend to cut myself off from credit dealings with such a creditor [as the body], for that is a sin which could forfeit everything: I ought not, and will not, cleave to it. And if some low vices have flourished in me I do not wish to tarry with them but to put a stop to them, and first and foremost, so as to end these misdoings, I wish to humbly betake myself to the Mother of the Heavenly King and pray to her that she should wish to be an advocate and mediator for me with her Son who is the mediator of all things and who is the true abundant fire, overflowing with charity, to inflame and kindle hearts.)

In the passage from the *temps de comprendre* to the *moment de conclure* we see the alternate fall, rise, and fall of the subject as it is born or fades with the rhythms of its interactions with others.

* * *

Supposing, then, that it is helpful to look at initiation in the light of Lacan's essay, what can it tell us about the initiation specifically to love? Comparing the versions of subjective experience recorded in the two *dits* suggests that the subject's truth is highly malleable, indeed that it can adopt incompatible forms. For although there is some sense in which the *Espinette* and the *Buisson* recount the same initiation – in both the subject is led by Venus to love the identical lady, to declare his love to her, and to encounter a mixture of setbacks and success – what is most striking about the experiences related in the two poems is their systematic divergence. The *Espinette* opens with evocations of childhood, the *Buisson* with those of old age. The *Espinette* begins in May, the *Buisson* in November. In the *Espinette*, Venus takes the young Froissart to a little thorn tree; in the *Buisson* she takes him to a vast cosmic bush, and this divergence is of course reflected in the titles of the respective *dits*. In both poems the lover gazes at a picture of his lady but in the *Espinette* he does so in a dream whereas in the *Buisson* it is what provokes the dream. In both dreams his lady assures him of her love, but in the *Espinette* she ascribes her earlier apparent indifference to fear of slander whereas in the *Buisson* she sees inherent value in love being withheld and the lover compelled to wait. This latter difference is symptomatic of a pervasive contrast between the two poems. In the *Espinette*, the obstacles in the way of successful courtship seem to be above all external events, whereas in the *Buisson* they are rather internal dispositions. Thus in the *Espinette* Froissart is discouraged when he learns that his lady is to be married; he falls sick with a fever for three months; he has to absent himself on a long journey; later he is involved in several unsatisfactory social situations with his lady and is further hampered by the death of their *confidante*; her behaviour towards him proves difficult to interpret. In the *Buisson*, by contrast, there is no real-world depiction of social relations and instead the lady, like the rose in Guillaume de Lorris's poem, is surrounded by a variety of personified abstractions. The lover is helplessly intimidated by the three most repellent of them, the lady's Refus, Escondis and Dangier, but with the help of Jonece and Desir obtains from the lady a softening of their hostility towards him. The whole drama seems to have been recast as internal and psychological. The outcomes of the two works are radically different too, given that following the dream in the *Espinette* the lady's reassurances are to some extent fulfilled and the lover continues to pursue his love. By contrast the dream which makes up the *Buisson*, even though his lady again reassures him of her love (ll. 4556–60), nevertheless leads to his renouncing it. These differences can perhaps be summarized by saying that *Espinette* entertains an 'if only' relationship to love – it posits love as something that could work if only such and such conditions could be met – whereas the *Buisson* takes the more radical step of recognizing that this love is inherently incapable of fulfilment.

I have argued that the relation in the *dits* between *le temps de comprendre* and *le moment de conclure* resembles Lacan's essay in that the subject's truth is reached through what he gleans from the misrepresentations of others. We now see how far this truth is itself susceptible to radical difference. Although the *Buisson* attempts to repeat the *Espinette*, there is in fact a yawning gap between them. This gap implies that any attempt to seek to define the nature of initiation to love is doomed to fail. It has no constant, positive content. Retrospection captures what it can from the perspectives available to it. The narrator of the *Espinette* writes as one still under Venus's influence whereas the narrator of the *Buisson*, although only four years older in 'real' time according to the dates commonly ascribed to the two texts, has passed in his *temps de comprendre* through several more of life's ages. Whatever his biological age, he writes as a man who, in his imagination, is close to death. It is striking how the *Buisson*, the poem of the two which sets out deliberately to re-experience love, is also the one which finds that experience most elusive.

A return to the passage from the prologue, discussed above, will enable us more precisely to focus the sense of deadlock which prevails in this *dit*. Here are the relevant parts of it again:

> Diex par sa grasce me deffende
> Que ja Nature jamés n'offende!   60
> Ja fu uns temps que l'offendi,
> Mais le guerredon m'en rendi,
> Car elle qui eslevet m'ot
> Sans ce qu'onques en sonnast mot,   64
> Elle me fist – chi se miron –,
> Descendre ou piet dou somiron.
> [. . .]
> Mes tous seuls, pour oster l'esclandle
> Dont je voel ores qu'on m'escandle   80
> Me mesfis, dont moult me repens,
> Car j'ai repris a mes depens

Ce que de quoi je me hontoie;
Dont grandement m'abestioie,   84
Car mieuls vaut science qu'argens.   (*Le Joli buisson de Jonece*)

(May God by his grace defend me from ever again offending Nature. For offend her once I did, but she paid me back for it. For she who had raised me up dashed me down without a word from the summit to the foot – let everyone take example from this! [. . .] But in order to avoid the scandal which I now seek out I erred in secret, and I repent of this greatly now, and so I have publicly reproved on my own account my degeneration into bestiality, for knowledge is worth more than money.)

Froissart is feeling guilty at having failed to write. By describing his crime as one committed against Nature (ll. 79–81), he attributes a sexual dimension to this guilt. The reference to having sinned in solitude suggests a parallel between his wrongdoing and masturbation. Life without poetic activity, it is implied, again with echoes of the *Rose*, is onanistic, whereas writing for others is like 'natural' sex. At the end of the passage his confession to bestiality continues the sexual innuendo; its insinuations are checked only by the enigmatic reference to money.

Perhaps Froissart's point is that writing is to be equated with loving and so not writing means offending against Nature; or perhaps writing, like reproductive sex, is seen as a socially creative and productive act. But whatever his fault may have been, Froissart plunges into his dream in an attempt to restore his fallen Nature in the only way he knows: by recourse to the subject matter of love. Between the beginning and end of the *dit*, then, the subject's impasse emerges starkly: love is both compulsory and impossible. By the same token, poetic composition, which is likewise compulsory, also seems to be impossible – until a solution is found in religion. It is not surprising, then, that love in the *Buisson* is also experienced as excruciatingly painful, far more so than the *Espinette*.

The pressure of pain in both *dits* is, indeed, something that reading them through Lacan's essay on 'Le Temps logique' has distracted me from. It points to a 'cause' of a different order from the logical conundrum facing Lacan's prisoners, and to a 'reality' more perilous than a coloured disk fastened to one's back. In writings subsequent to this essay, the 'real' ground and cause of our subjectivity identified by Lacan becomes both more perilous and more abstruse.[18]

For Lacan, as Žižek explains, the ultimate causes of our behaviour are indeed real, inflecting what we do. In this sense, Lacan is not to be regarded as a 'constructionist', that is, as one who conceives of reality as constructed by

18 Interestingly, it is in his seminar on love and sexuality that Lacan observes the connection between the 'Temps logique' essay and his later account of the real: see J. Lacan, *Le Séminaire livre XX: Encore. 1972–3* (Paris, 1975), p. 47. Trans. B. Fink as *Encore: The Seminar of Jacques Lacan Book XX. On Feminine Sexuality, the Limits of Love and Knowledge, 1972–3* (New York, 1998), pp. 48–9.

language. On the contrary, for Lacan the real as cause cannot be captured in language, it is refractory to rationalization and remains unconscious. But because we are speaking subjects, we of necessity use language to explain our situation to ourselves and thus we constantly produce what we represent to ourselves as 'causes' after the fact. Moreover, since the language we use to do this is itself already inflected by the real – by the way it haunts the limit of thought, tugging and distorting it – the explanations that we forge are already themselves affected by these real causes of our acts. Indeed, we become aware of the 'reality' of causation when we are reminded of its traumatic dimension by some triggering disturbance in our lives. As a result, unbeknownst to ourselves, our rationalizations are both spurious and authentic; the cause is both an effect of, and prior to, the subject's understanding; and intense suffering always has the value of a repetition. As Žižek puts it,

> This paradox of trauma *qua* cause that does not pre-exist its effects but is itself retroactively 'posited' by them involves a kind of temporal loop; *it is through its 'repetition', through its echoes within the signifying structure, that the cause retroactively becomes what it always-already was.*
>
> (*Metastases of Enjoymyent*, p. 32, emphasis in the original)

Žižek's account of Lacanian causality and interpretation, which is based largely on Lacan's Seminar on *The Four Fundamental Concepts of Psychoanalysis*,[19] will provide the framework for the next part of this paper.

* * *

I have shown that initiation to love in the *Espinette* and the *Buisson* is not so much a positive content as a set of gaps and divergences. Between them these two *dits* convey the sense of an inevitable failure either to experience or narrate love which, in the *Buisson*, reaches a state of impasse as love, and narrating love, are represented as simultaneously compulsory and impossible. I shall now argue that this impasse and the suffering that accompanies it are, as the passage from Žižek which I have just quoted puts it, 'repetitions' and 'echoes within the signifying structure' of an absent cause. These deadlocks and sufferings can, of course, be spoken of – fourteenth-century love poets speak of little else – but the language which speaks them also carries the traces of a disturbance that underlies them. That is, Froissart's very rationalization of the impossibility of love – his impulse retrospectively to ascribe 'causes' for love's failure – also points to a traumatic deadlock which is the 'real' cause beyond language. Its effects are, I suggest, legible in the tropes of

---

[19] J. Lacan, *Les Quatre concepts fondamentaux de la psychanalyse* (Paris: Seuil, 1973) [Seminar XI, given in 1964]. Trans. A. Sheridan as *The Four Fundamental Concepts of Psychoanalysis*, Introduction by D. Macey (Harmondsworth, 1994).

his writing. I shall illustrate this by briefly tracing the vocabulary of burning, or searing, in these two *dits*.

In the *Espinette*, a recurrent image is that of the prick or thorn. The little hawthorn may have attractive flowers in May, but its thorns last all year. Sometimes the pain of this repeated pricking flares into a burning sensation and gives rise to the imagery of fire that will later dominate the *Buisson*.

> Pour vous, ma dame souverainne,
> Ai recheü tamainte painne
> Et sui encor dou rechevoir
> Bien tailliés. Je di de che voir
> Car, come plus vif, et plus m'enflame
> De vous li amoureuse flame.
> En mon cuer s'art et estincelle
> La vive et ardans estincelle
> Qui ja ne prendra ja sejour
> Heure ne de nuit ne de jour.   (*Espinette*, ll. 3881–90)

(For you, my sovereign lady, I have received much pain and am cut out to receive much more. I speak truly in this, for the longer I live, the more the flame of love for you sets me on fire. The live, burning spark burns and sparkles in my heart, and will never cease any hour of the day or night.)

This passage from the end of the *Espinette* is echoed at the start of the *Joli buisson de Jonece* when the narrator first looks at the picture of his beloved which he put away many years long ago:

> Quant je l'ymagine et regars,
> Le tamps passé me ramentoit
> Et tout ce que mon coer sentoit
> Lors que ma dame regardoie
> Pour laquele amour tous ardoie.
> Or ai le feu descouvert
> Et le petit pertuis ouvert
> Par ou les estincelles sallent
> Qui me renflament et rassallent
> Et ratisent cel ardant fu[. . .]   (*Le Joli Buisson de Jonece*, ll. 615–24)

(When I hold it in my thoughts and look at it, it reminds me of time past and of everything my heart used to feel when I used to look at my lady. Now I have uncovered the fire and opened up the hole through which the sparks fly which set me on fire again and leap up once more and stir up that burning fire.)

In the second of these two passages one can see how Froissart's sudden confrontation with the past as represented by the picture also induces retrospection at the level of the text. The repetitions within it of the vocabulary and imagery from the earlier passage retroactively make his expressions of suffering then appear to cause the intensity with which he can give vent to his suffering now.

167

The motif of fire persists through much of the *Joli buisson*. The dreamer feels as though he is on fire, and is burning in agony. This imagery dominates the episode of his encounter with Desir and continues right through to the end.

Burning is present not only as a repeated vocabulary, it also flickers through formal devices such as wordplay and versification. An example is the echoing structure, or *rime retrograde*, in the last *ballade* of which here are the first three lines of the first and third stanzas:

> D'ardant desir pris et atains
> Tains sui, et ceste ardeurs m'afine,
> Fine dame, je sui certains [. . .]
> Se par vous n'est chils feus estains
> Tains ardans, plus vermaus que mine,
> Minera mon coer; je m'en plains [. . .]
> (*Le Joli buisson de Jonece*, ll. 3996–8 and 4008–10)

(Caught and hurt by ardent desire I'm darkened yet this ardour purifies me, pure lady, and I am sure [. . .] If this fire isn't put out by you, its burning hue, redder than red lead, will consume my heart; I am suffering [. . .])

Metaphors of fire and its effects – refining, blackening, consuming – are here continued through the repetition of sounds as well as meaning; agony seems to be implanted in the signifying system that invokes it. In the concluding *lai* to the Virgin, however, these metaphor are metamorphosed into religious images of fire as purifying, most notably the burning bush; and a new set of associations is brought about through the use of rhyme. This extract is from stanza xi of the *lai*:

> C'est li Buissons resplendissans
> Non amenrissans
> Mais croissans
> Et edifians
> Tous biens par divine ordenance.
> Et ses Fils, ce dist sains Jehans,
> Est li feus plaisans
> Non ardans
> Mais enluminans
> Tous coers qui en Lui ont fiance,
> Qui descendi, ja fu li tamps
> Entre ses enfans
> Inspirans
> Et yauls alenans
> Et leur donna plainne possance
> De convertir tous coers errans
> Et les fist si grans
> Que parlans
> Et bien entendans
> Toutes langhes sans variance.
> (*Le Joli buisson de Jonece*, ll. 5402–21)

(It is the resplendent Bush which does not diminish but which grows and raises up all good things according to the divine plan. And its Son, as Saint John tells us, is the pleasant fire which does not consume but which illumines all hearts that put their trust in Him who came down once upon a time among his children, inspiring them and breathing upon them, giving them full power to convert all errant hearts, and made them so great as to be able to speak and understand well all languages, without distortion.)

Here *ardans* rhymes with a whole new set of positive terms. Far from being destructive it is now set upon increase, illumination and edification. The stanza ends with the promise of an inspired and irresistible language which will cure all who hear it of their worldly errors. The very motifs and language which had caused Froissart such anguish within the deadlock of the real now provide the means of escaping from it. The last lines of this stanza find a solution to the problems with which the *dit* began, the ones set out in its prologue, as the poet finds a subject matter in which love's language is not only freed from love's deadlock but the 'gift of tongues' is guaranteed. The terrors of love are sublimated as the bliss of the sacred, and Froissart is let off Nature's hook by Grace. The trauma of passion and language, of passion *in* language, is allayed.

* * *

I began reading Froissart's poems in the light of Lacan's essay on 'Le Temps logique'. This early work of Lacan's illumines their subjective, or rather intersubjective, structuring of time and their strange balance of sophistry and truth, but not the anguish attaching to the cause of the subject's thought processes. The prisoners really want to know what it is that is fixed to their back; this knowledge will bring them freedom. The lover-writer, however, is much better off not knowing the nature of love. To understand this situation, a look at Lacan's later writing is helpful. Love cannot be pinned down; the retrospective purchase on it, the only one available in Froissart's *dits*, leads to contrary conclusions; the pain of recognizing that erotic desire is inherently deadlocked is hard to endure. Such pain, I have argued, triggers the reverberations of the absent real, provoking Froissart to find in religion another way of writing altogether. This *moment de conclure* is, however, only a precarious moment that the *temps de comprendre* will open up and reverse in subsequent works.[20]

A psychoanalytical account, then, helps us to get to grips with two aspects of Froissart's treatment of initiation, which are bound together in a paradoxical unity. Our sense is enhanced that initiation is a 'real' development, yet also that

---

[20] For this reason I am unconvinced by the claim that the *Buisson* is a 'farewell to poetry': see M. Freeman, 'Froissart's *Le Joli Buisson de Jonece*: A Farewell to Poetry?', in *Machaut's World: Science and Art in the Fourteenth Century*, ed. M. P. Cosman and B. Chandler, Annals of the New York Academy of Sciences 314 (New York, 1978), pp. 235–347 (pp. 244–6, n. 3).

it is one which can nevertheless only be construed in retrospect, via the mediation of the Other, the symbolic and social order. The fact of having been initiated is an effect which generates its cause, which is not to say that the cause is not 'real'. On the contrary, the 'real' (in the psychoanalytical sense) nature of this cause lies precisely in its traumatic character, which is why initiation orchestrates itself around the terrifying challenges of birth, sex, and death. In the *Espinette amoureuse* Froissart views with some indulgence his painful initiation to love. In the *Joli buisson de Jonece*, however, when he has passed through more of the ages of man, the dread of his impending initiation to the age of death weighs retrospectively on his initiation to the age of youthful love. Hence the effects of his pain, reconstructed by him as the cause for love and poetry failing, are at the same time the trace of a real cause he can never hope to experience or express.

I have chosen to write this essay about poetry, but other modes of initiation could be approached from the same theoretical perspective. The experience of political initiation, viewed close up, would be likely also to provide evidence of collective collusion in misapprehension, the outcome of which could only be determined retrospectively. *Le temps pour comprendre* necessary to confirm a monarch, for instance, remains on shaky ground until *le moment de conclure* arrives and it is determined that the claimant always-already 'really' was a king. Lacan's thrust against Lévi Strauss warns against hypostasizing social institutions as if they were a pre-formed mould in which individuals were cast, and proposes instead a dialectical process in which 'truth' emerges through social interaction and through the constant re-evaluation and (mis)interpretation of social relationships. The ritualization of initiation might also be seen as a defensive manoeuvre aimed at defusing the potential for a 'real' political trauma. Lacan's conception of the 'real' as an absent cause legible only in its effects, and as a trauma perceptible only through its repetitions, is, indeed, one which has been taken up by Marxist theorists and thus already given historical and political resonance.[21]

Another area to which the ideas I have discussed can be extended is that of our knowledge of the past. Froissart's reputation as a writer is founded chiefly on his *Chroniques* in which the question of access to the past is played out on a much broader scale than in the *dits*. As is well known, the later volumes of the *Chroniques* cease any attempt to record history as though it were a series of objective facts and instead repeatedly stage the process of investigating memory through dialogue. Froissart's attitude to memory owes much to contemporary Scholastic thinkers,[22] whose preoccupations in turn present

---

[21] Louis Althusser's history 'as absent cause' owes much to his intellectual association with Lacan, while Fredric Jameson's definition of history 'what hurts' is informed by his reading of both Althusser and Lacan.

[22] P. J. Archambault, 'Froissart and the Ockhamist Movement: Philosophy and its Impact on Historiography', *Symposium* 28 (1974), 197–211. Scholastic influence on Froissart is also discerned in J. Pioche, *Le Vocabulaire psychologique dans les 'Chroniques' de Froissart* (Paris and Amiens, 1976 and 1984), and Kay, 'Mémoire et imagination'.

interesting analogies with Lacan's. Both hold that the past can only ever be reconstructed on the basis of the present, and yet that the conceptual apparatus which we turn on the past has, unbeknownst to us, been forged by our past experience of the world.[23] Thus in the famous Voyage en Béarn section of Book III of his *Chronique*,[24] Froissart collaborates with his informants to elicit the vicissitudes of the house of Béarn, a process of collusion in which the past becomes entwined with, and filtered through, Ovidian myths like that of Actaeon. 'Memory', then, is at once a connection to past horrors and a fabrication from within contemporary discourses and exchange.

It is impossible for us to evaluate the element of collective collusion in our own (mis)understanding of the past but we can be sure that there is one. A volume such as this bears witness to the strength and intellectual fecundity of our social (mis)construal, as well as of the power of the past to motivate it.

---

[23] Simply put, medieval theories of memory needed to reconcile two conflicting tenets: on the one hand, that memory is of singular occurrences; and on the other, that we cannot have direct knowledge of singulars, since our knowledge is located in universals. The act of memory thus becomes an act of revisiting the experience by which we formed a conceptual understanding of the singular occurrence which provided the memory trace, but is not preserved within it. Here for example is Coleman's account of how memory works in Duns Scotus: 'When a man reminisces, he actively seeks to recall a mental image that corresponds with his continuously present universal understanding of something. He does not remember past *things* in themselves; he remembers past acts of knowing the formal aspects of things through sensible and intelligible species which represent those things in modes peculiar to active mind. He remembers only that which had and still has intelligible being for him.' See J. Coleman, *Ancient and Medieval Memories: Studies in the Reconstruction of the Past* (Cambridge, 1992), p. 497. I also found J. Marenbon's account of memory in Scotus very helpful in *Later Medieval Philosophy* (London, 1987), pp. 160–8.

[24] Froissart, *Le Voyage en Béarn*, ed. A. H. Diverres (Manchester, 1953). On the intertwining in Froissart of history, memory and poetry, see also C. Thiry, 'Allégorie et histoire dans la *Prison amoureuse* de Froissart', *Studi Francesi* 61 (1977), 15–29. Thiry suggests that Froissart, in attributing importance to chance contingency, has an Ockhamist bent.

INDEX

YORK MEDIEVAL PRESS: PUBLICATIONS

God's Words, Women's Voices: The Discernment of Spirits in the Writing of Late-Medieval Women Visionaries, Rosalyn Voaden (1999)

Pilgrimage Explored, ed. J. Stopford (1999)

Piety, Fraternity and Power: Religious Gilds in Late Medieval Yorkshire 1389–1547, David J. F. Crouch (2000)

Courts and Regions in Medieval Europe, ed. Sarah Rees Jones, Richard Marks and A. J. Minnis (2000)

Treasure in the Medieval West, ed. Elizabeth M. Tyler (2000)

Nunneries, Learning and Spirituality in Late Medieval English Society: The Dominican Priory of Dartford, Paul Lee (2000)

Prophecy and Public Affairs in Later Medieval England, Lesley A. Coote (2000)

The Problem of Labour in Fourteenth-Century England, ed. James Bothwell, P. J. P. Goldberg and W. M. Ormrod (2000)

New Directions in later Medieval Manuscript Studies: Essays from the 1998 Harvard Conference, ed. Derek Pearsall (2000)

Cistercians, Heresy and Crusadse in Occitania, 1145–1229: Preaching in the Lord's Vineyard, Beverly Mayne Kienzle (2001)

Guilds and the Parish Community in Late Medieval East Anglia, c. 1470–1550, Ken Farnhill (2001)

The Age of Edward III, ed. J. S. Bothwell (2001)

Time in the Medieval World, ed. Chris Humphrey and W. M. Ormrod (2001)

The Cross Goes North: Processes of Conversion in Northern Europe, AD 300–1300, ed. Martin Carver (2002)

Henry IV: The Establishment of the Regime, 1399–1406, ed. Gwilym Dodd and Douglas Biggs (2003)

Youth in the Middle Ages, ed. P. J. P Goldberg and Felicity Riddy (2004)

The Idea of the Castle in Medieval England, Abigail Wheatley (2004)

York Studies in Medieval Theology

I   *Medieval Theology and the Natural Body*, ed. Peter Biller and A. J. Minnis (1997)

II   *Handling Sin: Confession in the Middle Ages*, ed. Peter Biller and A. J. Minnis (1998)

III *Religion and Medicine in the Middle Ages*, ed. Peter Biller and Joseph Ziegler (2001)

IV   *Texts and the Repression of Medieval Heresy*, ed. Caterina Bruschi and Peter Biller (2002)

York Manuscripts Conference

Manuscripts and Readers in Fifteenth-Century England: The Literary Implications of Manuscript Study, ed. Derek Pearsall (1983) [Proceedings of the 1981 York Manuscripts Conference]

Manuscripts and Texts: Editorial Problems in Later Middle English Literature, ed. Derek Pearsall (1987) [Proceedings of the 1985 York Manuscripts Conference]

Latin and Vernacular: Studies in Late-Medieval Texts and Manuscripts, ed. A. J. Minnis (1989) [Proceedings of the 1987 York Manuscripts Conference]

Regionalism in Late-Medieval Manuscripts and Texts: Essays celebrating the publication of 'A Linguistic Atlas of Late Mediaeval English', ed. Felicity Riddy (1991) [Proceedings of the 1989 York Manuscripts Conference]

Late-Medieval Religious Texts and their Transmission: Essays in Honour of A. I. Doyle, ed. A. J. Minnis (1994) [Proceedings of the 1991 York Manuscripts Conference]

Prestige, Authority and Power in Late Medieval Manuscripts and Texts, ed. Felicity Riddy (2000) [Proceedings of the 1994 York Manuscripts Conference]

Middle English Poetry: Texts and Traditions. Essays in Honour of Derek Pearsall, ed. A. J. Minnis (2001) [Proceedings of the 1996 York Manuscripts Conference]